The Regulation of Gender Stereotypes in Advertising

This book provides an innovative and policy-oriented analysis of gender stereotypes in advertising regulation from a socio-legal perspective.

Examining the law and policy of the European Union and three case studies in Sweden, Spain and the UK, the book draws on interviews, focus group data and desk research to critically assess the legislation and regulation on the use of gender stereotypes in advertising. Its focus is on the largely neglected question of the EU's competence in the area of gender. And to assess this, the book considers various forms of 'good practice' through legislation, regulation and policy. It also explores the proscribing of gender stereotypes in advertising through 'soft law' measures such as self-regulation at state level, and action programmes and roadmaps at EU level. Finally, it critiques the lack of progress in achieving a unified code on the regulation of gender stereotypes whilst imagining what such a code might look like.

The book will appeal to academics with research and teaching interests in EU law, gender equality and comparative law, as well as academics and practitioners involved with media and advertising regulation, anti-discrimination law and freedom of expression.

David Davies is a lecturer in criminology at the University of Sussex, UK.

The Regulation of Gender Stereotypes in Advertising

Law and Policy in Europe

David Davies

Routledge
Taylor & Francis Group
a GlassHouse Book

First published 2025
by Routledge
4 Park Square, Milton Park, Abingdon, Oxon OX14 4RN

and by Routledge
605 Third Avenue, New York, NY 10158

Routledge is an imprint of the Taylor & Francis Group, an informa business

A GlassHouse book

British Library Cataloguing-in-Publication Data
A catalogue record for this book is available from the British Library

Library of Congress Cataloging-in-Publication Data
Names: Davies, David (Writer on law and sociology), author.
Title: The regulation of gender stereotypes in advertising: law and policy in Europe / David Davies.
Description: Abingdon, Oxon [UK]; New York, NY: Routledge, 2025. | Includes bibliographical references and index.
Identifiers: LCCN 2024044215 (print) | LCCN 2024044216 (ebook) | ISBN 9781032372457 (hardback) | ISBN 9781032372488 (paperback) | ISBN 9781003336037 (ebook)
Subjects: LCSH: Advertising laws—European Union countries. | Advertising laws—Great Britain. | Stereotypes (Social psychology) in advertising—European Union countries. | Stereotypes (Social psychology) in advertising—Great Britain. | Sex role in advertising—European Union countries. | Sex role in advertising—Great Britain.
Classification: LCC KJE6580.D38 2025 (print) | LCC KJE6580 (ebook) | DDC 343.2408/2—dc23/eng/20240919
LC record available at https://lccn.loc.gov/2024044215
LC ebook record available at https://lccn.loc.gov/2024044216

ISBN: 978-1-032-37245-7 (hbk)
ISBN: 978-1-032-37248-8 (pbk)
ISBN: 978-1-003-33603-7 (ebk)

DOI: 10.4324/9781003336037

Typeset in Sabon LT Pro
by Apex CoVantage, LLC

For the holy trinity: Vida, Moira & Sarah

Contents

Acknowledgements

I would like to thank everyone at Routledge, in particular Colin Perrin for his thorough advice from the very first draft proposal until the end.

Thank you also to friends and colleagues at the University of Sussex for your kindness and support throughout the process. Tarik Kochi for his encouragement and sincerity in the early stages and Nuno Ferreira for taking the time to read and comment on my early ideas. I would also like to thank Susie Scott for our endless conversations about dogs, Buxton and Goffman (not in that order!) and Sue Millns for inspiring me on my socio-legal journey.

Finally, thank you Sarah for putting up with my diva-esque performances during the writing and re-writing of this book.

Abbreviations

ASA	(UK) Advertising Standards Authority
AVMSD	The Audio-Visual Media Services Directive
BPfA	Beijing Platform for Action
BCAP	The UK Code of Broadcast Advertising
CAP	Committee of Advertising Practice
CEDAW	Convention for the Elimination of All Forms of Discrimination against Women
CJEU	Court of Justice of the European Union
EASA	European Advertisings Standards Alliance
EESC	European Economic Social Committee
EC	European Commission
ECHR	European Convention of Human Rights
ECtHR	European Court of Human Rights
EP	European Parliament
EEC	European Economic Community
EU	European Union
EWL	European Women's Lobby
FEMM	The Committee on Women's Rights and Gender Equality
MEQR	Measure having equivalent effect
OIM	Women's Image Observatory (Spain)
OfCom	Office for Communication (UK)
PSOE	Spanish Socialist Party
RO	Reklamombudsmannen (Sweden's advertising regulator)
SDP	Swedish Social Democrat Party
SRO	Self-Regulatory Organisation (i.e. the UK's ASA)
SWL	Swedish Women's Lobby
TEU	Treaty on the European Union
TFEU	Treaty on the Functioning of the European Union
TWFD	Television without Frontiers Directive

Chapter 1

Gender stereotypes

A contemporary legal problem

Recent literature suggests that harmful gendered content and gender stereotypes[1] in advertising are problematic, especially in influencing gendered expectations and gender norms in society (Antoniou and Akrivos, 2020; Roth-Cohen et al., 2023). Stereotypical representations of women and men frequently reinforce attitudes or behaviours which can contribute to restricting individuals' choices and aspirations. Advertisements that disproportionately sexualise, objectify and dehumanise women and girls are increasingly more pervasive, and this can pose a multitude of risks to harm such as violence against women and girls, eating disorders, body dysmorphia and self-harm (Capella et al., 2010; Wen et al., 2017; Raj et al., 2022). The mode in which audiences habitually and ritualistically consume media in their everyday lives (e.g. on smartphones, through social media apps or on-demand TV) compounds these risks and further increases the frequency of exposure to harmful gendered content and gender stereotypes. Over the last decade, advertising has rapidly shifted from an analogue to a digital landscape, and with that shift, so too has the use and development of algorithmic decision-making systems that generate 'targeted' or 'personalised' advertisements. Relying on mass data aggregation based on audiences' identity and personal interests (age, gender, ethnicity, location, lifestyle, taste and consumption habits), algorithmic advertising has become a ubiquitous and everyday part of most web users' experience (Bishop and Kant, 2023). As online advertising advances, the emergence of algorithmic discrimination or algorithmic bias has raised many concerns relating to algorithms' tendency

1 'Harm' in this context has a broad definition: for example, women and men portrayed in traditional professional or domestic roles whereby women are represented disproportionately as mothers or care providers carrying out gendered chores such as cooking and cleaning and men in manual work or business settings. Other examples of harm may be where women and girls are disproportionately portrayed in a sexualised, objectified or in dehumanised way; women disproportionately portrayed as neurotic or infantilised; and non-conforming identities mocked or ridiculed.

DOI: 10.4324/9781003336037-1

to discriminate based on, amongst other traits, race, socioeconomic status and gender (Blass, 2019). Algorithmic advertisements produce a confluence of ethical and legal issues, particularly in relation to social identity, privacy, data bias and, most significantly, its ability to categorise individuals into a reductive male/female binary and diminish audiences to a single statement or gender stereotype (e.g. 'mother of two' or 'young girl interested in make-up'). The extensive use of gender stereotypes in advertising raises the question of how suitable the current EU legal framework is for protecting audiences from these new forms of personalised/targeted advertising and the harmful gender stereotypes they produce. Literature suggests that the current legal frameworks are insufficient and calls for tighter regulatory responses to gender stereotypes in advertising more broadly (Adams-Prassl et al., 2023; Antoniou and Akrivos, 2020).

Current EU legislative framework

Gender stereotypes both inside and outside the workplace have been a persistent concern for the European Union (EU), and attempts to curb their usage can be felt in the Court of Justice of the European Union's (CJEU) early anti-discrimination case law. In the two landmark anti-discrimination cases of [1972] *Sabbatini* and *Defrenne*, the Court of Justice of the European Union (CJEU) were proactive in challenging outdated gender norms. Both cases foreground the same overarching issue: how outdated gender stereotypes both present a persistent problem and have a direct effect on women in the workplace. Since [1972] *Sabbatini* and *Defrenne* 1978, the CJEU has, on the one hand, reinforced gender stereotypes, particularly in cases relating to accessing rights during pregnancy and maternity leave and, on the other, contested their usage in employment, parenting and reconciliation (Timmer, 2016). Under the guise of free movement, the CJEU has also intervened when member states' regulatory codes have breached free movement rights (Kraft, 2007), notably in the cases of *De Agostini* [1997], *Leclerc-Siplec* [1995] and *Keck* [1993].

The EU has in the past attempted to address the issue of harmful content and gender stereotypes in advertising by incorporating advertising (along with media and education) in secondary legislation. The initial drafting of the Goods and Services Directive on equal access treatment to services 2004/113/EC (GSD) was, at the time, heralded as the first EU legal instrument intended to eliminate gender-based discrimination across numerous fields, including advertising. Unfortunately, after intense lobbying from some of the larger member states, the final GSD excluded advertising and the media from its scope. The failure to include these provisions was, according to some scholars at the time, a missed opportunity (Carraciolo Di Torella, 2005; Masselot, 2007a). The EU has since then sought to tackle the issue through piecemeal, ad hoc 'soft law' measures, such as action programmes, gender strategies, roadmaps, opinions and parliamentary reports.[2] In recent years, the European Commission have reignited this goal through the development of Gender Equality Strategy 2020–2025 (The Gender Equality Strategy, COM/2022/151) and campaign to tackle harmful gender stereotypes and the limitations they (re)produce. Current EU anti-discrimination legal framework lags behind and is yet to return to the issue of tackling gender stereotyping beyond the workplace. Despite efforts via soft law and secondary legislation, harmful gender stereotypes in advertising remain a powerful instrument in (re)producing a reductive binary in individuals' lives. Tackling harmful gender stereotypes, sexist content or misogyny in advertising is regulated at state level, predominantly through self-regulatory organisations (SROs) and ethical codes (Edström and Svensson, 2023). Amongst numerous flaws, SROs generally lack clear guidelines on specific types of gender stereotypes and avoid clear guidance on terms such as sexualisation, objectification, dehumanisation, nudity, body image and violence against women and content linked to eating disorders, such as fat shaming adverts.

In addition to the exclusion of advertising from the GSD 2004/113/EC, there are no EU law measures that tackle the evolution and pervasiveness of gender stereotypes in digital algorithmic advertising, which permeates social media platforms. The Audio-Visual Media Services Directive 2018/1808/EU (AVMSD) addressed some of these concerns but has so far remained redundant in achieving a unified code on regulation of harmful gendered content in advertising or providing a useful definition of what the commission deems harmful. The recent Regulation 2022/2065, also known as the Digital Services Act (DSA), introduces new mandatory due diligence obligations for large online platforms to address a range of societal risks posed by their services. As online platforms rely on advertising revenue, the DSA has sought to regulate the use of advertising through the guise of transparency and risk to harm to minors. From a gender equality and anti-discrimination perspective, the DSA prioritises online gender-based violence, cyber violence, cyber bullying and targeted advertising as fundamental risks for women and girls. The DSA also provides some scope on how member states should ensure new regulatory codes for advertising content prohibiting targeted advertisements to minors and advertising based on sensitive data (e.g. gender, sexuality, race). Despite the DSA's attempt at formulating regulatory code, scholars

2 See, for example, part 5.3 in the Roadmap to Equality (2006–10), the Opinion of the European Economic and Social Committee and follow up-strategy (2010/C354/0) Advisory Committee on Equal Opportunities for Women and Men Opinion 'Breaking Gender Stereotypes in the Media', the Parliament resolution (3 September 2008) on how marketing and advertising affect equality between women and men (2008/2038) and 'The Liotard Report' on eliminating gender stereotypes in the EU (2012/2116 (INI) 06.12.12).

have criticised the lack of regulation of algorithmic advertising and harmful gender stereotypes (Turillazzi et al., 2023).

Excavating the past: the Goods and Services Directive 2004/113/EC

This book therefore looks at the enduring use of harmful gendered content and gender stereotypes in advertising and provides a socio-legal analysis of the EU's attempts to combat their usage both online and offline. In doing so, it evaluates various forms of good practice from three national legal perspectives—Sweden, Spain and the UK—focusing on primary legislation, self-regulation, soft law and policy in order to conceptualise what a European unified code of regulation might look like. This book is rooted in the European Commission's drafting of the Goods and Services Directive 2004/113/EC and what feminist legal scholars have indicated was a failure to incorporate an article that tackles gender stereotypes outside the workplace (Caracciolo Di Torella, 2005). The Directive's original aim was partly a symbolic one: a move to tackle the entrenched and numerous forms of institutional sexism and discrimination that individuals encounter whilst pursuing access to services such as education, advertising and media. At the time of drafting of the directive, some member states, most notably the UK and Germany, were heavily involved with the overall tone and outlook of the legislation and subsequently lobbied for the removal of any language that sought to prohibit gender stereotypes in advertising (Masselot, 2007). Since the removal of education, advertising and media from the directive, the European Commission and European Parliament have retreated on the omission and persevered in challenging gender stereotypes in advertising through soft law measures. The political arm of the EU has dominated the discourse on regulation of the portrayal of gender in advertising for the past decade, but there has been limited progress in terms of substantive law. National governments, advertising regulators and non-state actors alike have postured on tighter controls on regulating harmful gendered content and gender stereotypes in the traditional (offline) forms of advertising, yet there has been little substantive progress in the UK and many other EU member states. Moreover, there has been less focus on the evolution and pervasiveness of online algorithmic advertising which permeates social media, video on demand and catch-up TV. The AVMSD went some way towards addressing some of these concerns but has so far remained redundant in achieving a unified code on regulating gender stereotypes or providing a useful definition as to what the European Commission deems 'harmful' advertising.

This book readdresses the gaps left by these two directives by evaluating how three different states combat gender stereotypes and imagines what a European code of best practice might look like. The gap in EU legislative framework will be constructed by evaluating three national and diverging perspectives through assessing each state's national legislation, policies, regulation and self-regulation of advertising. The first national perspective, Sweden, has shown reluctance in legislating on the issue due to its strong tradition of respecting the principle of freedom of expression (Svensson and Edström, 2016). When compared to its Nordic counterparts, Sweden's reluctance to legislate on the issue is an interesting position and highlights the conflict of legal principles such as gender equality, anti-discrimination and freedom of press and expression. Conversely, the second nation, Spain, has passed legislation Ley Organica 2004/1 (BOE-A-21740) that tackles issues related to gender-based violence and includes provisions on harmful gender stereotypes in advertising. The legislation links the use of harmful gender stereotypes and sexist content in advertising to numerous gender equality issues in Spain, including femicide and domestic violence, gender-based violence and misogyny (Martin-Llaguno, 2016). In tandem with this law, the Spanish advertising regulator, Autocontrol, amended its ethical code to prohibit the sexualisation, objectification and reification of women and girls in advertising. Finally, the UK's evolving self-regulatory advertising framework contrasts with Spain's firm legislation. Instead of providing legislation to tackle the issue, the SRO (advertising standard authority) recently adopted new rules that prohibit certain forms of gender stereotypes in advertising. Legal analysis will be bolstered by empirical research from the three national perspectives that informs the social context and the affect harmful gendered content and gender stereotypes in advertising have on teenagers. The empirical evidence is an assemblance of focus groups with teenagers from across the three case studies documenting their experiences through visual diaries of adverts that they kept during the research. The data from these groups develops richer insight of emotions and attitudes towards advertising, exploring how teenagers' interaction with advertising shapes their sense of self, gender and identity.

Concepts, themes and frameworks

Legal frameworks

The main legal analysis is positioned at the confluence of two EU competences—anti-discrimination and media. These two competences are discussed together with the jurisprudence from the CJEU and its role in shaping wider media and anti-discrimination law. The second area of literature concerns the two main directives discussed earlier, the GSD and the AVMSD. Commentators have criticised the former, including the controversial lobbying process and the exclusion of advertising from its implementation (Calvero and Galligan, 2012; Masselot, 2007, Carraciolo Di Torella, 2005). Equally, legal scholars have criticised the drafting process of the AVMSD (Little, 2008; Micova and Jacques, 2019). The remainder of the legal literature falls within 'soft law' approaches to combatting gender stereotypes. The final chapters are the three national perspectives: how each European state has sought to combat harmful gendered content and gender stereotypes in advertising through legislation (and case law), self-regulation and prominent rulings from the self-regulatory bodies or relevant courts.

Conceptual and theoretical frameworks

Drawing on the works of Erving Goffman and Judith Butler, this book is assembled by theorisations of gender, identity and performativity. Goffman's concepts of dramaturgy, frame analysis and gender display help form the visual representations of gender in advertisements (Goffman, 1959, 1974, 1979). Butler's theorisation performativity is deployed throughout the book (Butler, 1990). I locate and fuse Butler and Goffman's concepts within a broader social constructionist framework in which gender is (re)produced through cycles of ritual and repetition of gendered performances based on accepted gender stereotypes gleaned from everyday life. By revisiting and reimagining Goffman's 'gender display' typologies (Goffman, 1979), I work with the notion of 'commercial realism'—how advertisers attempt to (re)present gender to audiences through familiar yet truncated codes, rituals or displays. Throughout this book, I argue that adverts 'make the familiar strange', advocating the applicability of Goffman's typology schema and 'commercial realism' in contemporary forms of advertising in which displays or performances of gender are familiar yet peculiar. By returning to Goffman's typologies, I wish to highlight the unnatural representations of gender stereotypes in advertisements. The book revisits the following typologies: *feminine touch*, *ritualisation of subordination* and *licensed withdrawal* and measures them against legislative and regulatory standards in advertising. The empirical data collected from teenagers from across three case studies test Goffman's coding schema by mapping it onto contemporary modes and methods of advertising. The aim of revisiting Goffman's typologies is to (re)assess and (re)adjust the codes to emphasise that the subtleness of how gender stereotypes appear in advertisement and how this subtlety amounts to discrimination. The data collected from the fieldwork across the three case studies is a snapshot of emerging forms of advertising through new digital platforms and social medial and its pervasiveness and frequency through new technologies. This data therefore tests the applicability of Goffman's typologies to the new online advertising landscape.

Socio-legal methods

This book is located within socio-legal methodology, which brings together the two disciplines of law and sociology. On the face of it, the two may seem odd bedfellows as they not only seek different ends (Cowan and Wincott,

2016) but also approach the understanding of society in very different ways. One might argue that law is concerned with the practice of masculine language (Gilligan, 1982) or of rules and principles (Dworkin, 1985) that seek to (re)shape society by establishing (or amending) and then applying legislation. As John Rawls claims, the lawyer's 'concern is solely with the basic structure of society and its major institutions and therefore with the standard cases of social justice' (Rawls, 2009: 58). In practice, lawyers may often be somewhat over-zealous or righteous in trusting that their sole drive is to amend legislation and the legal system to bring about social change, regulate behaviour or radically shift opinion, whereas the sociologist is driven by a curiosity of society and their attempts to understand what social reality is (Hacking, 1999), whereas the sociologist's aim and influence are akin to Michael Burawoy's conceptualisation of 'public sociology' (2005)—to engage with non-academic audiences, promote and inform public debate and influence public and social policy. The connection between law and sociology is therefore perhaps the desire to bring about change, wishing to transform the lives of others and reacting to the vicissitudes of society. Thus, the two disciplines are not altogether dissimilar but are different in their approach to bringing about that social change.

Socio-legal research amalgamates these two disciplines and, by doing so, captures various elements of each of the subjects, borrowing concepts, ideas and methods from both. Untangling the wider definition of the ever-expanding interdisciplinary method of socio-legal research is troublesome (Fitzpatrick, 1995). As Banakar and Travers (2005) suggest, socio-legal research can mean different things to different researchers, depending on the nature of the research, their politics and what they wish to achieve by encountering the method. Ultimately, the researcher may pick and choose what parts of the method they employ. Socio-legal research as method employs sociology not so much for its substantive analysis of epistemological questions, such as 'What is social reality?' (Gane, 2004: 32) but as a tool for the collection of data used in sociological research. Banakar and Travers (2005) propose that legal research could benefit from more dialogue with sociology, specifically the methods used in this field. Wheeler and Thomas provide a similar suggestion, that the 'socio' in socio-legal represents the 'interface with a context within which law exists' rather than the study of sociology or social science (2000: 267). It is the latter statement by which I interpret the socio-legal research method. Law does not and cannot operate in a vacuum—it is the product of the society and a reaction to the social and cultural norms and values that prevail in that society. Rather than ascertaining what a socio-legal approach *is*, it is perhaps more helpful to note what socio-legal research is *not*. One common understanding amongst scholars is that socio-legal analysis diverges significantly from traditional 'black-letter' legal analysis as it attempts to understand law as a reflection of the society from which it emerges (Cownie, 2004). If 'black-letter law' researchers are concerned with analysing technical legal text and its routes, amendments and progress, then socio-legal research is about 'law in action' rather than 'law in books' (Banakar and Travers, 2005).

This books therefore follows the strong tradition of socio-legal methodology and the empirical study of the individuals onto whom the law is projected. As Lacey notes, socio-legal research aims to 'scrutinize not merely the legal articulation of the relevant rules and processes but the meaning and effects of those rules and processes as interpreted and enforced, and as experienced by their subjects' (Lacey, 1996: 132). Unpicking definitions of socio-legal methods is no easy task due to their ambiguity (Svensson, 2013) and the fact that they are still not fully recognised, developed or respected as the correct apparatus for legal research (Banakar and Travers, 2005). Socio-legal research is therefore criticised for its haziness and what some researchers would call its 'tawdry' approach to solving legal problems (Abel, 1980; Hunt, 1978). However, I wish to argue that socio-legal research methodology strives for deeper critical reasoning behind rules, or, for this book, the reasons behind the regulation and ethical codes that govern advertising. A further common distinction can be made between the two: black-letter law is law asking questions about itself: the internal questions, the suitability or limits of legal rules and ideas. This inward-looking process in black-letter law research is limiting and does not allow external critics from other disciplines to critique the problems within law from a different perspective. Finally, I argue that socio-legal methods are functionalist in their approach, seeking to understand the law's purpose in society and how it fits into the wider context of other institutions. It looks beyond the detailed analysis of legal rules and attempts to locate those rules 'within the context of the other social practices which constitute their immediate environment' (Lacey, 1996: 132). I wish to present how law does not—and cannot—operate in a vacuum; rather, it advances through interaction with the norms and values that prevail in society. By their nature, socio-legal studies observe law for its purpose and function in society, the questions that the law asks of society and the reasons that society needs law—in this case, a comprehensive legislative or regulatory code of harmful gender stereotypes in advertising. At the same time, this book intends to be both evaluative and reform oriented (Dodinson and Johnson, 2010), seeking to assess shortcomings of the GSD and AVMSD, identifying strategies to overcome gaps omitted in the drafting and looking towards new ways of regulating the use of harmful gender stereotypes in advertising. As much as socio-legal methodology acts as a buttress for this book, the analysis is a mixed-method approach. The majority of the book scrutinises the EU legislative framework, national perspectives, legislation, regulatory systems and high-profile cases. The empirical research element of the book is researcher-led focus groups which aim to engage with the teenagers onto whom the law is projected and to assess the shortcomings of laws and regulation already in place. As Lacey (1996) states, socio-legal research aims to scrutinise how law is felt and experienced by society.

Images and imaginations

I use the voices of teenagers from across the three national perspectives (Chapter 5) to underscore the problem of harmful gender stereotypes in advertising. I take a feminist approach to using focus groups (Kitzinger, 1994; Oakley, 1981) and draw on visual sociology methods (Rose, 2022) by using graphic diaries (screenshots/videos of adverts), a semi-autoethnographic method (Chaplin, 2011) to help understand what gender stereotypes are deemed harmful by the participants. The empirical research consists of three sets of focus group sessions with mixed-gender teenagers 13 to 18 years old across the three case studies: Sweden, Spain and the UK. The main purpose of the focus groups was to discuss the effects advertising had on the participants and explore how the participants interact with advertising in their everyday lives. The focus groups were mixed (age and gender) in order to widen the scope of diversity of discussion, leading to normative understandings of the subject matter, and to reduce the often pre-existing and problematic hierarchical structures that exist: in this case, secondary education (Bloor et al., 2001). The focus groups met for a second and third meeting to unravel the initial unfamiliarity of the subject matter and how advertising uses gender stereotypes to promote certain goods and services. The main objectives of the initial session were to create a 'visual diary' (Nind and Vinha, 2016), in which participants could document their own personal experiences and interaction with advertising and bring with them to the next session. The first session was also a space to confirm basic definitions such as 'gender' and 'stereotyping', providing the participants with traditional images (for example, a 1950s tomato ketchup advert) alongside contemporary banned adverts (for example, the 'Beach Body Ready' advert 2015–16). The one-to-two-week reflexive period between the first, second and third meetings allowed participants time to reflect on definitions (e.g. 'sex', 'gender' and 'stereotypes') and also to observe advertising through a new lens based on the discussions in the first session. At the second focus group session, all three focus groups provided evidence of advertisements that had appeared either online, on social media or in magazines and oral accounts of adverts they had viewed during the break. The benefits of using images and videos in focus groups is well documented in contemporary studies. For example, in Shirani and Henwood's research (2011), the researchers found that participants found it difficult to discuss abstract ideas such as fatherhood and masculinity without images. When the participants were provided with an image of fatherhood and/or masculinity, the discussion that followed was more fruitful than when a photo was absent. Images can often act as an anchor to address perceptions, ideas and feelings as well as grounding the research questions (Harper, 2002). Using photos, videos and other media serves three further roles for this book. First, it helps the participants ground the research question(s) and stimulate discussion. Secondly, images encourage the participants to engage with the familiar (or make the familiar strange) and help them think beyond taken-for-granted assumptions. This notion correlates with Goffman's 'commercial realism' observation that advertisements do not look 'bizarre' to the observer when, in fact, they really ought to (Goffman, 1979; Giaccardi, 1995). Finally, images help stimulate the participants into remembering or imagining similar ideas, events, feelings or situations in their everyday lives that they have otherwise overlooked or forgotten about. The reawakening of the senses applies to advertising, particularly when most adverts are viewed passively (Leiss et al., 2013). For example, Harper (2002), whilst interviewing farmers, suggested that some images can often appear as too familiar and do not lead to further discussion. However, when using images historical images of farms or images from other angles (e.g. bird's-eye view), the participants were far more engaged and willing to talk. The sociological research methods used in this book are employed as means to comprehend social reality and the 'the strange in the familiar' or to 'place the individual in the social context' (Macionis, 2001: 2). The focus groups with teenagers are used to discover these ideas: making the familiar (advertisements) strange and locating recipients' views of those adverts. The focus groups unravel two key questions: how do gender stereotypes in advertising affect young people, and what can be done to regulate advertising ensuring that rights are safeguarded? Embedded in the focus groups is commentary on the visual diaries the students kept during the research. The focus groups give voice to teenagers but also help explain how gender stereotypes manifest with data through their visual diaries. This visual data informs what is considered problematic, sexist or misogynist advertising and what forms of advertising resonate with young consumers' digital content.

Beyond the two-way mirror: developing a feminist perspective

The focus groups as a marketing and research practice are not too dissimilar to one popularised in the television series *Mad Men*. In one scene, a group of women are asked to visit the advertising agency's office to discuss beauty products with the sales and marketing team. The women talk about their beauty techniques, how they are passed down generation to generation and what works best for them individually. Beyond a two-way mirror in the adjacent room, the advertising agents observe the women, taking notes and joking that the future of the company's sales depends on a group of 22-year-old women. The two-way mirror, synonymous interrogation, experimental psychology and Foucauldian- or Orwellian-infused reality TV shows conjure up notions of surveillance, drawing out information, underhand tactics and general deceitfulness. Ironically, the focus group—or group interview (Hardy and Bryman, 2004)—stems from a somewhat misogynistic *Mad Men* era when advertising agencies employed the method to develop techniques to entice the consumer, drawing on gender stereotypes in the home and the sexualisation and objectification of women. I wish to counter this and claim that the focus group circumvents the exploitative nature of two-way mirror power dynamics (researcher-participant but also participant-participant) and allows for critique of the original consumer-capitalist values and the motives of the method. Turning this notion on its head, this book draws on feminist arguments (Oakley, 1981) that speak to the focus group's undertones of solidarity, of cohesiveness and camaraderie. Drawing on feminist frameworks that seek to garner life stories and experience (Oakley, 1981; Kitzinger, 1995), the methodological approach in the focus groups moves away from the 'predominantly masculine model of sociology and methodology' (Oakley, 1981: 32) of objectification.

As Bryman (2016) notes, the focus group begins life as an advertising agent's tool but is critiqued by counter-culture sociologists in the USA. Calder's research (1977) on participant's responses to ideas behind advertising demonstrates the transition from marketing research to sociological theorisations of method. Calder's approach provides that exploratory group discussions can unravel the 'everyday knowledge', experience and understanding of a certain group or a class of people. Merton et al. (1956) state that focus participants are complicit in the 'teasing' out of knowledge, aware of the arrangement that the researcher has selected them for the knowledge that they possess as 'valid' and their experience as 'legitimate' and, most importantly, that the researcher must work hard to obtain it. Merton's work on focus groups 'with a certain experience' have been conducted via new modes, particularly unstructured or semi-structured discussions, guided only by topic guides, themes or ideas (Merton et al., 1956: 155). Since Merton and Calder's work, researcher-led group interviews have gained prominence and recognition and been used widely in sociological methodology (Fern, 2001). During the 1990s, the focus group returned to its roots and became popular in research that considers mass media and advertising (Soar, 2000) and how audiences consume, digest and make sense of consumerism and marketing. For Morgan (1997), the focus group diffuses power relations and allows the researcher to take a step back and attempt to understand why people feel the way they do about a certain subject. Others within that group are able to question one another, taking power relations away from the interviewer/ee. This, Morgan argues, is the opposite of what occurs in a standard one-to-one semi-structured interview, in which the researcher wields asymmetric power in directing the interview's trajectory and, subsequently, the interviewee's answers. As group dynamics play a central role in the outcome of the focus group, the researcher can manipulate (to an extent) what they wish to interrogate and what should remain stifled. For example, one participant may state their perspective on a subject and then change their view once they have heard the rest of the group's views. The notion of dissent within the focus group is also an important and telling characteristic as arguments allow for a more realistic answer to the research question. Understanding a complex issue results from continuous interaction and discussion as opposed to the insular interview. As Bryman puts it, focus groups reflect the 'processes which meaning is constructed in everyday life and to that extent can be regarded as more naturalistic' (Bryman, 2016: 504).

Social interaction within the focus group is paramount for the success of 'drawing out' answers from the participants, moving away from asymmetrical power dynamics, building rapport and building a safe environment (Hennink, 2013). This is reflected in feminist theorisations of the focus group, whereby symmetrical power dynamics lead individuals to negotiate their own views on their own terms and in their own language (Kitzinger, 1995). Puchta and Potter (2004) argue that focus groups allow space for free will, autonomy and language control to formulate opinions and narratives that are too often absent in both questionnaires and structured interviews. Madriz (2000) posits that that discussions amongst marginalized groups, in particular women, leave space for shared empowerment, shared life experience and shared biography. Similarly, Ritchie et al. (2013) have highlighted that the 'back and forth' dimension is an important facet, allowing participants to hear one another's views, reflect in light of the group's wider discussion and (re)consider/develop their own positions further. Overall, the dynamic in focus group work is often a process of cohesion, prompting others to reveal more through similar experiences, seeking clarification and recognising ideas that are not always initially apparent. A 'spontaneity' derives from the participant's social context and can often lead to their own 'framing', which is less likely to occur in in-depth one-on-one interactions where the participant may be influenced by the interviewer or 'nudged' by normative influences (Oakley, 1981). Kitzinger (1994) notes that although there is very little research on social interaction in focus groups, there are two types of social interaction. First, complimentary—a broad agreement on the social world, understanding the framing of the phenomenon with each participant building on the previous remark, which eventually leads to consensus. Munday (2006) calls this consensus 'collective identity', which more frequently occurs in 'elite' or professional focus group sessions. The second—argumentative—occurs in the focus groups in this book, where participants disagree, and then it is paramount for the researcher to observe and highlight the disagreements no matter how trivial they may appear. The amplification of the disagreement can lead the participants to reconsider and revise what they have already said. Wilkinson (1999) suggests that feminist perspectives on social interaction are helpful in the focus group setting, where participants can often take control, and the researcher, at some point, must reassert their authority. I take up the feminist framings of the focus group, allowing for a disagreement/argumentative co-constructionist approach but also a space for negotiation, reflection and solidarity.

National perspectives and legal cultures

Methodologically, this book draws on a comparative legal method 'toolbox' (Van Hoecke, 2015) when exploring and framing what 'best practice' might look like in Chapters 6, 7 and 8. Throughout these chapters, I am critical of positivist 'mainstream' legal comparisons which lack reflexivity and disregard the politics, ethics, culture, economy, norms and values that underpin any given state (Frankenberg, 2016: 6). Instead, I advocate David Nelken's socio-legal comparative method (2007: 3) of borrowing ideas, collaborating on transnational legal problems or amending one element of a legal system in light of another. As with the broader framing of socio-legal research methods, this approach replaces black-letter method—which is usually symbiotic with traditional comparative legal scholars—with legal culture. Although often cited as vague (Legrand, 2003; Cotterrell, 2006), the concept captures the 'socio-legal' component, which is concerned with the scholarship of 'law in action' and not 'law in books' (Nelken, 2004). Legal culture is not necessarily about the active 'doing' but includes the general public's attitudes and feelings towards the laws that govern them. This is synonymous with the notion that law is part of society and is developed by Friedman's concept of external/internal legal cultures (1975): i.e. those who produce the laws and codes for advertising (legislators, regulators) and those who are recipients of it (the general public but critically, the most vulnerable: for example, minorities, children etc.). The term also refers to the wider methods of achieving and maintaining social order, beyond institutions, legislative procedures and the personnel who maintain the law (Nelken, 2007: 11). Socio-legal comparative law is therefore interested in the Hobbesian informal modes of social control: the social structures, customs, social norms and values, rather than formal and traditional modes. Legrand and Cotterrell's notion of 'legal culture' is the law as 'embedded within culture' (Cotterrell, 2006: 110) rather than an isolated notion apparent only in law textbooks. Thus, as Frankenberg argues with the 'Cinderella Complex' (2016: 6), it is not necessary for the comparatist be a specialist or 'insider' of the legal culture to pass comment on a wider legal problem: for example, how do different states understand and code what is sexist, misogynistic, degrading, harmful or in 'poor taste' when regulating the advertisements.

Legal culture(s) inevitably differ(s) across legal families and individual states. The legal style, the constitution, the courts, the personnel and, most importantly, the political framework shape legal culture reflecting social norms and values. This book borrows heavily from Banakar and Travers's cyclical notion that laws reflect the society they produce—reflect a nation's history, its principles and morals and the political and economic philosophy that underpins the system (Banakar and Travers, 2005). Law reflects the current society as well as the past; it reacts to social change or shifts technologically and therefore is not a stagnant set of rules (Graziadei, 2009).

References

Abel, R.L. (1980) 'Redirecting social studies of law', *Law and Society Review*, 14, pp. 803–829.
Adams-Prassl, J., Binns, R. and Kelly-Lyth, A. (2023) 'Directly discriminatory algorithms', *The Modern Law Review*, 86(1), pp. 144–175.
Antoniou, A. and Akrivos, D. (2020) 'Gender portrayals in advertising: Stereotypes, inclusive marketing and regulation', *Journal of Media Law*, 12(1), pp. 78–115.
Banakar, R. and Travers, M. (eds.) (2005) *Theory and method in socio-legal research*. Bloomsbury Publishing.
Bishop, S. and Kant, T. (2023) 'Algorithmic autobiographies and fictions: A digital method', *The Sociological Review*, 71(5), pp. 1012–1036.
Blass, J. (2019) 'Algorithmic advertising discrimination', *Northwestern University Law Review*, 114, p. 415.
Bloor, M., Frankland, J., Thomas, M. and Robson, K. (2001) *Focus groups in social research*. London: SAGE.
Bryman, A. (2016) *Social research methods*. Oxford University Press.
Burawoy, M. (2005) 'The critical turn to public sociology', *Critical Sociology*, 31(3), pp. 313–326.
Butler, J. (1990) *Gender trouble*. Routledge.
Calder, B.J. (1977) 'Focus groups and the nature of qualitative marketing research', *Journal of Marketing Research*, 14, pp. 353–364.
Calvero, S. and Galligan, Y. (2012) 'Justice, democracy and gender', in Galligan, Y. (ed.) *Deliberative processes and gender democracy*. Case Studies from Europe.
Capella, M.L., Hill, R.P., Rapp, J.M. and Kees, J. (2010) 'The impact of violence against women in advertisements', *Journal of Advertising*, 39(4), pp. 37–52.
Caracciolo Di Torella, E. (2005) 'The GSD: Limitations and opportunities', *Feminist Legal Studies*, 13, pp. 337–347.
Chaplin, E. (2011) 'The photo diary as an autoethnographic method', in *The Sage handbook of visual research methods*. Sage Publishing, pp. 241–262.
Cotterrell, R. (2006) 'Comparative law and legal culture', in Reimann, M. and Zimmermann, R. (eds.) *The Oxford handbook of comparative law*. Oxford: Oxford University Press.
Cowan, D. and Wincott, D. (2016) *Exploring the 'legal' in socio-legal studies*. Palgrave Macmillan.
Cownie, F. (2004) *Legal academics: Cultures and identities*. Hart Publishing.
Dodinson, I. and Johnson, F. (2010) 'Qualitative legal research', in McConville, M. and Chue, W.H. (eds.) *Research methods for law*. Edinburgh: Edinburgh University Press, pp. 20–33.
Dworkin, R. (1985) *A matter of principle*. Harvard University Press.
Edström, M. and Svensson, E.M. (2023) 'Promoting gender equality in media content: A limitation or extension of freedom of expression?', in *The handbook of gender, communication, and women's human rights*. Wiley online, pp. 193–211.

Fern, E.E. (2001) *Advanced focus group research*. SAGE.
Fitzpatrick, P. (1995) 'Being social in socio-legal studies', *Journal of Law and Society*, 22(1).
Frankenberg, G. (2016) *Comparative law as critique*. Edward Elgar Publishing.
Friedman, L.M. (1975) *The legal system: A social science perspective*. Russell Sage Foundation.
Gane, N. (2004) *The future of social theory*. A&C Black.
Giaccardi, C. (1995) 'Television advertising and the representation of social reality: A comparative study', *Theory, Culture & Society*, 12(1).
Gilligan, C. (1982) *In a different voice*. Harvard University Press.
Goffman, E. (1959) *The presentation of self in everyday life*. New York Press.
Goffman, E. (1974) *Frame analysis: An essay on the organization of experience*. Harvard University Press.
Goffman, E. (1979) *Gender advertisements*. Macmillan.
Graziadei, M. (2009) 'Legal transplants and the frontiers of legal knowledge', *Theoretical Inquiries in Law*, 10(2), pp. 723–743.
Hacking, I. (1999) *The social construction of what?* Harvard University Press.
Hardy, M.A. and Bryman, A. (2004) *Handbook of data analysis*. SAGE.
Harper, D. (2002) 'Talking about pictures: A case for photo elicitation', *Visual Studies*, 17(1), pp. 13–26.
Hennink, M.M. (2013) *Focus group discussions*. Oxford University Press.
Hunt, A. (1978) *The sociological movement in law*. London: Palgrave Macmillan.
Kitzinger, J. (1994) 'The methodology of focus groups: The importance of interaction between research participants', *Sociology of Health*, 16(1), pp. 103–121.
Kitzinger, J. (1995) 'Introducing focus groups', *British Medical Journal*, 311.
Kraft, D. (2007) 'Advertising restrictions and the free movement of goods – The case law of the ECJ', *European Business Law Review*, 18, p. 517.
Lacey, N. (1996) 'Normative reconstruction in socio-legal theory', *Social & Legal Studies*, 5(2), p. 132.
Legrand, P. (2003) 'The same and the different', in Legrand, P. and Munday, R. (eds.) *Comparative legal studies: Traditions and transitions*. Cambridge University Press, pp. 240–311.
Leiss, W., Kline, S., Jhally, S. and Botterill, J. (2013) *Social communication in advertising: Consumption in the mediated marketplace*. Routledge.
Little, V. (2008) 'Audiovisual media services directive: Europe's modernization of broadcast services regulations', *The Illinois Journal of Law, Technology & Policy*, p. 232.
Macionis, J. (2001) *Sociology*. New Jersey: Prentice Hall, Pensyvannia University.
Madriz, E. (2000) 'Focus groups in feminist research', in *Handbook of qualitative research*, Vol. 2. Thousand Oaks, CA: Sage.
Martin-Llaguno, M. (2016) 'Regulating sexist advertising in Spain', in Edström, M., Kenyon, A.T. and Svensson, E.M. (eds.) *Blurring the lines: Market driven and democracy driven freedom of expression*. Nordicom.
Masselot, A. (2007) 'The state of gender equality law in the European Union', *European Law Journal*, 13(2), pp. 152–168.
Merton, R., Fiske, M. and Kendall, P. (1956) *The focused interview: A manual of problems and procedures*. New York: Free Press.
Micova, S.B. and Jacques, S. (2019) *The playing field in audiovisual advertising: What does it look like and who is playing?* Centre on Regulation in Europe (CERRE).
Morgan, D.L. (1997) *Focus groups as qualitative research*. 2nd edn. London: SAGE.
Munday, J. (2006) 'Identity in focus: The use of focus groups to study the construction of collective identity', *Sociology*, 40(1), pp. 89–105.

Nelken, D. (2004) 'Using the concept of legal culture', *Australian Journal of Legal Philosophy*, 29, p. 1.
Nelken, D. (2007) 'Comparative law and comparative legal studies', in *Comparative law: A handbook*. Oxford: Hart.
Nind, M. and Vinha, H. (2016) 'Creative interactions with data: Using visual and metaphorical devices in repeated focus groups', *Qualitative Research*, 16(1), pp. 9–26.
Oakley, A. (1981) 'Interviewing women: A contradiction of terms', in Roberts, H. (ed.) *Doing feminist research*. London: Routledge.
Puchta, C. and Potter, J. (2004) *Focus group practice*. SAGE.
Raj, R., Arashpreet, A., Devedi, D., Pantho, S.F.H., Bara, P. and Agnihotri, B.K. (2022) 'Body dysmorphia and social media impact', *International Journal of Health Sciences*, pp. 3725–3735.
Rawls, J. (2009) *A theory of justice*. Harvard University Press.
Ritchie, J., Lewis, J., Nicholls, C.M. and Ormston, R. (eds.) (2013) *Qualitative research practice: A guide for social science students and researchers*. SAGE.
Rose, G. (2022) *Visual methodologies: An introduction to researching with visual materials*. SAGE.
Roth-Cohen, M.O., Kanevska, H.S. and Eisend, M. (2023) 'Gender roles in online advertising', *Journal of Gender Studies*, 32(2), pp. 186–200.
Shirani, F. and Henwood, K. (2011) 'Taking one day at a time: Temporal experiences in the context of unexpected life course transitions', *Time & Society*, 20(1), pp. 49–68.
Soar, M. (2000) 'Encoding advertisements: Ideology and meaning in advertising production', *Mass Communication & Society*, 3(4), pp. 415–437.
Svensson, M. (2013) 'Norms in law and society: Towards a definition of the socio-legal concept of norms', in *Social and legal norms: Towards a socio-legal understanding of normativity*. Routledge.
Svensson, E.M. and Edström, M., (2016) 'Market-driven challenges to freedom of expression and the interaction between the state, the market, and the media'. *Nordicom Review*, 37(2), pp. 1–16.
Timmer, A.S. (2016) 'Gender stereotyping in the case law of the EU Court of Justice', *European Equality Law Review*, 1, pp. 37–46.
Turillazzi, A., Taddeo, M., Floridi, L. and Casolari, F. (2023) 'The digital services act: An analysis of its ethical, legal, and social implications', *Law, Innovation and Technology*, 15(1), pp. 83–106.
Van Hoecke, M. (2015) 'Methodology of comparative legal research', *Law and Method*, pp. 1–35.
Wen, N., Chia, S.C. and Xiaoming, H. (2017) 'Does gender matter? Testing the influence of presumed media influence on young people's attitudes toward cosmetic surgery', *Sex Roles*, 76, pp. 436–447.
Wheeler, S. and Thomas, P. in Hayton, D. (2000) *Law's future(s)*. Bloomsbury Publishing.
Wilkinson, S. (1999a) 'Focus groups in feminist research: Power, interaction, and the co-construction of meaning', in *Women's studies international forum*. Pergamon, Vol. 21, No. 1, pp. 111–125.
Wilkinson, S. (1999b) 'How useful are focus groups in feminist research?' In Barbour, R. S. and Kitzinger, J. (eds.), *Developing focus group research: Politics, theory and practice*. Sage Publications Ltd., pp. 64–78.

Case law

Case C-20/71 *Sabbatini (Nee Bertoni) v European Parliament* [1972]

Case CC-149/77 *Gabrielle Defrenne v Société anonyme belge de navigation aérienne Sabena* [1978]
Cases C-34–46/95 Konsumentombudsmannen v De Agostini (Svenska) Forlag AB [1997]
Case C-412/93 Leclerc Siplec Société d'Importation v TFI Publicite & M6 Publicite [1995] ECR I-00179
Case C-267 and 268/91 Bernard Keck and Daniel Mithouard [1993] ECR I-6097

Legislation

Council Directive 2004/113/EC of 13 December 2004 implementing the principles of equal treatment between men and women in the access to and supply of goods and services [2004] OJ L 373
Council Directive 2018/1808/EU on the coordination of certain provisions laid down by law, regulation or administrative action in Member States concerning the provision of audio-visual media services (Audio-visual Media Services Directive) [2018] OJ L95/1
Regulation (EU) 2022/2065 of the European Parliament and of the Council of 19 October 2022 on a Single Market For Digital Services and amending Directive 2000/31/EC (Digital Services Act)
Communication from the commission to the European Parliament, The Council, The European economic and social committee and the committee of the regions A Union of Equality: Gender Equality Strategy 2020–2025 COM/2020/152 final
Ley Organica 1/2004 Medidas de Protección Integral contra la Violencia de Género. 28th December 2004 (BOE-A-2004-21740)

Chapter 2

EU competences

Introduction

For the last 60 years, the EU has acted as a vanguard in the battle against gender discrimination, and a comprehensive legal framework now exists in this field (Guerrina et al., 2023; Dustin et al., 2019). However, despite progress in many areas, including maternity and employment rights, much work is needed in addressing the use of harmful gender stereotypes that help (re)produce entrenched inequalities between men and women across Europe (Timmer, 2016; Frańczak, 2022). The EU's development of anti-discrimination and gender equality law therefore remains limited in scope, residing predominantly in the market and public sphere with progress limited to the workplace and childcare. Beyond the these sites for anti-discrimination law, the EU has been less successful, and little progress has been made in tackling an array of issues that women face in their day-to-day lives: for example, women are more often than not the victims of all forms of violence; more likely to be single parents; and at risk of poverty, social exclusion, precarious living arrangements and worse levels of physical and mental health (The European Institute for Gender Equality (2024)). Cook and Cusack (2010) have argued that one of the predominant causes of these issues is harmful gender stereotypes in society, in which women are increasingly portrayed in limiting and derogatory ways. These representations of women manifest via different cultural channels: through primary socialisation at childhood, in the home, and through parenting and the family through to secondary socialisation in school, from peers and from wider influences such as media and advertising. It is at this juncture that the book begins. The portrayal of men and women in the media and, more specifically, digital and analogue advertising is perceived as a problematic area for lawyers, sociologists and psychologists alike. These fields of study share the same overarching questions: how should the state regulate content on new forms of media, what safeguarding should be put in place and at what age?

I begin this chapter by introducing the two main interlocking competences that will inform the rest of the book: media and anti-discrimination. These

DOI: 10.4324/9781003336037-2

two competences will provide some context for how the regulation of gender stereotypes in advertising became an issue that the EU wished to tackle. The discussion will also chart EU's route into the Services Directive 2004/113/EC and show how and why advertising was excluded from the final directive. As with many of the competences that have slowly been carved out by the EU, there was no mention of gender equality, media or advertising regulation in the founding Treaty of Rome in 1957. These areas have developed as the EU has enlarged over the last 70 years and has been compelled to respond to social and technological shifts. Regardless of when, how or why the competences have evolved, it is worth noting at the start that there are fundamental issues at the heart of the term itself. As Barnard and Peers (2023) note, there are numerous problems with the term 'competence', in particular issues around *ultra vires* and subsidiarity: who has the capacity to introduce new legislation, the member state or the EU? This often results in further issues, such as 'turf wars' denoting questions such as which of the director generals of the EU Commission has the authority to draft secondary legislation or policy (Mastenbroek, 2005)? For example, when drafting legislation concerning gender equality, is it for the Directorate General of Social Affairs or Employment to provide secondary legislation? There are also problems with the semantics of the term: does competence indicate 'power' or 'legal authority', or is it something much broader (Barnard and Peers, 2023: 104)? These issues have been somewhat rectified by the Treaty of Lisbon (2009) provisions which provide guidance on who does what by introducing a 'competence catalogue' (Zeitlin, 2005). In the second part of the chapter, I turn my focus to the role of the ECtHR and the CJEU and how they have shaped the media (and, inherently, advertising) competence by looking at the jurisprudence of both courts.

Anti-discrimination competence

Gender equality was by no means intended to enter the social level of EU (Masselot, 2007; Sarikakis and Nguyen, 2009). Instead, this competence has developed, in part, as an economic consideration from the Treaty of Rome. The now-famous 'equal pay for equal work' emerged during the drafting of the treaty, when France single-handedly argued that it was necessary to include the principle in order to circumvent competition from the founding member states. At the time, France was the only founding member state in which workers were entitled to equal pay and therefore was afraid its businesses would be under-priced by companies based in other member states that did not enjoy the same equal treatment principle.

Since then, the EU has slowly managed to play a progressive role in ensuring that gender equality is safeguarded in its member states through the use of Article 119 (now 157 TFEU) of the Treaty of Rome, which is firmly anchored in the treaty's labour market provision. Article 157 provides that the then–European Economic Community (EEC) would promote 'equal pay for men and women for work of equal value'. The intention of this treaty provision, however, is not one based on protecting fundamental rights; as Millns states, Article 157 should not be mistaken for an effort to actively promote gender equality—rather, it should be read as a principle to ensure fair competition within the common market amongst the original founding member states of the EU and curb wage inequality (2017: 253). This has since provided a green light to the commission—and, more importantly, to the CJEU—to play a more active role in developing gender equality policy from the 1970s to present day. Article 157 TFEU was quickly picked up and developed by the CJEU through the single-market ideology of the provision. In *Defrenne v Sabina* (1976), the CJEU argued that the article acted as both a social *and* an economic objective.

The European Commission were equally quick to grasp the potential ramifications of Article 157 TFEU and did so by adopting secondary legislation. In the 1970s, the commission initiated two directives on equal pay and social security (Council Directives 75/117EEC and 79/7/EEC). During the 1990s, further secondary legislation provided more rights for citizens, covering pregnant workers and parental leave (Council Directive 92/85/EEC). In 2002, the EU provided a consolidation of the equal treatment directives and adopted the Equal Treatment in Employment Directive (2000/78/EC 2000), which extended the legislation to cover sexual harassment in the workplace and indirect discrimination. In 2004, for the first time, the commission sought to tackle discrimination outside the workplace by introducing the Goods and Services Gender Council Directive 2004/113/EC (2004). As Millns notes, the EU's policy surrounding gender equality is 'rather like the development of the Treaties underpinning EU law, a piece-meal, ad-hoc and incremental process' (2017: 252). This assessment was a commonly held view amongst most EU gender equality commentators at the time of the drafting of the GSD (Masselot, 2007; Walby, 2004) as well as legal feminist critiques that the EU is yet to fully tackle gender equality outside the workplace and in the private sphere (Kantola, 2010). The 'amending' treaties of Amsterdam (1996) and Lisbon (2009) help in remedying this criticism but, more importantly, further ossify the anti-discrimination competence.

Gender equality competence

Between the amending treaties, the EU sought to strengthen its anti-discrimination competence. There was also a shift in the semantics of the competence, with the 'limited language' of sex discrimination replaced with the language of human rights and gender equality (Millns, 2017). It could now be argued that the gender competence had become burrowed amongst the broader system of human rights protection of EU/ECHR. Since 1999, the EU has had powers to take appropriate action to combat discrimination based on sex, racial or ethnic origin, religion or belief, disability, age or sexual orientation. The Treaty of Amsterdam positioned gender equality as a priority, and it now enjoys an elevated position amongst the other EU goals and values.[1] The promotion of gender equality has had an important effect on the initiation of representation in advertising policy which is rooted in the wider scope of Article 19 TFEU (ex 13 EC). Rather than the neutral reactive tone of the directives of the past, the Treaty of Amsterdam worked towards a proactive stance to help shape future secondary legislation and EU policy, with the notion that equality is only achievable if individuals claim their rights by reacting to a discriminatory issue. In contrast, the proactive model of gender mainstreaming (2020 EU Gender Action Plan) provides that all EU institutions at all levels are obliged to promote equality. The action plan concludes the promotion of gender equality in all EU development projects, policies and EU institutions that may affect the rights of girls and women.

From a theoretical perspective, the EU has shifted towards a more substantive approach in achieving gender equality since the Treaty of Amsterdam, with top-down positive action and further engagement with NGOs, women's groups and other non-state actors. A good example of this shift in approach can be seen when comparing the *reactive* Equal Pay Directive 75/117/EU (1975) and the *proactive* and substantive 'Women on Boards' Council Directive 2022/2381 (2022). The introduction of Article 19 can therefore be seen as a reborn 'new' non-discrimination gender competence that has the scope to prohibit discrimination beyond the economic limitation of the internal market (Carraciolo Di Torella, 2005). Equally, it can be seen as an extension of Article 157 (ex 141), and there are some understated differences that shall be discussed now.

Between the bookends of the Amsterdam and Lisbon treaties, the EU had made further attempts to constitutionalise gender equality through the creation of the Charter of Fundamental Rights and the failed Constitutional Convention (with its ensuing Constitutional Treaty) of the European Union. With both came the repositioning of gender equality and women's rights, further cementing the notion of a solid gender competence. The initial aim of the EU was to showcase the disorganised 'shopping list' style of fundamental rights that had accumulated over the previous decades into a single coherent document. The charter's third chapter is devoted to equality, and Article 23 clearly specifies that equality between men and women shall be ensured 'in all areas' with the quasi-limitation 'including employment and pay'. Although this is

1 Gender equality is now perceived as an 'aim' and 'task' of the EU under Article 8 TFEU (ex-Article 3 EC). Article 10 TFEU confirms this approach by applying gender equality principle horizontally: 'in defining and implementing its policies and activities, the union shall aim to combat discrimination based on sex, racial or ethnic origin, religion, belief, disability age or sexual orientation'.

a departure from the traditional setting of gender equality that has historically been tied in to the workplace, the charter appears to regurgitate a mere statement of equality that does not create a specific legal right (Millns, 2017). Moreover, Article 23 provides for vague 'positive action' and is merely a repeat of Article 157 TFEU. The Constitutional Treaty, on the other hand, has a slightly different pathway. As a reaction to the EU enlargement of 2004 with ten new member states, the EU sought to further augment women's rights by providing a European Constitution that would reinforce the core values of the Union. The drafting of the original European Constitution initially omitted the term 'gender equality', but it was eventually included after intense lobbying from then–UK Commissioner Viviane Reding. Both France and Netherlands returned a 'no' vote in respective referendums, and so the brakes were firmly pulled on project. From the ashes of the failed Constitutional Treaty came the Treaty of Lisbon, including very similar content as the Constitutional Treaty and the core values of the EU in Article 2. According to Masselot (2007), during the period between the constitutionalisation of Europe and Lisbon, there was some concern and confusion on the positioning of the gender equality as a right and shared value of the EU. Furthermore, for some time, there had been loud criticism of 'competence creep' from member states—that the EU, by any means, always manages to legislate or act in areas in which there is no conferred or a specific competence (Weatherill, 2014; Garben, 2019). To remedy this problem, a clear competence catalogue was produced to provide guidance on EU powers. The catalogue inclusion is one of the most substantial shifts towards a constitutional approach to gender equality, particularly with regards to providing for a clear gender competence. Lisbon delivers a wide-ranging list of competences that are to be enjoyed by the EU institutions and a clear set of rules on demarcation of competences that shall be enjoyed by the EU member states (De Witte, 2012). Prior to Lisbon, competences were not entirely explicit, and the EU previously relied on the principle of conferred power (Rossi, 2012).

Competences and the principle of conferral in a post-Lisbon Europe raises more questions than it provides answers when it comes to EU involvement with gender equality. The principle of conferral is a chaotic subject; however, Article 3–5 TEU sets out guidance on whether it is the EU or the member states that wield the competence to legislate on certain issues. Article 5(1) and 5(2) provide that there are limits to what can be acted on under the EU treaties and where the member states retain their own competence. Article 26–197 TFEU provides for further specific areas or the 'nuts and bolts' of what the EU can do (Weatherill, 2014: 35). Article 3 TEU lists exclusive competences (areas in which the EU alone has competence to act: e.g. customs union, competition rules and fisheries), Article 4 lists shared competences (internal market, consumer protection public health) and Article 5 lists 'supporting' competences (those in which the EU can intervene to support member states). Hence, there is a clear 'precedent' of the EU acting in gender-related issues, and it is for the legislative arm of the EU to define where gender 'fits' amongst the conferred competences. For example, the regulation of gender stereotypes in advertising can fit in numerous (shared) competences: sexist or harmful content advertising could potentially be 'dressed up' as a health issue, an internal market issue or a consumer protection issue. This notion is addressed in Chapter 3 when considering the drafting of GSD.

Post Lisbon: new and old inequalities

When considering the wider anti-discrimination policy or 'institutional gender regime' (MacRae, 2006: 530; Walby, 2004) of the EU, there remain numerous challenges both inside and outside the labour market, with the latter a priority for those concerned with gender justice. This manifests in a visible and segregated gendered job market where 'women's work' is paid less and women disproportionately working as carers and primary educators and make up the majority of the primary healthcare sector (Eurostat). This segregation is augmented by a pan-European pay gap which, despite half a decade of secondary legislation covering equal pay and equal treatment at work,[2] currently stands at 18.2%. The trilogy of economic crises (the 2008 economic crisis, austerity measures and the COVID-19 pandemic) and their far-reaching consequences have disproportionately affected women's lives and widened the pay gap. Each overlapping crisis has pushed more women into part-time and/or precarious work, reliant on social welfare provisions, and further ossified gender norms both at home and in the workplace, leaving women outside national social security policies, with smaller pensions and at higher risk of poverty or socially exclusion (Rubery, 2015; Karamessini and Rubery, 2014; Cook and Grimshaw, 2021; Guerrina and Masselot, 2018; Meraviglia and Dudka, 2021; Guerrina, MacRae and Masselot, 2023). Equally, political inequality still remains prevalent throughout Europe, in underrepresentation in cabinet, government and national parliaments (The European Institute for Gender Equality or acronym EIGE, 2024; UN Women, 2023). Inequalities beyond political, economic and social rights are increasingly linked to civil rights: for example, domestic violence, gender-based violence, reproductive rights and sexual orientation remain issues in the EU member states. The symbiotic relationship between the economy and equality remains unchallenged in European law, in which little attention is paid to

2 See, for example: Council Directive 75/117/EEC on the approximation of the laws of the member states relating to the application of the principle of equal pay for men and women (1975) OJ L045; Council Directive 2000/78/EC of 27 November 2000, establishing a general framework for equal treatment in employment and occupation; OJ L/303 and Council Directive 2006/54/EC of the European Parliament and of the Council of 5 July 2006 on the implementation of the principle of equal opportunities and equal treatment of men and women in matters of employment and occupation.

why business trumps the 'leftover' or 'residual' inequalities that face women across the European Union (Fredman, 2022: 36)

Harmful gender stereotypes in advertising fall within the 'residual' categorisation, and, as an anti-discrimination competence issue, it has been for the last decade part of the EU's wider 'wish list' of contemporary forms of gender inequality. These new(er) societal, private-sphere inequalities can be seen as a departure from what can be deemed as the old(er) EU legislative agenda that has espoused a lengthy list of directives, action programmes and policy frameworks that ensure gender equality through an economic prism. The recognition of new forms of gender inequality in itself would seem to denote progress. The 'old' and 'new' inequalities are two sides of the same coin; one cannot be solved without the other. With this in mind, gender stereotypes in advertising are a form of discrimination promoting traditional conservative gender roles that markedly affect education, career choices and a segregated job market, increasing the pay gap between men and women throughout Europe. Although legally and habitually considered a private-sphere issue, gender stereotypes in advertising have a direct effect on the market-based gender equality concerns of the EU. In Chapter 3, I further discuss the slow acknowledgement and incorporation of gender stereotypes in advertising as a 'new' policy area of the EU gender regime by locating the heightened role and influence of social partners in the legislative process and the enhanced and strengthened use of 'soft law' that has gained ground in recent years.

The EU has been relatively successful in carving out an anti-discrimination competence, and it is yet to be fully realised or reached its limits. EU institutions have been effective in gently coaxing its member states to promote gender equality, both as a political and legal endeavour that has accumulated a catalogue of secondary legislation. It is clear that the EU has come a long way in creating a stable competence: for example, eradicating sex discrimination in the workplace is dominated by EU law. However, concerns such as trafficking are yet to be fully realised. As a result, the gender competence is limited and is resilient only in certain areas: namely, those that are unambiguously inclusive in their economic competence, with sex discrimination predominantly fought in the workplace through equal pay, social security and maternity measures.

The EU's commitment to gender equality also shifted in both the Charter of Fundamental Rights and the Lisbon Treaty, which have sought to bolster the principle of gender equality and gender mainstreaming, allowing the EU to further promote and ensure gender equality in its member states (Guerrina, MacRae and Masselot, 2023). Yet this commitment is very much based on the political goodwill of the Union and its institutions. Political will is too often a fragile affair, and as the fallout of Brexit comes more into focus, it is evident that the UK risks losing a layer of rights that has protected its citizens for the last 50 years. Without the safety net of the EU's anti-discrimination competence, it would seem that UK citizens are potentially at serious risk of losing the protection that the EU has fought to achieve (Sanders and Flavell, 2023). As Guerrina and Masselot (2018) concede, it is both difficult to forecast the full extent of the damage that Brexit will cause to the wider EU gender regime or, indeed, fully envisage what a post-Brexit gender regime may look like. The most significant and inevitable factor is that as Brexit begins to dismantle the scaffolding provided in the foundations of treaties, it may become evident that the soft law approaches that have the biggest impact on the UK will be diminished.

The emerging European media competence

Unlike the anti-discrimination competence, European law has sought to regulate cross-border broadcasting since the inception of the European Convention of Human Rights in 1949 and the Treaty of Rome in 1957. The overarching uncertainty back in those early days was which body would act first. Neither document contained an explicit reference to media, nor, understandably, was there any reference to advertising. For the initial phase of the ECHR, early cross-border broadcasting case law found itself in the European Court of Human Rights (ECtHR) with legal questions from signatory states on censorship and the restriction of 'ideas and information' (Barendt et al., 2013). At this point, there were few cases on the issue, except cross-border broadcasting of radio, and it was not until the late 1980s, with improved access to satellite broadcasting, that cross-border broadcasting (including advertising) regulation began to formulate. The early case law on freedom of information and radio broadcasting did, however, remind parties to the convention that they must ensure they could justify any legislation that hindered or restricted freedom of expression (Article 10 ECHR). Through the development and expansion of satellite television and cable TV operators, the European Court of Human Rights' piecemeal approach buckled, and a common television framework was initiated through the European Convention on Trans-Frontier Television (Television Convention). Nevertheless, the bulk of the effort towards regulating cross-border broadcasting—and, specifically, competence on advertising—has been initiated by the EU's jurisdiction.

The ECHR intervention is partly due to technological changes and shared languages between European states. The traditional printed press and radio were the most popular formats of 1950s, with television for the masses still in its infancy. Up to this point, it was common courtesy between the states to share the radio waves. As more countries with common languages joined the European community, the notion of media regulation became ripe. Germany and Austria, the Benelux, France, Portugal and Spain had always enjoyed cross-border broadcasting and printed presses, but due to satellite technology and customer subscriptions, cross-border broadcasting became an obvious oversight. The case law throughout the late 1980s and early 1990s—which runs somewhat parallel to the jurisdiction of the CJEU—doesn't just expose the change in media consumption but equally highlights the courts' insistence on reminding European governments that they must justify any legislation that would restrict cross-border technology and broadcasting. In *Groppera Radio AG* [1990] *and Others v Switzerland* [2011], the applicants challenged a national ban on a radio station that featured advertisements, claiming that such a ban would infringe on freedom of expression rights and overstep the right to 'impart information and ideas regardless of frontiers' under Article 10 ECHR. In *Autronic*, the court found that the Swiss government's prohibition on broadcasts received in an un-encoded format also contravened Article 10 ECHR, highlighting that it is not merely the content but equally the means of transmission. Almost twenty years later, in *Khurshid Mustafa*, the ECtHR held that a tenant's private tenancy agreement, which prohibited the applicant from positioning a satellite dish on the front of his flat, contravened Article 10. In parallel to the ECtHR case law, the European Convention on Trans Frontier Television (1989) began the process of a common framework on European Broadcasting, ensuring freedom of expression in broadcasting. In brief, the convention lays down a legal framework ensuring the free circulation of TV programmes and advertising in Europe. The convention provided, for the first time, some common minimum standards and rules; most importantly, it opened the door to advertising sponsorship (product placement) and the protection of certain groups (e.g., women and children) from harm. The convention's main friction lies between the freedom of expression rights and the rights of individuals (e.g. incitement to hatred/protection of minors). This friction will be discussed further in subsequent chapters that analyse national perspectives on combatting gender stereotypes in advertising. In terms of advertising standards, the common rules are basic and feature very little towards women's rights. Tobacco, gambling and medicine are the three main products and services in play. Simultaneously, the EU was working on this same area and some of the gaps in the convention are now plugged by EU secondary legislation and soft law across both the gender and media competences.

EU media and advertising competence

As television and satellite technology generated case law and consensus grew amongst its signatory states, the EU media competence became a much more strained affair as it moved beyond the language of freedom of expression rights of Article 10 ECHR and its complainants (Castendyk et al., 2008). Media and advertising are now—broadly speaking—secured within the EU's competence catalogue despite the two terms not being mentioned in the original Treaty of Rome. The EU's capacity to legislate in this field is 'considerably controversial' (Barendt et al., 2013: 201) due to the initial lack of competence, and, unlike the EU's anti-discrimination competence, there was no mention of media regulation in the establishing treaty. Media and advertising entered the lexicon of EU law through what was then the European Economic Community's (EEC) efforts to establish a common market and four freedoms (Articles 34–56 TFEU: goods, services, persons and establishment). With the increase of cross-border trade and free movement of persons and workers, it was inevitable that the CJEU would be forced to react to member states that were seen to be contravening the four freedoms. As previously outlined, the ECtHR were forced to act on market forces and cross-border advertising, and the CJEU would likewise be coerced into reacting to free-market principles and an ever-enlarging European Union. As member states joined the EU, competition within the media and broadcasting industries increased, and in 1974, the CJEU received its first preliminary question from Italy on the issue. *Sacchi* [1974] is now regarded as the beginning of the court's involvement in the area. Sacchi, the owner of a cable company that received transmitted TV programmes in Italy, refused to pay the Italian state licence fee. At the time, the Italian government had provided Radio Audioszione Italiana (RAI) a monopoly on broadcasting, and in refusing to pay, Sacchi argued that such a monopoly in the market restricted the reception of foreign TV shows in Italy and therefore acted as a barrier to the free movement of goods. The CJEU rejected Sacchi's argument but acknowledged for the first time that advertising was a service and consequently covered by the then–EEC treaty provision. Under EU law, media products are now generally covered as services or goods and scrutinised by the free movement principles that underpin EU law. *Saachi* solidified the link between the media, law and EU competences; however, it left some areas wide open. For example, there has been a wider discussion of whether domestic goods and services can directly discriminate against foreign goods/services. Case law in this area is guided by Articles 36 TFEU (goods) and 52 TFEU (services). The dominant discourse in both advertising and media (and also the internal market more broadly) is whether something is a good or service and will be looked at later in the chapter. Articles 36 and 52 TFEU both allow for member states to justify their measures; for example, in the case of *Rewe*, foreign products may be legitimately banned if they can objectively be perceived as contravening public health or morality. For such a justification to be accepted by the court, it must be shown to be proportionate. In *Bond Van Adverteeders* [1988], the Dutch government argued that the aim of limiting the number of foreign satellite channels that were broadcast in the Netherlands was justifiable. The Dutch argument was based on ensuring plurality: that political, cultural and social strands of Dutch society were guaranteed a certain amount of public airtime on television. Dutch authorities ensured this through the regulation of TV airtime and arranged advertising time limits across the different services providers. Cable and satellite network providers considered the state's advertising code far too strict, and, to circumvent their adverts, the broadcasters decided to leave the Netherlands and operate out of neighbouring Luxembourg and Belgium where the regulatory code and state measures were more relaxed.

EU media law has not only sought to catch discriminatory measures and national laws that impede free movement of TV services, but it has also caught rules that apply without discrimination to foreign or domestic services. For example, it has caught rules on the limitation and length of advertising that appears on terrestrial television as well as measures that ensure the broadcaster allots a certain amount of time and the programmes are in the national language or autonomous dialect/language. Such examples could fairly easily hinder free movement rights across EU televisions and satellite markets. The CJEU has also ruled on 'indistinctly applicable' measures: rules that are effectively indiscriminate, affecting both domestic and foreign advertising. In such instances, member states are allowed a certain amount of flexibility to justify their laws or advertising codes and regulatory standards. The most notable case from this area is on the protection of children. In *De Agostini* [1995], the court agreed with Sweden's total ban on children's television advertising, which the state justified on public health grounds. The facts of the case involved television advertising relayed via the UK to Sweden by state satellite television company TV3. The content was then broadcast on TV3, TV4 and the Home Shopping Channel in Sweden. The claimant, the Swedish advertising regulator, argued that the advertising consortium's adverts breached the Swedish advertising regulatory code. At the time, the Swedish regulator scrutinised the content of adverts that could be shown to children. The advert in question was a weekly 'collect them all'–style magazine in which subscribers (children) were sold a magazine that included a different part of a dinosaur each week. At the time, the Swedish code specifically prohibited advertising that was directly aimed at children under the age of 12. The Italian magazine producer De Agostini argued that the state regulatory code had breached EU free movement of services provisions by effectively blocking an Italian company from penetrating the Swedish children's magazine market. The CJEU held that the Swedish ban on advertising aimed at minors did amount to a breach of free movement rights but agreed with the Swedish ombudsman's claim that such restrictions were justifiable on public health grounds relating to the protection of minors.

Post-*Sacchi* [1974], *Bond Van Adverteeders* [1988] and *De Agostini*, the EU has focused on harmonising member states' regulatory standards and principles. This was galvanised by both the European Parliament[3] and, later, the commission through its Television Without Borders Green Paper.[4] The commission set out some basic hopes (harmonisation and standards) but also highlighted some fears (the US satellite completion) and was therefore not altogether about harmonisation but had more to do with competition law. The harmonisation of EU standards is well known for its complexity and

3 European Parliament Report drawn up on behalf of the Committee on Youth, Culture, Education, Information and Sport on radio and television broadcasting in the European Community. Working Documents 1981–1982 Doc 1013/81.

4 Television Without Borders Green Paper COM (84) 300 FINAL.

co-ordinating rules across a diverse media and broadcasting landscape that has within it conflicting regulatory standards; the commission at the time were left with a near-impossible task. Like other harmonisation programmes, the EU imposed minimum standards which all member states had to abide by but could—if they wished—impose higher standards, including banning certain goods or services (e.g. certain forms of advertising) from other member states that did not conform to the host's regulatory code. For example, certain member states may choose to set higher standards for their domestic services (e.g. the UK and the BBC) than for imported services (cable/satellite TV). In 1989, simultaneous with the Television Convention, the EU's Television Without Frontiers (TWFD) sought to regulate EU member states' satellite broadcasting and advertising. The TWFD received stark criticism from academics who suggested that the directive was regulating European television but also watering down cultural difference amongst and within the member states (Kleinsteuber and Sonnenberg, 1990). They were also criticised by individual member states with media lobbying, such as the UK and Germany, whose criticism came at a time when both were seeking to liberalise the market at a much faster speed (Gibbons and Humphreys, 2012).

Overall, the move towards harmonisation ought to be read through the prism of technological change, a political-economic shift towards the neoliberalisation of the market (particularly UK, Germany and Luxembourg) and increased competition from the US. Gibbons and Humphreys have argued that the TWFD is a 'classic piece of negative [EU] integration' (2012: 37), blaming member states such as the UK (which strongly supported the directive) for the neoliberalisation of media and advertising markets. The timing of the TWFD, which came into force in 1990 (one year after the Television Convention), is also relevant as the two instruments covered same areas: advertising and the protection of minors.[5]

With the foresight and power of the internet, catch-up TV and online services, the TWFD was radically amended and renamed the Audio-visual Media Services Directive 2018/1808/EC (revised in 2023). The AVMS directive will be looked at more closely when scrutinising secondary legislation (Chapter 3). However, it is worth noting a few of the transitions from TWFD to AVMS and the current media law that now operates as a regulatory framework in the EU. Unlike the TWFD, the AVMS directive covers audio-visual content and, more importantly, covers content irrespective of the technology that is used to deliver it. This is a significant transformation as there had been a gap in EU and international media law on this specific area. In the face of new technology and new emerging platforms, the EU have been keen

5 In 1997, the TWFD was amended to clarify on the rules protecting minors. See Directive 97/36/EC Amending Council Directive 89/552/EEC on the co-ordination of certain provisions laid down by law regulation administrative action in member states concerning the pursuit of television broadcasting activities [1997] OJ L 202/60.

to protect younger audiences through the AVMS directive. The current directive's net is has been cast wider in recent years, and the content regulated by the legislation can be audio-visual in nature but may be accessed through smartphone, tablet or TV and now covers video-sharing platforms (VSPs) and social media. The directive also regulates live, catch-up and video-on-demand (VOD) TV. It is at this juncture that the AVMS directive makes a clear distinction—catch-up TV and VOD are now covered by the AVMS directive along with traditional broadcast services. In terms of advertising regulation, the directive has also simplified the rules (Article 3(e)) on sponsored content. The monitoring of advertising, particularly product-placement adverts, has been a major concern for the commission, and the AVMS directive goes some way in regulating such advertisements.

Advertising regulatory standards and free movement case law

So far, I have demonstrated how the EU's media competence was initially manufactured through the ECtHR, involving satellite transmission and cross-border broadcasting. It is also the case that the CJEU has been equally instrumental in shaping media competence through its decisions on cross-border advertising regulation and policy (Kraft, 2007). Under the guise of free movement provisions in Articles 34 and 56 TFEU, the court has been involved in a number of cases concerning minors and advertisers. As the single market has expanded, member states have restricted certain forms of advertising content to certain times of the day and placed limitations on length and frequency and, more recently, personalised advertisements. Advertising regulation is diverse across the EU member states; some states have legitimate justifications in place to protect the public for different reasons: public health, promotion of ethics and moral standards, taste and decency, culture and language and the protection of children. Over time, these justifications—or regulatory standards—have been deemed not just obstacles to free trade but also a distortion of competition between member states and within the advertising market, favouring domestic over foreign goods. Member states such as Sweden have sought to protect children and young adults through their advertising ombudsman, as opposed to to other member states with more neoliberal approaches to advertising. In these instances, the CJEU has shown little reluctance in intervening if a member state's advertising code has hindered free movement. In the next section, I provide a brief overview and some analysis of the free movement rules that govern the single market and case law that dissects free movement, advertising regulation and justifications that the CJEU have considered.

Article 34 TFEU prohibits quantitative restrictions (QRs) on imports and all measures having equivalent effect (MEQRs) with the supplementary Directive 70/50 EEC providing a fuller definition of an MEQR: all measures that 'prohibit or limit publicity in respect of imported products only, or totally or partially confine publicity to domestic products only'. Article 3 of the directive also controls measures governing the marketing of products which apply to domestic and imported goods alike. According to Kraft (2007: 517), the CJEU has thus made clear that Article 34 catches all rules and regulations (measures) which place additional burdens on the marketing of imported goods, whether they discriminate on their face or in their effect (distinctly and indistinctly applicable rules). In addition to secondary legislation, the CJEU has over the years pursued the task of defining an MEQR, ensuring that any barrier to trade is removed to ensure the free movement treaty provisions operate fully.

The case of *Dassonville* [1974] provides the seminal definition that an MEQR covers 'all trading rules . . . capable of hindering, directly or indirectly, actually or potentially, intra community trade'. In the famous case of *Cassis de Dijon* [1979], the court developed the definition further, providing legal tests for the national courts to apply ad hoc. *Cassis de Dijon* involved a piece of German legislation which prescribed a minimum alcohol content of 25% ABV on fruit-based liqueurs and, in doing so, prevented German importers and supermarkets from selling French liqueur (marketed and advertised at 15–20% ABV). The German rule was found to be 'indistinctly applicable' to both the domestic and imported goods alike. The court, as was the case in *Dassonville* [1974], found that the German measure fell within the scope of the article and therefore amounted to an MEQR. The ruling established two vital concepts: first, the principle of mutual recognition of regulatory standards, whereby if a product has been subjected to one set of regulatory standards in the country of origin, it should then be allowed access to the importing country without another set of regulatory standards applied. Any additional statutory or regulatory controls were therefore deemed contrary to EU law and caught by Article 34. Secondly, *Cassis de Dijon* opened the door for member states to objectively justify their advertising regulatory restrictions. Although eventually rejected by the court, the German defence argued that the measure served to protect public health, signalling to the average German consumer that fruit liqueurs have high alcohol content, and a lower ABV would mislead the consumer. Notwithstanding the justification, the court was forced to acknowledge that Germany's advertising and labelling law was genuinely aimed at protecting the consumer rather than restricting trade and distorting competition in the drinks market. The German argument did not pass the proportionality test as better labelling or guidance for consumers would be sufficient. This argument has been successfully applied in other cases: for example, *Commission v Germany* [1987], in which a German regulatory standard prohibited the marketing of beer hops, barley and water only. Similarly, in *Commission v Spain* [2003], the regulation prohibited the marketing and advertising of bleach with chlorine greater than 35g per litre. As Kraft notes, national advertising and labelling measures 'aimed at protecting ill informed, unobservant or reckless consumers were rendered incompatible with the single market' (2007: 517).

The legacy of *Cassis de Dijon* [1979] is found in the Misleading Advertising Directive 84/450/EEC and Unfair Consumer Practices Directive 2005/09/EC. Both pieces of legislation introduced harmonisation and minimum standard measures for advertising, aiding companies wishing to penetrate new markets whilst balancing the protection of consumer rights. The broad definition (and justifications) built into *Dassonville* [1974] and *Cassis de Dijon* have equally caused a lot of uncertainty in the jurisprudence of free movement, specifically the reach of Article 34 (Steiner, 1992). Post–*Dassonville* and *Cassis de Dijon*, the courts were awash with free movement litigation with larger companies testing whether or not national laws amounted to a hindrance to free movement provisions, which left the CJEU unaware of how to deal with trade complaints made by or against national regulatory bodies.[6] The jurisprudence and rules that derived from *Keck* [1993] acted as a sieve and remedied the relentless case law flooding the court. Paragraphs 16 and 17 of the decision rupture the original definition of an MEQR by providing that national laws or regulations that are seen to restrict or prohibit 'certain selling arrangements' that apply to traders 'operating within the national territory' will not be caught by article 34. *Keck* [1993] has had a profound effect on advertising rules and regulation and has since found advertising cases under the banner and categorisation of 'selling arrangements'. For example, in *Gourmet International Products*, the Swedish advertising ombudsman placed a blanket ban on adverts featuring alcohol with more than 2.5% ABV (except at point of sale) on radio and TV and in print. A total ban clearly restricted free movement provisions; if the state prohibited non-national producers of alcoholic beverages, the consumer would be less aware and therefore less likely purchase non-Swedish alcohol.

Advocate General Jacobs's opinion in *Leclerc-Siplec* [1995] is often regarded as a shift in the courts' argument or the 'beginning of a different interpretation of Article 34 in relation to advertising' (Enchelmaier et al., 2010: 158) as it acts as an important tool in developing a free market economy that allows for fairer competition. Prior to the landmark ruling in *Keck* [1993], the CJEU in the case of *Oosthoek* [1981] had always held that advertising restrictions should be caught by Article 34 as indistinctly applicable measures unless they could be justified. For example, in the joint cases of *Angonesa* [1990], restrictions on advertising of alcoholic drinks were viewed as contravening single-market principles and, accordingly, a breach of Article 34. The *Keck* [1993] decision did not reverse the jurisprudence of the court entirely; rather, Advocate General Jacobs's opinion marked a shift in the reading of Article 34 by emphasising that rather than a hindrance, advertising was an aid to competition and free trade ideology by allowing new products and services to penetrate untapped markets and, consequently, accessing trade in

6 See, for example, cross-border price fixing advertising case C-362/88 *GB-INNO-BM v Confederation du Commerce Luxembourgeois* [1990] I ECR 667.

new member states. According to Jacobs, advertising provides variety and mobility for the single market, and member states that seek to regulate or prohibit certain forms of advertising are directly or indirectly hindering free movement within the single market and also limiting the consumer's habits and behaviour. *Leclerc- Siplec* [1995], *Keck* [1993] and AG Jacobs's opinion have been influential in the CJEU jurisprudence. Thus, advertising regulatory standards is generally considered as 'selling arrangements' (i.e. the way in which a product or service is sold rather than the products' characteristics or qualities). Or, as the courts states in *Keck* [1993], selling arrangements fall outside Article 34 if they affect 'in the manner in law and in fact, the marketing of domestic products and those from Member States'.

In the late 1980s and early 1990s, the CJEU found numerous national measures that amounted to 'selling arrangements', and the jurisprudence of the time provides a broad definition of the term. For example, in the case *Puna Casa* [1993], national legislation limiting the time at which goods can be sold may not amount to a selling arrangement and, therefore, is not a breach of Article 34. Other examples include the opening of petrol stations (*Tankstation*), Sunday trading times (*Semeraro*), retail sale licences (*Burmanjer* [2003]) and measures that ensure infant milk is sold in public pharmacists (*Commission v Greece* [1995]). At this stage, the court suggested that national measures which place certain advertising restrictions (or regulation that is higher than already guaranteed at EU level) on advertising amounts to a selling arrangement and falls outside Article 34. Examples of advertising as a selling arrangement are somewhat dated but wide ranging: for example, German advertising regulation prohibiting private pharmacies from advertising para-pharma products outside the shop (*Hünermund* [1993]) and a Swedish blanket ban on advertising of alcohol across all forms of media (*Gourmet International Product*). In the case of *Karner* [2004], the court clarified its view on advertising, claiming that '[P]rovisions and advertising of those products as well as certain marketing methods are provisions governing selling arrangements', and in *Gourmet International Products* (prohibition of advertising alcohol), the Swedish regulator raised questions as to whether the state could protect its consumers from other member states' advertising when it did not meet national regulatory standards. In *Gourmet*, the blanket ban on alcohol advertising was found to be a clear breach of Article 34 because a total ban has a disproportionate impact on non-national/foreign imports accessing the market. The consumer will be less aware and therefore less likely to purchase non-national products. In both cases, the court stated that, whilst bans on advertising space and airtime would potentially breach Article 34, Sweden's public health justifications could be accepted but only if the national court found the measure to be proportionate, and there were no less restrictive ways of achieving the public health objectives of the bans. AG Geelhoed's opinion in *Douwe Egberts* [2004] appeared to be a slight departure from the *Keck/Leclerc* interpretation as the court abandoned selling arrangements altogether (Enchelmaier et al., 2010) and yet still argued that advertising should be caught by Article 34 TFEU.

Conclusion

This chapter has introduced the two main EU competences that bind this book together, anti-discrimination and media, and investigated the core question of if, when and where the EU has the capacity to regulate harmful content and gender stereotypes in advertising. The answer to this lies in what Sylvia Walby (2004, 2020) calls the 'gender regime' of the EU and the changing landscape of EU law from the very early notion of gender equality at the Treaty of Rome to the patchwork of legislation that the institutions developed from the 1970s onwards. Through the emergence of the EU's 'competence catalogue', the two competences have ossified over the years, allowing the EU to legislate in both areas, taking advantage of the political and technological shifts that have taken place since the 1990s across Europe. The EU has taken considerable steps to safeguard women's rights in all manner of areas, starting within the workplace but, more recently, in the private sphere where soft law approaches seem *de rigueur*. The Lisbon Treaty has encouraged EU institutions (in particular the CJEU and Parliament) to take a more hands-on approach in these areas, especially with gender equality; the use of gender stereotypes in (and outside) the workplace is seen as a threat to gender equality equal to that of substantive barriers such as work-based discrimination.

This chapter has also hinted at how 'soft law' options may remain the EU's most realistic tool for accelerating the regulation of gender stereotypes in advertising, especially within the anti-discrimination competence. As underlined in the final section of the chapter, the CJEU have not hesitated in shaping advertising regulation in the guise of a single market concern via the free movement articles of TFEU and through the wider remit of free movement case law. However, this is an area of case law that is currently dormant and has been since the rise of AG Jacobs's 'market access test'. It is apparent that the EU certainly have the capacity and political will to legislate on gender stereotypes in advertising as both areas have dominated the EU agenda for some time, and, as I will show in the following chapter, the EU have taken considerable steps to push for the removal of gender stereotypes in advertising through soft law approaches. Chapter 3 will move on to a more critical discussion of how gender stereotyping in advertising as a policy area has been pushed further up the EU agenda and an examination of the actors who have played a part in bringing this issue to the fore.

References

Barendt, E., Hitchens, L., Craufurd-Smith, R. and Bosland, J. (2013) *Media law: Text, cases and materials*. Pearson Higher Ed., pp. 195–196.

Barnard, C. and Peers, S. eds., (2023) *European Union Law*. Oxford University Press.
Carraciolo Di Torella, E. (2005) 'The Goods and Services Directive: Limitations and opportunities', *Feminist Legal Studies*, 13, pp. 337–347.
Castendyk, O., Dommering, E.J. and Scheuer, A. (2008) *European media law*. Kluwer Law International, p. 18.
Cook, R. and Cusack, S. (2010) *Gender stereotyping: Transnational legal perspectives*. University of Pennsylvania Press.
Cook, R. and Grimshaw, D. (2021) 'A gendered lens on COVID-19 employment and social policies in Europe', *European Societies*, 23(sup1), pp. S215–S227.
De Witte, B. in Ripley, S. (2012) *EU law after Lisbon*. Oxford: Oxford University Press.
Dustin, M., Ferreira, N. and Millns, S. (eds.) (2019) *Gender and queer perspectives on Brexit*. Springer.
Enchelmaier, S., Jarvis, M., Johnston, A. C., Norberg, S., Oliver, P. J., Stothers, C., and Weatherill, S. (2010) *Oliver on Free movement of goods in the European Union*. Bloomsbury Publishing.
The European Institute for Gender Equality or acronym EIGE, (2024) https://eige.europa.eu/publications-resources/publications/gender-balance-politics-november-2023
Frańczak, O. (2022) '(Stereo) typical law: Challenging the transformative potential of human rights', in Guney, G., Davies, D. and Lee, P.H. (eds.) *Towards gender equality in law*. Palgrave Macmillan, pp. 15–33.
Fredman, S. (2022) *Discrimation law*. Oxford University Press.
Garben, S. (2019) 'Competence creep revisited', *JCMS: Journal of Common Market Studies*, 57(2), pp. 205–222.
Gibbons, T. and Humphreys, P. (2012) *Audiovisual regulation under pressure: Comparative cases from North America and Europe*. Routledge, p. 37.
Guerrina, R., MacRae, H. and Masselot, A. (2023) 'Between a rock and a hard place: The EU's gender regime in times of crisis', in *Women's studies international forum*. Pergamon, Vol. 99, p. 102722.
Guerrina, R. and Masselot, A. (2018) 'Walking into the footprint of EU law: Unpacking the gendered consequences of Brexit', *Social Policy and Society*, 17, pp. 319–330.
Kantola, J. (2010) *Gender and the European Union*. Bloomsbury Publishing.
Karamessini, M. and Rubery, J. (2014) 'The challenge of austerity for equality: a consideration of eight European countries in the crisis'. *Revue de l'OFCE*, (2), pp. 15–39.
Kleinsteuber, H.J. and Sonnenberg, U. (1990) 'Beyond public service and private profit: International experience with non-commercial local radio', *European Journal of Communication*, 5(1), pp. 87–106.
Kraft, D. (2007) 'Advertising restrictions and the free movement of goods—The case law of the ECJ', *European Business Law Review*, 18, pp. 517–527.
MacRae, H. (2006) 'Rescaling gender relations: The influence of European Directives on the German gender regime', *International Studies in Gender, State and Society*, 13(4), pp. 522–550.
Masselot, A. (2007) 'The state of gender equality law in the European Union', *European Law Journal*, 13(2), pp. 152–168.
Mastenbroek, E. (2005) 'EU compliance: Still a 'black hole'?', *Journal of European Public Policy*, 12(6), pp. 1103–1120.
Meraviglia, C. and Dudka, A. (2021) 'The gendered division of unpaid labor during the Covid-19 crisis: Did anything change? Evidence from Italy', *International Journal of Sociology*, 51(1), pp. 64–75.
Millns, S. (2017) in Irving, H. (ed.) *Constitutions and gender*. Edward Elgar Publishing.

Rossi, L.S. (2012) in Ripley, S. *EU law after Lisbon*. Oxford: Oxford University Press, p. 107.
Rubery, J. and Karamessini, M. eds., (2013) *Women and austerity: The economic crisis and the future for gender equality*. Routledge.
Rubery, J. (2015) 'Austerity and the future for gender equality in Europe', *ILR Review*, 68(4), pp. 715–741.
Sanders, A. and Flavell, J. (2023) 'The direction of gender equality policy in Britain post-Brexit: Towards a masculinised Westminster model', *Journal of European Public Policy*, 30(11), pp. 2303–2325.
Sarikakis, K. and Nguyen, E.T. (2009) 'The trouble with gender: Media policy and gender mainstreaming in the European Union', *European Integration*, 31(2), pp. 201–216.
Steiner, J. (1992) 'Drawing the line: Uses and abuses of article 30 EEC', *CML Review*, 29, p. 749.
Timmer, A. (2016) 'Gender stereotyping in the case law of the EU Court of Justice 2016', *European Equality Law Review*, 1(16).
UN Women (2023) https://www.unwomen.org/en/what-we-do/leadership-and-political-participation/facts-and-figures
Walby, S. (2004) 'The European Union and gender equality: Emergent varieties of gender regime', *Social Politics: International Studies in Gender, State & Society*, 11(1), pp. 4–29.
Walby, S. (2020) 'Varieties of gender regimes'. *Social Politics: International Studies in Gender, State and Society*, 27(3), pp. 414–431.
Weatherill, S. (2014) *Cases and materials on EU law*. Oxford: Oxford University Press, p. 291.
Zeitlin, J.H. (2005) in De Búrca, G. (ed.) *EU law and the welfare state: In search of solidarity*. Oxford: Oxford University Press.

Cases

Groppera Radio AG and others v Switzerland App no 10890/84, A/173, (1990) 12 EHRR 321
Autronic AG v Switzerland, Merits and just satisfaction, App no 12726/87 (A/178), (1990) 12 EHRR 485
Khurshid Mustafa And Tarzibachi v Sweden ECHR (Bailii, [2011] ECHR 1277
Case C-155/73 Italy v Sacchi [1974] ECR I-409
Case C-43/75, Defrenne v. Sabena, 1976 European Court Reports 1 455
Case C-120/78 Rewe v Bundesmonopolverwaltung für Branntwein [1979] ECR I
Case C-25/85 Bon Van Adverteeders and Others v The Netherlands [1988] ECR I-2085
Case C-34/95 Konsumentombudsmannen (KO) v De Agostini (Svenska) Forlag [1995] ECR I-179
Case C-8/74 Procureur de Roi v Dassonville [1974] ECR 837
Case C-120/78 Rewe-Zentral AG v Bundesmonopolverwaltung für Branntweinv [1979] ECR I 649
Case C-178/84 Commission v Germany 1987 ECR 1227
Case C-385/01 Commission v Spain [2003] ECR I-13145
Case C-412/93 Leclerc Siplec Société d'Importation v TFI Publicite & M6 Publicite [1995] ECR I-00179 [1981] ECR 4575
Case C-286/81 Oosthoek's Uitgeversmaatschappij BV.
Join cases C-267 and 268/91 Bernard Keck and Daniel Mithouard [1993] ECR I-6097
Joined Cases C-69/93 and C258/93 Puno Casa [1993] ECR I-02355
Case C-20/03 Marcel Burmanjer and Others [2003] ECR 687

Case C-391/92 Commission v Greece [1995] ECR I-01621
Case C-292/92 Ruth Hünermund and others v Landespothekerkammer Baden Wüttemberg [1993] ECR I-06787
C-1/90 and C-176/90 Angonesa de Publicidad Exterior SA and Publivía SAE v Departmento de Sanidad y Seguridad Social de la Generalitat de Cataluña
Para 38 of Case C- 71/02 Herbert Karner Industrie-Auktionen GmbH v Troostwijk GmbH. [2004] ECR I-0302
Case C-239/02. Douwe Egberts NV v. Westrom Pharma NV and Others [2004] ECR I-07007
Council Directive 2000/78/EC of 27 November 2000 establishing a general framework for equal treatment in employment and occupation OJ L 303
Council Directive 2004/113 EC 3 implementing the principles of equal treatment between men and women in the access to and supply of goods and services OJ L 373
Council Directive 2022/2381 of the European parliament and of the council of 23 November 2022 on improving the gender balance among directors of listed companies and related measures

Chapter 3

EU gender regime

Gender stereotypes as a new form of discrimination

Introduction

This chapter provides an overview and evaluation of the two international instruments that seek to prohibit gender stereotyping in advertising: the Convention for the Elimination of All Forms of Discrimination against Women (1979) and the Beijing Platform for Action (1995). In this chapter, I continue analysing EU secondary legislation in this field. First, I focus on the shortcomings—and potential reprisals—of the Goods and Services Directive (113/04/EU 2004), and how both the AVMS Directive (1808/18/EU 2018) and the Digital Services Act (Regulation (EU) 2022/2065 2022) seek to protect children from online harmful content. I then provide further analysis of the numerous 'soft law' approaches that have been adopted by the EU institutions. In doing so, I argue how the adoption of soft law by the EU institutions has kept gender stereotypes on the agenda and, more importantly, why and how it is a more viable, palatable option for member states.

International law

There are numerous international human rights instruments that oblige state parties to address gender stereotypes in society. These range from the Istanbul Convention (adopted by the European Council) to the Maputo Protocol (African Union) and the Convention of Belem do Para (Organisation of American States). This would indicate that the international community believe that law is a suitable device to address gender stereotypes. However, not one of these legal instruments provides a definition of the term, and, as will become clear in the remainder of this book, providing a definition of the term comes with numerous disadvantages. A narrow definition of the term will limit what is caught by the legal instrument (or regulatory code); if defined broadly, the legal instrument will catch all manner of gender-related issues. The Council of Europe Gender Equality Strategy 2018–2023 provides a definition of gender stereotyping, but, unlike CEDAW, it is not legally binding. State parties to CEDAW, on the other hand, are obliged take action

DOI: 10.4324/9781003336037-3

towards ending the practice of gender stereotyping. As with the aforementioned international legal instruments, CEDAW does not define the term. The document has nonetheless been highly influential and interpreted in many ways throughout the international community. As discussed in the previous chapter, the founding treaty of the EU showed no indication of a gender equality competence or the roots of recognising gender stereotypes as a legal and societal problem in CEDAW. CEDAW provides a 'bill of rights' for women, and although the EU is not formally a signatory, the majority of member states are, which, in recent years, has steered the EU towards a heavily human rights–based approach to tackling sex discrimination and gender discrimination (Holtmaat and Tobler, 2005). According to Frańczak (2022), CEDAW establishes the connection between harmful gender stereotypes and discrimination and violence against women. Articles 2(f), 5(a) and 10(c) of CEDAW oblige state parties to address gender stereotypes, their persistence and the effect they have on the wider society. This issue will become more apparent later in the book when discussing regulatory codes. Article 5(a) of CEDAW of has two broad aims: first, it obliges parties to eliminate harmful gender stereotypes that are based on superiority and inferiority. The second requires state parties to eliminate the pretext that women's role is somehow fixed: for example, the family and home. Fundamentally, the article attempts to 'modify gender stereotypes and fixed parental gender roles in order to realise full equality of women and men' (Holtmaat and Tobler, 2005: 422). In the CEDAW Burundi opinion (CO Burundi CEDAW/CBDI/CO/4 (2008)), the committee stated that Article 5(a) is a tool that should be used to remove gender stereotypes in *all* structures of society, therefore rendering its reach limitless. As discussed in previous chapters, legal academics have consistently argued that gender stereotypes remain embedded in structures across society: namely, in education, healthcare, criminal trials, media and advertising (Cook and Cusack, 2011; Cusack and Timmer, 2011; Cook and Weiss, 2016; Holtmaat and Naber, 2011; Frańczak, 2022). For example, in curricula and education, gender stereotypes influence the courses and interests that young boys and girls select, impacting education, employment options and income, leaving women with a narrow range of possibilities in work. CEDAW perceives the eradication of gender stereotypes in education similar to media and advertising: both industries harbour harmful stereotypes that are damaging to all ages, particularly the young. In CEDAW's Finnish opinion (FIN CEDAW/C/FIN/5 (2008)), the committee identified the eradication of gender stereotypes in advertising and the media as a priority, specifically advertising that uses sexualised and objectified bodies to promote goods and services. The committee found that these advertisements were linked to increased rates of violence against women, segregation in the labour market, eating disorders, low self-esteem and deteriorating mental health. According to Burrows (1985) and Kathree (1995), CEDAW's overarching tactic is threefold: to bring complete equality, improve the position of women in society and combat negative gender stereotypes. There is evidently difficulty in ascertaining how state parties could implement the obligations set out in Article 5(a), and it is perceived as one of the most difficult articles of CEDAW to implement (Cook, 1990).

The second United Nation legal instrument, the Beijing Platform for Action (BPfA) contains comparable aims and aspirations for greater opportunities for women and the removal of all obstacles to women's participation in economic, social and political decision-making. The removal of gender stereotypes features as one of BPfA's 12 critical areas of concern, and as technical and communication systems advance, this area of concern is aimed at government, non-governmental organisations and the private sector. In its 11 areas of concern, the BPfA promotes actions aimed at removing and/or regulating gender stereotypes by raising the awareness of the media's responsibility by promoting non-stereotypical images of women and men, encouraging the media to look at the influence and impact of gendered stereotypes in advertisements which cultivate gender-based violence, the removal of gender stereotyping of men and women in the media and, finally, encouraging the media to develop guidelines, self-regulation and ethical codes to promote non-stereotyped images of women.

The main issue with the BPfA is that it is not legally binding. However, the BPfA does commit its signatory states to exercising due diligence to prevent and sanction through legislation. The BPfA places emphasis on NGOs and non-state actors playing active roles, and it is the primary responsibility of national parliaments and governments to implement the actions of the 12 critical areas for concern and related objectives. The European Parliament's subsequent 'follow-up' resolution implementing the BPfA in May 2000 began the Parliament's acknowledgment, albeit a weak one, that effort must be made to combat gender stereotypes and adopted the measure to 'strongly support[] a more positive and realistic portrayal and image of women in the media' (EP resolution on the follow-up to the Beijing Action Platform 2000/2020 (INI)).

The Goods and Services Directive

In the previous chapter, I outlined how the bulk of EU anti-discrimination legislation has centred on employment law, setting a high standards in a range of work-related directives. However, secondary legislation has not reflected some of the third-wave feminist goals, such as violence against women, trafficking, body image and the 'pornification' of the media. The Goods and Services Directive (Council Directive 2004/113/EC) sought to plug this gap, or at least during the drafting process, the European Commission's goal was to tackle issues beyond the labour market. The directive's history begins with the Treaty of Amsterdam (1997), which positioned gender equality as a priority, and it now enjoys an elevated position (gender equality is now perceived as an 'aim' and a 'task' of the EU under Article 8 TFEU (ex-Article 3 EC)) amongst the other EU goals and values. This promotion had an important impact on the initiation of gender stereotyping as policy, which is rooted in wide scope of Article 19 TFEU (ex–Article 13EC). Article 19 allowed the Council of the European Union to 'take appropriate action to combat discrimination based on sex, racial or ethnic origin, religion or belief, disability, age or sexual orientation'. The Treaty of Amsterdam provided the much-needed 'proactive' stance, as opposed to the previous 'reactive' tone of the directives that had derived from the treaties in previous years. This reactive/proactive shift is seen in the early years of equality with the notion that gender equality will only be achieved if individuals claim their rights by responding to a specific discriminatory problem, whereas the proactive stance, on the other hand, provides that all EU institutions at all levels are obliged to achieve equality. From a theoretical perspective, the EU has moved towards a more substantive approach to achieving equality, with 'top-down' positive action with further engagement with NGOs, non-state actors and women's groups.

The commission had previously used Article 19 for the employment (Council Directive 2000/78/EC (2000)) and race (Council Directive 2000/43/EC (2000)) directives. The introduction of Article 19 at Amsterdam can be seen as a new non-discrimination competence that has the scope to prohibit discrimination beyond the economic limitations of the internal market (Carraciolo Di Torella, 2005). The article can also be viewed as an extension of Article 157 (ex–Article 141 TFEU), but there are some understated differences here which provide for the shortcomings of the Goods and Services Directive, which, in its final version, failed to incorporate gender stereotypes in media, advertising and education. First, there is a tangible link between gender and the market in Article 157 TFEU. Secondly, Article 157 TFEU is more effective as it refers to adopting measures that safeguard equal treatment between men and women, whereas Article 19 TFEU bears a more generic undertone to merely 'combat discrimination'. Finally, there are bureaucratic differences between the two articles. A measure adopted under Article 19 TFEU requires unanimity from the Council, whereas Article 157 TFEU requires a qualified majority vote, which increases the chance of any such adoption. Article 157 TFEU would also have benefited from the European Parliament's involvement, which is widely regarded as the 'guardian' of gender equality legislation. Accordingly, it is clear from the inception that the directive seems somewhat misplaced by the commission if gender stereotypes were in any way to be included in its final version.

Despite this procedural error, the commission initially sought to implement CEDAW-inspired goals in the directive: specifically, anti-discrimination outside the workplace. The commission's aim was a comprehensive piece of secondary legislation on the representation of gender in various areas, including education, the media, advertising, taxation and social security. Initiated by the Directorate General of Social Affairs (now DG of Employment, Social

Affairs and Inclusion) with guidance from NGOs and legal academics, the commission moulded the directive, taking inspiration from both CEDAW and BPfA provisions such as domestic violence, trafficking and gender stereotypes. The roots of the directive can be traced back to as early as 2000, when the commission consulted interested parties, including the European Women's Lobby (EWL). The EWL put forward ten particular areas of interest that should form part of the draft directive, including, amongst others, 'images of women and men portrayed in advertising and the media'. By February 2002, the EWL and the Advisory Committee on Equal Opportunities prepared an opinion with the majority of the original ten proposals from EWL—including advertising and the media—remaining unscathed. Simultaneously, the commission produced an alternative draft with a narrower tone and attenuated content. Nonetheless, both the opinion and the draft legislation preserved some of the core areas, such as education, taxation and gender stereotypes in advertising and the media. Inclusion of these areas is on par with the contents of the 'Race Directive' (Council Directive 2000/43/EC (2000)), the Goods and Services Directive's nearest comparable piece of secondary legislation. During the drafting process, the contents of the directive were leaked to the media and industry—namely media and insurance—and both expressed hostility towards the gender representation proposal (Carraciolo Di Torella, 2005; Masselot, 2007). In particular, the media industry provided the strongest reaction by claiming that the inclusion of gender stereotypes in the legislation was one step away from complete censorship that would inevitably clash with the fundamental principle of freedom of expression, a cornerstone of the EU. The insurance industry indicated that the proposal to remove sex difference as a factor in the calculation of car insurance rates would have a catastrophic effect on industries and consumers across the EU. Prominent commissioners such as Mario Monti and larger member states (UK and Germany) also raised strong opposition to the inclusion of advertising and the media in the directive for similar reasons. A coalition of members of the European Parliament—he Women's Rights and Gender Equality Committee (FEMM), the European Women Lawyers Association (EWLA), the EWL and the Association of Women in Southern Europe (AFEM)—clung to the core demands set out initially: insurance, social benefits, education, advertising and the media.

Despite persistent lobbying from interested parties, specifically the EWL's desire to retain the core areas covered in the Race Directive (education, taxation and advertising and the media), these were dropped, so the Commission was left with no choice but to draft a new directive and withdraw its initial proposals. The exclusion of education, advertising and the media is at odds with the Race Directive, which does not contain a similar limitation but goes as far as to explicitly list the areas that are covered. The reason for the exclusion of advertising is based on the limited the nature of the legislation, and the scope of the initial Goods and Services Directive was to be limited to the access and supply of goods and services only. The redrafted directive and narrow scope of its content were criticised by the Economic and Social Committee and the FEMM in the European Parliament, which disputed the decision to go ahead with the directive due to lack of proper consultation and not being informed of the changes.[1] During this period, the commission refused to accept any of the amendments, nor were they considered by the council, with the majority of discussion spent on the insurance policy question. The directive was finally agreed on by the commission, Parliament and the Council on 13 December 2004, with the requirement that all member states transpose the legislation into national law no later than 21 December 2007. After a flurry of leaks, exposes and lobbying in the UK and Germany, the final outcome of the draft resulted in a much-diminished directive.

Overall, the directive makes little effort to protect gender equality outside the workplace, where no such secondary legislation exists, and is merely confined to the access to and supply of goods and services. The directive falls short of its original intention to combat the representation of gender in educational materials, taxation, the media and advertising (Calvero and Galligan, 2012). Moreover, substantive equality appears to have been abandoned, in that Article 6 appears to be the only sufficient form of substantive equality, with reference to member states taking 'positive action'. Similarly, Article 12(1) has a more practical tone, ensuring that member states harmonize the implementation process of gender equality by creating bodies that 'may form part of agencies charged at national level with the defense of human rights or the safeguard of individuals' rights, or the implementation of the principle of equal treatment'. The directive is also not in line with the other equality directives that were born out of the Amsterdam initiative. By comparison, the Race Directive is marginally enhanced, including a provision on public bodies, social protection and education (Article 3(1)) which, in effect, establishes a hierarchy of discrimination. The Goods and Services Directive, as clearly stated in its preamble, is only linked to the access and supply of goods and services, which means two things: first, there must be an economic link to the market as defined by EU law, and secondly, it limits undertakings carried out by public bodies. Both of these limit the directive's use outside the workplace. Some commentators have stated that due to the failure of the commission to press ahead with the initial proposals, gender equality takes a back seat in the wider equality programme and is less important than other forms of discrimination (Brennan, 2003; Carracciolo Di Torella, 2005). Certainly, the removal of these provisions is particularly vexing as in the years after the adoption

1 See, for example, FEMM and EWL's Annual report 2003 (www.womenlobby.org). FEMM eventually proposed 34 amendments to the draft directive which received a strong backing in the European (2005) Parliament plenary session on 30 March 2004 (313 votes for, 141 against, 47 abstentions). Accessed 7 June 2023.

of the Goods and Services Directive, the commission, along with Parliament, persistently attempted to hang the idea of combatting gender stereotypes on adopting 'soft law' measures, which will be looked at in later in this chapter.

In recent years, there have been signals that the Goods and Services Directive will be revisited. The most significant indication is from the recent European Equality Law Network's report 'In search of the potential of a forgotten directive' (2022), which recommends revisiting the directive and expanding its scope, specifically in areas included in Article 3(3) of the directive: education, media and advertising. The report provides the commission with a raft of recommendations, ranging from providing member states examples of good self-regulatory practice to full inclusion of Article 3(3).

The Audio-Visual Media Services Directive

The Audio-Visual Media Services Directive (Council Directive 2018/1808/EU) (AVMSD) has a relatively limited effect on the regulation of advertising content, in particular harmful gendered content (Trzaskowski et al., 2015; Savin, 2020). The primary aim of the original AVMSD (2010/13/EU) was to co-ordinate national laws on all audio-visual media, incorporating traditional broadcast and contemporary services such as online/catch-up TV. The original wording derives from the commission's target in the Lisbon Agenda (2000–2010) to remain buoyant with the expanding market and demand for online, on-demand and 'catch-up' TV on smartphones, tablets and laptops as well as monitoring the free circulation of the audio-visual services that vary from one member state to another (Little, 2008). The contents of the AVMSD have since been overhauled, and the directive was revised in 2018. For the purposes of this book, the most significant element of the revised AVMSD is the inclusion of certain types of advertising that are deemed illegal. These are listed in the directive, and member states must protect minors, respect human dignity and ensure adverts do not promote or include sex discrimination. Article 9.1(c) now ensures that advertisements shall not prejudice human dignity or promote discrimination based on sex. This is a fairly broad approach, and protecting human dignity will vary from state to state. Although 'human dignity' is a universally recognised term, enshrined in international law and most European constitutions, the scope of the term and its meaning will diverge due to cultural and societal divergence across Europe (Cole and Etteldorf, 2023). Article 9.1(c) should be read conjunction with Article 29, which establishes a contact committee that is composed of member state representatives and chaired by a representative of the commission, who shall set guidelines on exchanges of information on advertising between the commission and the member state competent authorities. This commission can be viewed as the regulator of the transposition and implementation process of the AVMSD; however, the member state 'monitoring groups' will be paramount in reporting back to the commission with the findings of advertisements. The AVMSD is clear that the contact committee should also tackle issues related to gender equality and gender stereotypes, inviting experts to an exchange of views. Article 27 relates to the protection of minors but only in as far as protecting mental health and moral development, which has a clear link to pornography and violence but not explicitly to sexualisation and objectification. The wider aim of the AVMSD is reflected in the neoliberal or 'light touch' tone of the EU's approach in that it merely sets out to liberalise the media market, support self-regulation over autonomous regulation or legislation and then adjust the rules only when there is a market failure.

Up until 2004, gender stereotypical images were dealt with by the DG for Education and Culture, whereas now, the issue is predominantly dealt with by the DG Employment and Social Affairs. As Sarikakis and Nguyen (2009) have argued, the AVMSD merely follows on from the Gender Directive's outlook: the DG Employment and Social Affairs' neoliberal stance will inevitably limit the full potential of any draft legislation that wishes to tighten regulation, as the onus is more often than not placed on the consumer to complain rather than pre-emptive controls in the field of gender equality. This amplifies the distinction and void between soft law and legislative instruments that aim to tackle gender stereotypes in the media and advertising—the 'proactive' substantial equality that is stable throughout the 'soft' instruments such as the recommendations from the Committee on Equal Opportunities Opinion evaporates. The coerciveness of good practice and positive action is replaced by individual complaints through a self-regulatory system that reflects the formal 'reactive' gender equality.

The commission's first report in May 2012 (Commission to the European Parliament, the Council, the European Economic and Social Committee and the Committee of the Regions on the Application of Directive 2010/13/EU) on the AVMSD's implementation actively assesses gender stereotypes in two ways. Firstly, the AVMS directive's methodology of qualitative data is similar to previous monitoring techniques. (See Council Directive 89/552, Television Without Frontiers Directive, Recital, 1989 O.J. (L 298).) However, the AVMS directive sets out to assess the content and presentation of the advert and, more importantly, the effectiveness of implementation at member state level—acting as a watchman over state regulators. Secondly, the report sets aside the aims of Article 6.1(a) of the directive—that member states must respect human dignity, and services (including advertisements) ought not to incite hatred of or violence against a group of persons, as per Article 21 of the Charter of Fundamental Rights. The commission's analysis of 'advertising spots' (or advertisement periods/commercial breaks during TV programmes) across all 27 member states found that stereotyped representation amounted to 21% to 36% of all advertising time, with no member states resistant to the portrayal of gender stereotypes. The report also found that women fill the majority of 'subordinate' positions and 'sexual presentation'—the sexualisation of the product is characterised using a female body unconnected to the product itself, therefore rendering the female body the commodity itself. The amended AVMSD goes some way in obliging video-sharing platform providers (VSPs) to protect the general public from media (including advertising) that contains content that amounts to incitement of violence or hatred against a group of persons or a member of that group as referred to in Article 21 of the Charter of Fundamental Rights.

The final significant revision of the AVSMD is the widening scope of the directive to hold VSPs responsible for preventing harmful content. This is an important development as the hope of the commission at the time of drafting was to prevent social media platforms from inciting violence and hatred online (Kuklis, 2020). It still remains uncertain what digital platforms are deemed VSPs and regulated by the directive, and, indeed, it is unclear whether or not the AVMSD regulates all social media content. Moreover, whilst VSPs might be held responsible for such content, they're not liable for the harmful content. According to Kostovska and Micova (2021), the AVMSD defines VSPs through their functionality, and a platform will be deemed a VSP if its sole objective or purpose is to provide video content to the general public. Relevant harmful content is defined by the AVMSD as content that is likely to incite violence or hatred against a group of persons or a member of a group of persons based on particular grounds (e.g. sex). As with other media within the scope of the AVMSD, advertisements that appear on VSPs must respect human dignity and not include or promote discrimination based on sex, and finally, they must not cause physical, mental or moral detriment to persons under the age of 18.

The Digital Services Act

Like the AVMSD, the recent Digital Services Act (Regulation (EU) 2022/2065) (DSA) has a limited scope on the regulation harmful gender stereotypes in advertising. The DSA does, however, introduce new mandatory due diligence obligations for large online platforms (VLOPs) such as TkTok and Instagram and very large online search engines (VLOSEs) such as Google and Bing to address a range of societal risks posed by their services. Article 28 protects minors from online algorithmic advertising by prohibiting the use of data aggregation and profiling or targeting adverts towards children. The DSA also provides some scope on how member states should ensure new regulatory codes for advertising content, prohibiting targeted advertisements to minors and advertising based on sensitive data (e.g. gender, sexuality, race).

Soft law

As was mentioned at the start of the chapter, soft law has played a vital role in keeping the regulation of harmful gender stereotypes on the agenda. The next half of this chapter demonstrates how soft law has been used in different ways by the EU institutions to continue the pursuit of curbing the use of harmful gender stereotyping in advertising and influencing member states in the regulation of their use. Article 17(1) TFEU provides clear grounds for the use of soft law by stating that the commission shall 'promote the general interest of the Union and take appropriate initiatives to that end'. Soft law is well known for lacking what hard law upholds: 'obligation, uniformity, justiciability, sanctions, and/or an enforcement staff' (Trubek and Trubek, 2005: 343); nonetheless, soft law is effective in establishing 'objectives, guidelines to bring about changes in social policy, relying on shaming' (Shelton, 2009: 68). It is the pillory facet of soft law that is the most significant in this instance, as it has been most effective when it comes to influencing member states to regulate the use of gender stereotypes in advertising and media. The various soft law instruments reflect the commission's efforts to remain on course with the task of adopting measures to remove negative gender stereotypes in advertising. I wish to argue that these soft law instruments do not so much develop a new EU legal order as fill a void where EU secondary legislation has been relatively weak. Soft law is exhibited here as mechanisms beyond legislation that aim to make advancements in the subject of gender stereotypes, and, as Shelton notes (2009), soft law often hardens over time and paves the way for new EU endeavours.

The characteristics of soft law can be construed either widely, as a source of EU law (Article 288 TFEU)—endorsed by not just the EU institutions but also the CJEU—or narrowly, as 'complementary' to EU legislation (Senden, 2005). This latter interpretation is a problematic one as it is neither legally binding nor limited in the development of legal order (Dawson, 2013). Soft law measures vary throughout the EU but generally reflect the commission's long-term intentions on most policy areas and 'test the ground' in member states for future legislative measures (Beveridge and Velluti, 2016: 14). This generalisation of soft law's pre-emptive character is echoed in processes that are adopted by reluctant member states that initially reject entering into legally binding obligations but eventually agree to the wide-reaching goals, principles and targets (Snyder, 1993). Ultimately, soft law plays the perfect agent in the field of gender equality where very little action has been taken by the Council to shift policy from the economic to the social sphere. This void is where soft law's advantages flourish: it is encouraging rather than coercive, even towards the most reluctant of member states; it is self-regulatory in nature and provides for ample flexibility as well as the awareness that no single member state will face formal sanctions. Finally, and most importantly, the void between the economic and social sphere that soft law occupies is a mirror for the future of EU policy (Beveridge and Velluti, 2016).

The European Women's Lobby

In explaining the impact soft law has had on gender equality policy, a good place to start is the European Women's Lobby (EWL) and how the 'Roadmap to Equality Programme 2006–2010' reignited the regulation of gender stereotypes in advertising. Just one year after the Goods and Services Directive came into effect, the efforts to encourage progress in regulating gender stereotypes in advertising at a national level was placed at the heart of the EWL roadmap. Amongst the roadmap's six priority areas, the removal of gender stereotypes in advertising and media (6.2) is positioned alongside other EWL goals, such as the eradication of gender-based violence and equal representation in decision-making. The roadmap is advanced by the commission's Gender Equality Report (2008) and refers to the negative use of gender stereotypes and their barrier to gender equality. Listed in the report's challenges, 'tackling stereotypes, support for individuals' reflects the European Commission's intent to remove negative stereotypes in certain areas such as media and advertising. The commission also lays out significant (but vague) strategic actions—the removal of stereotypes at a very young age, access for men and women to non-traditional work roles (including decision-making positions), adopting two-way training schemes in which the guidance and the trainee disregard gendered roles and promoting realistic images of men and women in the media. In the same year, the Council adopted conclusions on Svensson report on 'Eliminating Gender Stereotypes in Society' (2008), assessing the influence gender stereotypes in advertising have on society, concluding that industry 'contributed in the reproduction of culturally transmitted stereotypes and images'. The Council concluded that the onus would be on the member states to improve education materials at all levels in schools and engage with the mass media (including advertising agencies) on the detrimental effects gender stereotypes have on young people. The Council's conclusions are on the one hand weakened by the uncertainty surrounding exactly how the right balance can be struck between fundamental principles of freedom of expression, the right to a free press and gender equality, nor is it clear how this can be achieved at the member state level. On the other hand, it is encouraging to see that the council places emphasis on the gender stereotypes that need to be tackled at a young age through children's toys, advertising and education, which cements the roadmap's assertion that the onus should be on educators rather than advertising agencies.

Parallel to the commission's and Parliament's efforts, EU presidencies have been instrumental in encouraging debate by providing a platform for research and transforming the issue into mainstream dialogue. Once again, in conjunction with the European Women's Lobby (EWL), the Slovenian Presidency Conference's 'Mission (Im)possible' (2008) presented the need for eliminating stereotypes in childhood and the advertising industry. The conference identified various forms of gender stereotypes that hinder gender equality and the link that harmful content has with gender-based violence, eating disorders and self-harm. The fundamental theme running throughout the EWL and Slovenian Presidency Conference is the need to combat stereotypes from the very beginning—from conception, birth, early childhood and then at the primary education level. The trend of placing the onus on educators rather than advertisers is once again sustained, and, not for the first time, discourse surrounding a ban on gender stereotypes used in the media and advertising takes a back seat, and early intervention is seen as crucial. The Czech Presidency Conference of 2009 and the EWL conference 'New Ways in Overcoming Gender Stereotypes' once again considered the role the advertising industry has in shaping gender stereotypes as well as the role soft law mechanisms can play in European education systems and advertising regulators' agencies. One of the main conclusions of the conference was the importance of self-regulation and increasing citizens' awareness of state self-regulation mechanisms. In 2024, as part of the Liechtenstein presidency, the Council ran a conference on 'Breaking down gender stereotypes in media and advertising', calling for member states to take action on advertising that 'tolerates and trivialises "everyday" sexism'.

The FEMM Committee

In 2008, the European Parliament overwhelmingly adopted a critical report by the Committee on Women's Rights and Gender Equality (FEMM) on how advertising affects women. The Parliament proposed four recommendations aimed at motivating EU institutions and member states to monitor harmful and degrading images of women in the media and advertisements. The report shifts responsibility to the advertising agencies, and paragraphs 9 and 25 call for better regulatory control by recommending national media monitoring bodies and an EU-wide 'code of conduct' set up by the commission. Paragraph 15 looks at sexual services advertising and its visibility and availability to young adults and children. Finally, paragraph 18 calls for education, training and employment of women and equal access for women in all areas of advertising and media. The report links the use of gender stereotypes and their significance to the functioning of the single market and how they contribute to gender pay gap and divide the labour markets and gender professions, with women earning less than men. Recital R criticises certain member states' weak national advertising codes and ethics, in which rules are either not respected or non-existent, and calls for more action in this area.

The second report from FEMM (2012/2116(INI)) (Liotard Report) provided the Parliament with a further opportunity to strengthen its position on combatting gender stereotypes in advertising and the media. The report included two major additions. First, it appealed to the EU to provide legislation to ensure equality between women and men in education and media and, secondly, urged the member states to develop ombudsmen and/or advertising authorities to ensure ethical codes of conduct are put in place to monitor media and advertising agencies. With cross-party support from the Parliament, the Liotard Report is one of the strongest positions that any EU institution has taken since the Goods and Services Directive. Compared to the first FEMM report, the draft resolution's content is much improved, emphasising the need for the advertising industry to take an active role. Embedded in the report are 12 areas that require attention from and action by the EU and member states. These areas include the removal of outdated gendered representations in advertisements (such as women providing domestic labour, housework, cleaning, cooking and childcare), advertisements that are aimed at young children that often feature outdated gender norms and values, the need for stronger educational content rather than self-fulfilling gender roles in adverts, the removal of gender stereotypes and sexualisation in advertising, how advertisements dehumanise women and promote violence against women and, finally, the pornification of advertising or 'mainstreaming of pornography' in advertising.[2] The theme that runs throughout the report is that national advertising regulators must acknowledge that gender stereotypes in advertising are linked to a multitude of economic and societal issues such as the gender pay gap and domestic violence. The language of the report is also very distinctive in comparison to other soft law measures from the same period. With firm undiminished targets aimed at member states and state actors, the report signals a change in how self-regulatory bodies operate to combat discrimination in the media and advertising to ensure effective sanctions on those who promote the sexualisation of women. Since the committee's referral in Parliament in June, the report has been somewhat overshadowed by the reference made to pornography in the draft version, and although this reference was eventually removed, the report has lost its original momentum.

European parliamentary opinions

Parliamentary opinions have played an equally important role in debating the topic and setting the future agenda. The first opinion delivered by European Economic Social Committee (EESC) in December 2010 (2010/C 334/01) provides economic-based recommendations to the commission on gender stereotypes in the media, education and advertising. None of the recommendations are unexpected or new and merely repeat previous communications: the need for education and training at all levels in the advertising industry, eradication of stereotypes in the workplace and the link between gender stereotypes and domestic violence against women. In the recommendations, the EESC dedicate an entire section to eliminating sexist stereotypes and provides further nuanced recommendations for the commission on how to tackle gender stereotypes in the workplace. Amongst other things, the EESC recommend the eradication of sexist stereotypes from the media and advertising industry with particular reference to 'the portrayal of violence and degrading images of women'.

2 'Pornification' or mainstreaming of pornography is the process by which advertisements aimed at young audiences feature quasi-pornographic or porn-themed content. This content is slowly normalised, accepted and idealised (Rossi, 2007).

The second, the Advisory Committee on Equal Opportunities for Women and Men, also provided an opinion for the commission on 'Breaking gender stereotypes in the media' (2010). Unlike the EESC recommendations and FEMM reports, the advisory committee's position provides a comprehensive analysis of how the media and advertising industries could work in collaboration with EU institutions rather than relying on a blanket ban on gender stereotypes. The opinion is more prescriptive, identifying how the media and advertising industries can learn from the good practices set by member states that are spearheading harmful gendered content and stereotypes in advertising. Part 5 of the opinion reflects this tone through proactive gender equality measures such as inclusion and the promotion of more 'realistic images' of women and men should be made through actively promoting womento senior positions in media and advertising companies. Throughout the opinion, the committee state that an EU-wide monitoring group should have the ability to set benchmarks for defining 'degrading', 'sexist' and stereotypical images with the competence to 'receive and consider' individual complaints from the general public as well as women's groups, NGOs and charities.

Both opinions unquestionably reignite the regulation of gender stereotypes in advertising and the media as part of the EU's remit. Equally, both opinions place some emphasis on the recognition that a comprehensive ban on gender stereotypes is unfeasible, considering the two industries' lack of desire and will to collaborate during the gender directive's drafting. This shift towards a more *laissez-faire* approach to regulating media and advertising practices is indeed appealing to EU institutions, governments and the advertising industry alike as it is speaks to a common ground on which advertisers can engage with contributing to the regulation rather than feeling obliged to eradicate harmful types of gender stereotypes. The tone of the opinions is also highly significant in that both centre on the self-regulation of the industries with calls for minimal legislative interference. This again can be traced back to the reality that the commission has no precedent of legislative competence with media or advertising content. The tone of the opinions and FEMM's reports chime with the theoretical approach that the gender regime has woven in the last two decades. The shift from reactive to proactive is reflected in some of the soft law instruments. For example, the technique of pillory, in which member states are 'named and shamed' poor regulatory practice or legislation on the area of gender stereotypes. However, the reality is a more humble mix of the recommendations, reports and opinions of formal equality (increased self-regulatory emphasis based on offended individual consumers) and substantive equality (gender databases)

The European Advertising Standards Alliance

The European Advertising Standards Alliance (EASA) is a not-for-profit co-ordination body for cross-border advertising complaints across Europe. Whilst its main purpose is to serve as a co-ordination point redirecting complaints between one state and another, it has in recent years become more influential, particularly in promoting responsible advertising and guidance to its 54 members. As the commission failed to include advertising (and the media) in the Goods and Services Directive, the EASA has incorporated 'gender portrayal' as one of its key issues. In June 2004 'portrayal of gender' featured as one of the ley issues in the EASA's first Self-Regulatory Charter (2004). The charter was presented to the commission and the EESC as a form of pan-European guidance for the growing emergence of self-regulation. Effectively, the charter is a set of commitments for all EU member states, endorsing moral and financial support for the creation of an advertising self-regulatory framework and network. The charter's commitments can be viewed as a code of conduct that reflects technological and societal changes across Europe. What is significant about the charter is that the commission is willing to accept, at least at this stage, the more palatable self-regulation framework as an instrument to combat gender stereotypes in advertising than the less malleable secondary legislation. The charter's code is furthered by the EASA's Portrayal of Gender Report (2008), which provides an overview of how the self-regulatory organisations (SROs) across the EU combat the issue of harmful gender stereotypes in advertising. The report targets four main issues that arise from the analysis of member states that participated in the report. Gender stereotypes, which falls under Article 2 of the International Chamber of Commerce code's 'social responsibility' heading, has been interpreted widely by the member states. Most states have 'taste and decency' and 'social responsibility' embedded in their national self-regulatory codes. The report has some interesting findings: increasing sexualisation and 'dumbing down' representations of men in advertising and the 'pornification, nudity and sexual innuendo' of women. The common themes present in all member states included in the report are objectification, sexualisation and outdated ideas around motherhood and caring.

The EASA Gender Portrayal Report throws out some other insightful observations that are common amongst member states. First, self-regulation is the norm in Europe, and there are few legislative initiatives with sanctions (with the exception of Finland, Denmark, Norway and Spain). Secondly, there are a significant number of complaints made against SROs on gender portrayal, the sexualisation/objectification of women and gender violence. SRO 2010 statistics place gender portrayal in 'taste and decency', which generated 21,825 complaints overall across the EU, with gender stereotypes amounting to 19%. In more recent years, the number of complaints jumped to 49% (2019) but has remained at 24% to 25% of since 2020. This is something that will be scrutinised in the book in the national perspectives chapters. Thirdly, most member state regulators appear to be sceptical not just towards EU legislative instruments but towards what constitutes 'taste and decency'. These findings from EASA are not surprising considering the lobbying process from the media and advertising industries during the drafting of the gender directive. Moreover, the hostility shown against the notion of an EU-level 'taste and decency' definition runs with the norm that the margin of appreciation test seems to be the standard recourse in the EU. However, what is interesting is the lack of complaints from consumers across all member states. This lack—and often fluctuation—of complaints received can be attributed to various theories. The most common concept, is that a taste and decency/ gender portrayal advert receives augmented attention from media outlets, which leads to further consumer complaints. The UK Asda Christmas advert of 2013 is a good example of this theory as it initially received very few complaints until reported widely on in the UK press and on social media. By the end of January 2014, the complaints reached a record of 620. Advertisements such as the Asda Christmas advert represent a further problem with SROs in the EU as some advertisements are rejected at the first hurdle and are therefore not formally registered in the annual EASA or national SROs statistics.

Conclusion

This chapter has offered an evaluation of international legal instruments and the EU's approach to eliminating gender stereotypes in advertising. This has been provided against the backdrop of its limited competences in this area but also the context of expanding soft law approaches to curtailing harmful gender stereotypes in advertising. The chapter provided a critical overview of secondary legislation in the field of advertising regulation: the Goods and Services and AudioVisual Media Services Directives and the Digital Services Act, which have both fallen short of tighter regulation. I have therefore argued that it has been left to the commission to strike a happy medium and compromise through 'soft law' approaches by cajoling member states and industry into submission, to pillorize or 'name and shame' those states that fall below the standard expected or establish pan-European regulatory advertising standards through the EASA. Soft law approaches from various EU institutions have kept the prospect of regulating gender stereotypes in advertising afloat, and the pursuit of such regulation has been kept alive—only just—on the fringes of the commission's agenda. Due to the inherent characteristics of soft law, most instruments possess ample political will but lack the sanction mechanisms required to be effective. The commission, it would seem, is at something of a crossroads: either it revisits and amends the Goods and Services Directive by reintegrating advertising (education and media) or continues with soft law signals and a pan-EU regulatory code.

I have discussed how the gender regime is made up of actors and organisations beyond the standard institutional framework, and by concentrating on action programmes, recommendations and opinions, I have shown that there are numerous dialogues and narratives that help frame gender stereotypes. Such framing reflects both the lack of political will and the neoliberal orientation of the EU, where industry and free-market ideology 'trumps' fundamental rights. This, along with the EU's low-level competence in gender equality, can be deduced from the gender directive's drafting in 2003 and 2004. The measures that transpired in the subsequent decade have dramatically advanced the position of gender stereotypes, and this has been developed thanks to the guidance of the Parliament. However, such committee recommendations and opinions are not binding and lack teeth, rendering the Council the opportunity to disregard any opinion. It would therefore seem apparent that the decade following the gender directive has acted as a sticky plaster rather than a call for regulation.

Nonetheless, the history of the gender regime and soft law approaches tells an encouraging story as 'soft' law tends to precede 'hard' law, laying the foundations for the future development. This has been seen in many EU gender-related policy areas: for example, the recent EU plight of regulating trafficking (Council Directive 2011/36/EU)—soft law pre-empts fundamental change and inevitably shapes future legislation (Kantola, 2010). Likewise, the effects that soft law has on member states should not be undervalued. When pressure has been applied in other areas of the gender regime, the results have led to shared practices and norms in response to the pan-European problems. Indeed, some scholars such as Guiraudon (2006) and Terpan (2015) argue that soft law can have more impact than secondary legislation. In the next chapter, following on from the analysis of the legal framework surrounding the regulation of gender stereotypes in advertising, I look towards the theoretical framework of the thesis, in particular, a theorisation of gender stereotypes and their problematic effects in advertising.

References

Beveridge, F. and Velluti, S. (2016) *Gender and the open method of coordination.* University of Lincoln.

Brennan, F. (2003) The race directive: recycling racial inequality. *Cambridge Yearbook of European Legal Studies*, 5, pp. 311–331.

Burrows, N. (1985) 'The 1979 convention on the elimination of all forms of discrimination against women', *Netherlands International Law Review*, 32(3), p. 419.

Calvero, S. and Galligan, Y. (2012) 'Justice, democracy and gender', in Galligan, Y. (ed.) *Deliberative processes and gender democracy: Case studies from Europe.* Arena, p. 28.

Carraciolo Di Torella, E. (2005) 'The Goods and Services Directive: Limitations and opportunities', *Feminist Legal Studies*, 13, pp. 337–347 at p. 339.

CEDAW Burundi opinion (CO Burundi CEDAW/CBDI/CO/4) (2008) https://www.ohchr.org/en/documents/concluding-observations/cedawcbdico4-concluding-observations

Cole, M.D. and Etteldorf, C. (2023) *Future regulation of cross-border audiovisual content dissemination: A critical analysis of the current regulatory framework for law enforcement under the EU audiovisual media services directive and the proposal for a European media freedom act.* Nomos Verlagsgesellschaft mbH & Co. KG, Vol. 84, p. 272.

Cook, R. (1990) 'Reservation to the convention on the eliminations of all forms of discrimination against women', *Virginia Law Journal*, p. 644.

Cook, R. and Cusack, S. (2011) *Gender stereotyping: Transnational legal perspectives*. University of Pennsylvania Press.
Cusack, S. (2011) 'Gender stereotyping in rape cases: The CEDAW Committee's decision in *Vertido v The Philippines 2011*'.
Cusack, S. and Timmer, A.S. (2011) 'Gender stereotyping in rape cases: The CEDAW Committee's decision in Vertido v The Philippines'. *Human Rights Law Review*, 11(2), pp. 329–342.
Dawson, M. (2013) 'Soft law and the rule of law in the European Union: Revision or redundancy?', in Vauchez, A. and De Witte, B. (eds.) *In lawyering Europe*. Bloomsbury Publishing, pp. 221–222.
Frańczak, O. (2022) (Stereo) typical law: Challenging the transformative potential of human rights. In *Towards gender equality in law*. Palgrave Macmillan, Cham., pp. 15–33.
Guiraudon, V. (2006) 'Anti-discrimination policy', in Graziano, P. and Vink, M. (eds.) *Europeanization: New research agendas*. Springer.
Holtmaat, R. and Naber, J. (2011) *Women's human rights and culture from deadlock to dialogue*. Intersentia.
Holtmaat, R. and Tobler, C. (2005) 'CEDAW and the European Union's policy in the field of combating gender discrimination', *Maastricht Journal of European and Comparative Law*, 12(4), pp. 399–425, p. 401.
Kantola, J. (2010) *Gender and the European Union*. Bloomsbury Publishing.
Kathree, F. (1995) 'Convention on the elimination of all forms of discrimination against women', *South African Journal of Human Rights*, 11(3), p. 42.
Kostovska, I. and Broughton Micova, S. (2021, June) 'Platforms within the AVMSD regulatory architecture: A VSPs governance model'. In *TPRC49: The 49th Research Conference on Communication, Information and Internet Policy*.
Kuklis, L. (2020) 'Media regulation at a distance: Video-sharing platforms in Audiovisual Media Services Directive and the future of content regulation', *MediaLaws-Law and Policy of the Media in a Comparative Perspective*, 2(2), pp. 95–110.
Little, V. (2008) 'Audio visual media services directive: Europe's modernization of broadcast services regulations', *Journal of Law, Technology and Policy*, pp. 223–236 at p. 232.
Masselot, A. (2007) 'The state of gender equality law in the European Union', *European Law Journal*, 13(2), pp. 152–168.
Rossi, L.M. (2007) 'Outdoor pornification: Advertising heterosexuality in the streets', in *Pornification*. Berg, pp. 127–138.
Sarikakis, K. and Nguyen, E.T. (2009) 'The trouble with gender: Media policy and gender mainstreaming in the European Union', *European Integration*, 31(2), pp. 201–216.
Senden, L. (2005) 'Soft law, self-regulation and co-regulation in EU law: Where do they meet?' *Journal of Comparative Law*, 9(1).
Shelton, D. (2009) 'Soft law', in Armstrong, D. (ed.) *Routledge handbook of international law*. Routledge.
Snyder, F. (1993) 'The effectiveness of European Community Law: Limitations, processes, tools and techniques', *Modern Law Review*, 56(1), p. 33.
Terpan, F. (2015) 'Soft law in the European Union—The changing nature of EU law', *European Law Journal*, 21(1), pp. 68–96.
Trubek, D.M. and Trubek, L.G. (2005) 'Hard and soft law in the construction of social Europe: The role of the open method of co-ordination', *European Law Journal*, 11(3), pp. 343–364.
Trzaskowski, J.J., Savin, A., Lindskoug, P. and Lindqvist, B. (2015) *Introduction to EU internet law*. Ex Tuto Publishing.

Commission to the European Parliament, the Council, the European Economic and Social Committee and the Committee of the Regions on the application of Directive 2010/13/EU Audiovisual Media Service Directive 7 May 2012 COM (2012) 203
Council Directive 2004/113/EC of 13 December 2004 implementing the principles of equal treatment between men and women in the access to and supply of goods and services [2004] OJ L 373
Council Directive 2018/1808/EU on the coordination of certain provisions laid down by law, regulation or administrative action in Member States concerning the provision of audio-visual media services (Audio-visual Media Services Directive) [2018] OJ L95/1
Council Directive 2000/78/EC of 27 November 2000 establishing a general framework for equal treatment in employment and occupation [2000] *OJ L 303*
Council Directive 2010/12/EU on the coordination of certain provisions laid down by law, regulation or administrative action in Member States concerning the provision of audio-visual media services (Audiovisual Media Services Directive) [2010] OJ L95/1
Council Directive 2000/43/EC of 29 June 2000 implementing the principle of equal treatment between persons irrespective of racial or ethnic origin [2000] OJ L180
Council Directive 89/552, Television Without Frontiers Directive, Recital, 1989 O.J. (L 298)
Council Directive 2011/36/EU of the European Parliament and of the Council of 5 April 2011 on preventing and combating trafficking in human beings and protecting its victims
FIN CEDAW/C/FIN/5 2008 https://documents.un.org/doc/undoc/gen/n04/257/97/pdf/n0425797.pdf
Opinion of the European Economic and Social Committee on the 'Communication from the Commission—Strategy for the effective implementation of the Charter of Fundamental Rights by the European Union' COM(2010) 573 final (2011/C 376/14)
Regulation (EU) 2022/2065 of the European Parliament and of the Council of 19 October 2022 on a Single Market For Digital Services and amending Directive 2000/31/EC (Digital Services Act)
European Parliament. (2012) *Report on eliminating gender stereotypes in the EU* 2012/2116(INI))
Committee on Women's Rights and Gender Equality
Advisory Committee on Equal Opportunities for Women and Men Opinion on "Breaking gender stereotypes in the media" 28th December 2010
European Parliament. (2008) Report by the European Commission on Equality Between Women and Men (2008) Directorate-General for Employment, Social Affairs and Equal Opportunities
Communication from the Commission to the Council, he European parliament, The European Economic and social Committee and the Committee of the Regions. 'A Roadmap for equality between women and men 2006–2010 (COM (2006) 92)

Chapter 4

Theorising gender stereotypes

Introduction

This chapter provides a discussion of the concept of gender, outlining the theoretical position of this book. I largely draw on Erving Goffman's catalogue of concepts: commercial realism (1976), dramaturgy, performance and identity (1959), gender difference (1977) and how adverts present a distorted versions of gender and reality (1976). I also adopt Goffman's 'gender display' typologies from *Gender Advertisements* (1976) to measure the subtle form gender stereotypes take on in advertising. Through pictorial analysis, Goffman scrutinises advertisements for their 'openly contrived scenes' and how they present a distorted version of gender and reality, or what he calls 'commercial realism' (1976: 15). Commercial realism is distinctly different from the way we live our day-to-day lives; whereas in the everyday, behaviour is highly ritualised through impression management (Goffman, 1959), in which we each do our best to present the best versions of ourselves to the world (Scott, 2015). In advertisements, this presentation is a hyper-ritualised (Baudrillard, 1988), amplified, augmented and often distorted version of behaviour through forced poses and unnatural expressions. Commercial realism is therefore the technicolour version of reality. In real life as much as in advertisements, we can live out our reified social ideals, performing the 'perfect family' having a wholesome Christmas or enjoying a picnic in the park. This may also be true in advertisements; the advert will reflect the perfect smiling family, a social ideal of what having a 'good time' is. Yet visually, it appears—or ought to appear—highly edited, hyper-ritualised and manufactured. Back in reality, according to Goffman, we are 'stuck with a considerable amount of dull footage' (1976) that cannot be corrected or revised. Beyond 'commercial realism' and 'gender display', I draw on the sociological theorisations of gender identity (Lorber, 1994), dramaturgy, performance (Goffman, 1959), performativity (Butler, 1990), 'doing' gender (West and Zimmerman, 1987 and frame analysis (Goffman, 1974) to locate these terms within the broader contexts of social constructionism (Berger and Luckman, 1966; Butler, 1990; Goffman, 1976).

DOI: 10.4324/9781003336037-4

At the heart of this chapter are the works of Erving Goffman and Judith Butler: how both discern gender as a phenomenon that is constantly and ritualistically being 'done' in the social world, an identity that is attained as opposed to something that is essential or innate. Therefore, the 'doing' of gender is part of a societal effort rather than an individual endeavour and takes place through interaction and social construction through social norms and values that allow individuals to take part in some actions but prohibit or 'police' others. As *Gender Advertisements* is one of Goffman's final works, there are a litany of Goffman concepts spanning his career that have influenced his work on gender display. Therefore, this chapter extracts Goffman's earlier concepts (frame analysis, impression management) that have shaped the gender display framework. The chapter then inspects Goffman's views on some of the coding and typologies of 'gender displays' that appear in advertisements: 'feminine touch', 'licenced withdrawal', 'family' and 'ritualization of subordination' (1976: 27–47).

Doing, performing and scripting

Social constructionism posits that gender is a product of society, so society defines what is deemed masculine or feminine, what is 'ladylike', what is 'macho' and what the expected roles of men and women are (Butler, 1990; Lorber, 1994; Hacking, 1999). The social construction of gender can be understood by declaring what it is not: essentialist, the 'common sense' notion of biological difference and mapping an individual's gender onto their body. Essentialism observes gender through the correlation of sex organs and gender—that maleness and femaleness are the consequences of genitalia, and an individual's sex determines their gender. Binary perceptions of gender based on sex assume there is something essential about the individual: desires, talents and needs. Through an essentialist prism, one will see what legal rights that individual will be granted, what opportunities should come their way, what role they will play in society and what labour they will perform. To base gender on sex or to map gender onto an individual's sex organs is to accept that gender is somehow innate; it is that individual's essence, their decisions are based on their sex, and their sex is their destiny.

Social constructionism, on the other hand is, suggests that gender is performance. There is a 'doing' of gender, or, as Judith Lorber suggests in the essay 'Night of His Day', gender is 'created and re-created out of human interaction, out of social life, and is the texture and order of that social life . . . that depends on everyone constantly *doing* gender' (1994: 55–56). The process of 'doing gender' chimes with socialisation and cognitive development theorists (Parsons and Bales, 1956; Wadsworth, 1996) while the 'doing to' commences at the very beginning of life; parents discover the child's sex, talk to the baby in the womb in a certain way or, later on, decide how to dress the baby in distinct binary colours (Paoletti, 2012; Frisoli, 2019). The 'doing to' continues through to the naming of the child and other gender markers (Lorber and Farrell, 1991), such as the appropriate length of hair, choice of toys and dress code (Fine, 2011). If these gender markers are missing, unknown or ambiguous then, as Butler observes, one might feel uncomfortable or raise questions such as 'Is it a boy or a girl?' until the gender is recognised or understood. Once the gender markers have made the child's gender identity apparent to the world, both the behaviour of the child and parents' responses to that behaviour are shaped (Lorber, 1994). Gender markers are simultaneously learnt to equip them and understand gender distinctions. Equally, for the adult, parenting is gendered, with different expectations placed on mothers and fathers, which, in turn, shapes the career and work that the parents perform outside parenting (Butler, 1990: 185).

I wish to avoid cognitive or psychoanalytical theorisations of gender and move towards a sociological framing of 'doing gender'. I want to question why gendering is 'done' or appears in a state of 'doing' from birth into early childhood and beyond and explore the conceptualisation of gender as a social institution and structure. In doing so, I consider how institutions and structures such as the media and advertising act as agents in this 'doing'. As a backdrop to this discussion, I have so far begun to apply Lorber's notion of 'doing' and will continue this through Butler's and then Goffman's similar framing of 'doing' for the remainder of this chapter. For Butler, the dismissal of essentialist legitimisations of gender through claims that it is mapped by physical difference between men and women is further dislocated by transgenderism and intersexuality (1990). Here, Butler suggests that gender is constructed and learned, and the gender boundaries of male/female and masculine/feminine are ruptured by individuals who shift from one gender to another: 'These odd or deviant or third genders show us what we ordinarily take for granted—that people have to learn to be women and men' (1990: 57). Similarly, Lorber's assertion dovetails with Butler's theorisation as well De Beauvoir's adage that 'one is not born but rather becomes a woman. . . . [I]t is civilization as a whole that produces this creature . . . which is described as feminine' (1949: 267). As I will later go on to discuss, these claims run parallel to Goffman's theorisations of gendered identity and performance. Similar theorisations of gender walk the same semantic pathway; as West and Zimmerman note, the 'doing' follows once a gender has been recognised and ascribed in early childhood (1987: 142). Throughout childhood, individuals test gender through interaction with either parents or siblings of the same and opposite gender through expressing 'gender appropriate behaviour' (1987: 143). In adolescents, the 'gendered script' formulates through social interaction at different institutions such as school, peers and mass media, all of which guide young adults into their gendered lives. These gendered scripts can extend as far as the norms, such as the way individuals walk, gesture and eat (1987: 14; Young, 1980), and the institutionalisation of gender occurs when 'doing gender' is performed appropriately: individuals 'sustain, reproduce, and render legitimate the institutional arrangements' (1987: 14). For Erving Goffman, gender is seen as a social (and faux-spontaneous) script which is a performed based on society's imagining of innate feminine/masculine assumptions and stereotypes. The social script is then played out 'onstage' for the real (or perceived) audience, who are equally refined in the language of performance and script. Taken together, these theorisations so far are concerned with the performativity of gender—taking on a role or acting in some way that we present or 'display' to the rest of society Goffman (1976). Each of these theorisations of gender will be analysed accordingly, but for now, the significance of this discussion is that, broadly speaking, social constructionists dispute sex/gender essentialist discourse and offer that individuals have to be shown how masculine or feminine is 'done'. With such notions of 'doing', performing and acting and the scripting of gender, I now turn to theorisations of performativity and dramaturgy.

We 'do' rather than 'are'

Echoing theorisations of 'doing', both Butler and Goffman conceptualise gender as performance, claiming that no one true identity or core essential self exists behind gender, and it is neither stable nor absolute (Scott, 2015; Butler, 1990). The claim here is that gender is not natural; it is merely naturalized through repetition, with individuals believing in the 'correct' performance of their own designated gender. Being of a gender is therefore the side effect of cultural and social constructions. Butler's extension of West and Zimmerman's 'doing' once again evokes de Beauvoir's locus that individuals have agency during the becoming, but gender is nonetheless mere performance. Butler considers gender performance as taking on a role which is an act that is crucial to the gender being presented to the world, but the presentation is not merely a performance as this would assume the existence of an actor who is 'doing' that performance—or 'doing gender'. Instead, Butler's assertion is that performance is everything and, most importantly, precludes the existence of the performer (Salih, 2002). This is something that will be discussed later through Goffman's work on identity and the 'core self' or the 'actor behind the character' (Scott, 2013).

At this juncture there, is divergence in Butler's interpretation of gender identity. Gender as performance and gender as *performative* are somewhat different; the latter is principally the 'process of invoking the subject, not a performance by a subject' (Brickell, 2005: 24). These are the ways in which individuals amalgamate the impression of being either a man or a woman. According to Butler, individuals act as though being (either a man or a woman) is an internal reality. Thus, gender identity is a phenomenon—an experience—that is ceaselessly (re)produced over time. Accordingly, to say gender is *performative* is to claim that, from birth, there is no gender identity. To substantiate the claim, Butler disputes hegemonic constructs of gender as binary and offers up subversive and disruptive examples from the third genders or identities that fall outside the 'heterosexual matrix' ('sissy boys'; 'tomboys'; or transgender, queer, pansexual, genderless etc.). In doing so, Butler demonstrates the performativity of genders that lie outside the heterosexual matrix.

Subverting gender, gender roles and stereotypes is a hard task, with at least the fear of being bullied or physical threats of violence being made. Butler substantiates performativity through Foucauldian 'policing' of gender norms and the nuanced inquiry of the social construction of gender: How do these gender norms manifest in the first place, how do they persist, how are they policed, and what are the ways to disrupt them or perhaps subvert the policing? Some answers come in the form of examples from the social constructionist literature: for example, social intervention in childhood and adolescence, grimacing at behaviour deemed outside the gendered norms, or psychological intervention: 'Maybe you should get some help' or 'Why can't you be normal?' Amongst these structural/institutional and informal practices (bullying, ridiculing and ostracizing) that keep individuals fixed in their gendered positions, media and, indeed, advertising are instrumental. Advertising takes on a structural position, providing gender(ed) codes, norms and values that appear innate for feminine/masculine boundaries and order. By providing stringent norms, the viewer can be left in a state of powerlessness, unable to resist the 'policing' of advertising. This is something that both Butler and Goffman refute. At least for Goffman, in his understanding, the micro-politics of power in the everyday focuses on—and interrogates—individual agency and posits the possibilities of resistance. I will now start to map out some of Goffman's fundamental claims on gender as performance and gender display (that features in advertisements) by beginning with dramaturgy, the metaphor of performance and the 'front' and 'back' stages of that performance.

All the world's a stage

In *Presentation of Self in Everyday Life* (1959), Goffman evokes William Shakespeare's 'Seven Ages of Man' from *As You Like It* to colour his dramaturgical approach. Goffman suggests that social life is theatre, and 'all the worlds a stage and all the men and women are merely players. . . . [O]ne man in his time plays many parts'. As agentic 'actors' on a stage, individuals try out various performances, with each actor perpetually performing the role for self-presentation, relying on other actors to maintain the performance(s) and to keep 'the show' going. Like Butler's, Goffman's observation is one of continuous (self) regulation of behaviour: painting the best version of ourselves by adapting and adopting different masks in diverse situations. Thus, 'impression management' is, according to Goffman, the name of the game in social life: tailor and ritualise certain moves, routines, scripts and gestures to fit the various settings and actors we encounter in our everyday lives. Ultimately, Goffman argues that it is quite difficult to ever truly know or understand the self as the actor struggles and staggers from one performance to another, thus never really knowing which persona is the 'true self'.

Butler's work on gender identity is theoretically distinct from Goffman's ethnomethodological approach to order and identity (Brickell, 2003); however, their ideas echo one another, and as Smith (2006) notes, branches of Butler's work on gender identity and performativity resonate with Goffman's work on dramaturgy, ritual, frame analysis and gender display. This Butler-esque tone in Goffman's work is testament to his reading of gender as performance:

> One might just as well say there is no gender identity. There is only a schedule for the portrayal of gender. . . . [T]here is only evidence of the practice between the sexes of choreographing behaviourally a portrait of relationship.
>
> (Goffman, 1959: 8)

Understanding Goffman's route into gendered identity and gender performance, the 'schedule' for the portrayal and choreography is rooted in his earlier work on performance, ritual and display (1959). Goffman highlights the importance of interaction between actors and how it is to be understood sociologically through the metaphor of a theatrical performance and stage. Goffman painstakingly categorises performances and codes which require cooperation from audiences and other 'performers' or 'actors' to 'define the situation'. The 'actors' involved in social life carve out their own sense of self, informed by other actors' impressions and performances as they simultaneously attempt to manage their own self impression. This next part of the chapter will map some of the key concepts that ground Goffman's work on performance. From there, the chapter will then move on to look at the links between performance, gender display and gender codes in advertisements.

Exit stage left

When approaching notions of (gendered) performance, Goffman turns the question on its head by asking *why* individuals perform rather than *where* that performance comes from or *what* that performance is saying about the person (1959). At the centre of this inquiry is the notion that social life is 'always and everywhere' as we consciously play a (gendered) role, obtaining a character, becoming individuals and donning various 'masks' depending on the situation and our audience. Seeking interaction, social life leaves space for individuals to gain stock knowledge through osmosis (Schutz, 1970); through the experiences and interactions, we encounter reality in our everyday lives. At worst, we could perhaps be labelled as con artists, devious in our 'acting' and personas as we seek to guide and control others. Or, at best, we paint ourselves in the best light for how we want others to perceive us and to influence the 'definition of the situation' (1971). The impression management of the self is therefore vital to gendered performance—the way we dress, walk and talk differently according to whom we are with. The metaphor is taken further when Goffman conjures the demarcation and imagery of the back stage and front stage. In these two very separate—yet interconnected—worlds, individuals learn to (re)present themselves in certain situations. Goffman's understanding of front is the performance we give on the stage or in a 'setting'; this fixed space/place is where we encounter our fellow actors. In contrast, the back stage is the private space/place where actors relax 'out of character' to rehearse their identity and scripts, mindful of what has just occurred at the front stage during their performance (Scott, 2015: 17). Back/front stage movements and spaces are omnipresent in everyday life.

It is paramount that we create the best presentation of ourselves if we are to obtain the fruits of life: friendships, jobs, careers—to be liked and loved. Accordingly, impression management is a tool for success; we ensure we are more appealing to other people whilst front stage. The dramaturgical metaphor helps us understand and shape the presentation by asking how we use the stage and the setting. What does this stage say to others, and what does it say about us? Goffman argues that when we find ourselves in a social setting, we are on the front stage behaving like actors, accessing and utilising impression management at will to ensure the best version of ourselves is projected on to the audience. Exiting the front stage may occur when we are no longer required or, indeed, when the other actors have exited, and we have no one else to interact with. Panic may ensue when we are faced with not enough material or lines to use for the interaction. But we are safe back stage; we can relax and learn how we should be on the front. Once here, with no one else to monitor us, our (gendered) performance is dropped, and we no longer need to perform as there is no one to interact with.

Parameters of performance

There are, of course, some limits to Goffman's conceptualisation of dramaturgy, performance front/back stage and the self and certainly how far this allegory can be taken. As I mentioned previously, the movement between the two worlds or the difference between spaces/places may lead to existentialist anxiety around the 'true self'. Similarly, Butler disputes the notional 'true self', and such back stage regions are rare privileges. Goffman too is lucid: there is no authentic self at the core of who we are, nor is there any notion maleness or femaleness—the self is born out of the individual's incessant management and self-impression towards other actors (Goffman, 1972: 26; Brickell, 2005).

The front stage is not entirely improvised; we have rehearsed it meticulously over the years, crafting a representation of ourselves and who we want others to think we are. Impression management and self-presentation can be viewed as an individual enhancing certain aspects of their character whilst muting other elements to achieve the desired result. The performance in this way is not entirely scripted in the back stage; it is at least part improvised or spontaneous due to the various roles we may select from the back stage. The repertoire of crafted roles is rooted in the experience of interaction that goes from early childhood through to adulthood. Thus, Goffman's conceptualisation of 'performance' has limitations as we can never really know what is going to happen when we go 'live' on the stage. One can never rehearse for every potential situation or eventual interaction. Goffman does, however, maintain the notion of a 'core self', and when referring to the relief that is felt back stage: 'Behind many masks and many characters, each performer tends to where a single look, a naked unsocialised look' (1959: 235).

It is at this point the success of impression management relies on a consensus and support from the other actors; they must keep the situation (as joint performance) alive and avoid embarrassment. If one of the actors puts a foot wrong, then the interaction has the potential of breaking down. Goffman calls this 'performance team' or, as Scott notes, 'teamwork' relying on the 'tact' of a collective 'defining the situation', ensuring that the routine performance appears effortless. The team may need to pull together to save face; a poor performer, a slip of the tongue—any back stage slippage must be brushed under the carpet. Like Butler's use of Foucauldian panopticon imagery, there is surveillance at play in Goffman's teamwork. The actor wants their audience to see consistency between the expected behaviour and the idealised gendered self. There is inevitable risk that if an idealised performance is inconsistent, the audience will see behaviour that belongs in the back stage enter the front stage, and the performance may collapse entirely. Again, Goffman's notion of the performance, self-presentation and the theatre metaphor are not wholly synonymous. Theatre is an illusion; audiences know that real actors have time to perfect performance, to rehearse their roles back stage before they play out their parts (Scott, 2017). In real life, one can prepare their own personal role for the best performance they want to achieve, but the performance is constantly evolving, improving based on previous experiences and knowledge. Goffman's work chimes with Butler's framing of performativity; there is improvisation and spontaneity, which suggest room for autonomy of the performance, independent of the actor.

Front stage as gender(ing) performance

The 'front stage' is an important place when understanding the latter works of *Gender Advertisements* on which this book is based. The front is where gender identity is performed, where it is negotiated and where it can become fixed. The front stage can be broken down into three interlocking parts: setting, appearance and manner. The static setting (i.e. the physical arrangement) might be a living room, comprising furniture, décor and scenery that assist the performer's role and also props: remote control, newspapers, books (1959: 32). The appearance and manner make up the 'personal front', the expressive equipment that informs the audience of the performer's gender: clothing, looks, size, posture, speech patterns, facial expressions, bodily gestures. The personal front appears fixed, but some elements can and will change over one's lifetime. As Goffman notes:

> [D]ifferent routines may employ the same front. . . . [A] social front tends to become institutionalized in terms of abstract stereotyped expectations to which it gives rise and tends to take on a meaning and stability apart from the specific tasks which happened at the time to be performed in its name. The front becomes a 'collective representation' and a fact in its own right.
>
> (1959: 35)

The front is therefore a selection of performances designed to avoid embarrassment, taboo or breaching social norms and so not entirely agentic. Due to fear of breaching societal norms, the actor is forced into selecting a social/personal front, and, as these are chosen rather than created, certain performers may run into trouble when they are obliged to select a front appropriate for the specific moment. There are correct ways to act, and 'acting out' will result in others 'saving' the actor to avoid embarrassment or shame (1959: 266). Goffman's use of the props, scenery, manner and appearance also helps shape fundamental Western stereotypical idealisations of gender: for example, hair (length, style, colour), make-up, handbag, voice and, as will become apparent, pose, posture and height—each takes on a meaning to provide stereotypical gendered expectations.

This motif is extended in Goffman's work in *Frame Analysis*, in which performances are involuntary or constrained by the 'principles of organization which govern events' (1974: 10). The metaphorical framing (structures) that helps understand the picture (context) is invoked here and draws on notions of cognitive organisation of experience and the process of deciphering what is happening (and what is significant) in any given experience to build frames to produce our perception of reality. Drawing on phenomenology and notions of stock knowledge (Schutz, 1970; Husserl, 2013), Goffman claims that individuals 'frame' experiences in order to organise current understandings of the world but also to guide future actions. However, individuals are not wilfully manufacturing these frames; they are unconsciously adopted and adapted, depending on the social situation.

Reading gender as a social front, the performer can present some statements for their audience and shape their performance of gender accordingly. In this regard, the performance is a presentation that is 'moulded and modified' to idealised 'expectations of the society in which it is presented to' (1974: 45). Goffman's works on gender display in *Gender Advertisements* (1976) amalgamate the aforementioned ideas surrounding dramaturgy, performance, impression management, front stage and framing with the guiding notion of gender as social front. Goffman asserts that gender is interactionally consequential, and the consequences of repeated gendered practices formulate gender as a social institution. In gender display, through an analysis of gender as difference, Goffman arrives at the anti-biological essentialist pathway and endorses the view that gender is socially produced through interaction:

> Women do, and men don't gestate, breast-feed infants, and menstruate as part of their biological character. So, too, women on the whole are smaller and lighter boned and muscled than men. For these physical facts of life to have no appreciable social consequence would take a little organizing, but, at least by modern standards, not much.
>
> (1977: 301)

Just as Lorber, Butler and West and Zimmerman question why social difference should reflect 'natural' differences, Goffman similarly asserts that gender does reflect sex in society, and it is unnatural when a society claims it as truth or natural. Social difference therefore defines an individual's role, traits and social position. Goffman evokes 'institutional reflexivity': 'a newish phrase for an old social anthropological doctrine' (1977: 301), which requires the individual to perceive themselves as an agent within a wider structure that is open to the socialisation of that social structure (Giddens, 1991). The more reflexive the agent, the more inclined they are to shape their structure. In contrast, the less reflexive one is the more malleable they are and thus shaped by the structure. Thus, reflexivity shows how society treats men and women differently based on myths and gender stereotypes. Applying institutional reflexivity, Goffman refers to it as 'whenever an environment is manipulated so that it exaggerates sex differences in order to justify gender inequalities' (1977: 323). Differential treatment is vindicated and normalized by 'folk beliefs' (Cohen, 1972) about what is essentially known about the two genders (biology, physiology, temperament, traits etc.). Physiological and biological differences do not account for the social difference or disparate treatment that men and women receive in their everyday lives. The notion of biological difference rationalises and (over)simplifies difference via the use of gender-based stereotypes, and so the question is, why should it account for the unequal social and legal treatment of the two genders—e.g. status, rights and opportunities? It is here that Goffman contributes to the social constructionist/essentialist debate, maintaining that there are numerous institutionalised social practices (that are justified, excused and deemed 'natural' through the essentialist differences between the sexes) at play, and these practices (re)produce gender differences. The crux of the theory rests on a simple question: If the biological difference is *x*, why does this account for social difference? Goffman's answer is that institutionalised social practices (institutional reflexivity) present themselves as natural or normal and are used to produce and honour social difference. To sum up, repetitive social practices through interaction order produce gender (1977: 313).

The response to the cultural difference versus natural debate is an account that describes how social environments are constructed to amplify and exaggerate gender difference. Differential treatment is a result of this process, and the differential treatment is justified or excused through reference to innate biological differences between the sexes. Goffman offers five examples of institutional reflexivity: gendered division of labour, siblings as socialisers, the gendered division of toilet arrangements, selective job placement and, finally, the identification system: an actor being 'gendered' by their audiences through sight, tone of voice, title, clothes etc. (1959: 301–314). According to Smith, this analysis is critically overlooked by feminists (Smith, 2006) and is crucial to understanding social difference and also gender stereotypes in advertising. In each of these five examples, Goffman stresses that biological and essentialist discourse disguise the phenomenon they produce; gender difference is the production of institutionalised reflexivity. It is therefore (re)produced through institutionalised social practices via folklore, long-held unshakeable beliefs and myths on the differences between men and women, the interactions that take place, sustain and endure. It is these beliefs that are the real source of the presumed differences between the sexes. These practices are problematic when they are projected onto interactional fields, and the resulting scenes 'do not so much allow for the expression of natural differences between the sexes as for the production of that difference' (1977: 324). Needless to say, one of the institutions that project these practices is advertising.

I have so far outlined some of the broad(er) similarities and differences between Goffman's and Butler's theorisations of gender, exploring gender as dramaturgical, formed in dialogue between back and front stage as performative and constituted through 'repetitive attempts of being'. Butler's concept of performativity offers up similarities and parallels to Goffman's emphasis of performance within the theatrical characteristics (dramaturgy) of social life and behaviour. There are some differences and limitations to these theorisations of gender that are worth briefly discussing before moving on to the next section, where I will outline the specifics of Goffman's coding of advertisements. Unlike Goffman's interpretation of gender, Butler leaves little room for notions of agency:

> My argument is that there need not be a 'doer behind the deed', but that the 'doer' is variably constructed in and through the deed.
>
> (1990: 195)

Butler's claim 'there is no doer behind the deed' or no performer behind the act limits possibilities for change. Since *Gender Trouble* emerged, critics of Butler remain sceptical of the conceptualisation of performativity and whether it instils or excludes notions of agency in the subject. Benhabib has questioned the underlying argument that draws Butler and Goffman together: whether or not that there is a 'self' behind the mask, and if there is no gender identity behind the 'the expressions of gender', then how can women change these expressions? (Salih, 2002: 60).

> If we are no more than the sum total of the gendered expressions we perform, is there ever any chance to stop the performance for a while, to pull the curtain down, and let it rise only if one can have a say in the production of the play itself?
>
> (Benhabib, 2017: 21)

Benhabib's critique of the ability to transform with little (or no) agency in the process is taken further by Salih:

> Butler is not suggesting that the subject is free to choose which gender she or he is going to enact. 'The script', if you like, is always already determined within this regulatory frame, and the subject has a limited number of 'costumes' from which to make a constrained choice of gender style.
>
> (2003: 56)

This is where Goffman and Butler diverge. The backstage 'script' indicates agency; though sometimes spontaneous, it is constructed and crafted. The (im)possibility of change in Bulter's work has been critiqued by Nussbaum (1999), who argues that Butler's notion of identity is unstable, relying on the constitutive outside, thus removing the possibility of one desiring and subscribing to an identity-based subject in terms of formulating social relations As Benhabib argues, this impossibility for change is problematic for the subject:

> Given how fragile and tenuous women's sense of selfhood is in many cases, how much of a hit and miss affair their struggles for autonomy are, this reduction of female agency to 'a doing without the doer' at best appears to me to be making a virtue out of necessity.
>
> (2017: 22)

The question is whether Butler and Goffman deny agency through the deconstruction of the self, or their contribution is a critique of normative constructions of agency, in which claims to an 'I' are always claims of power and therefore inherently relational—I can only claim an identity through the constitution of an unspeaking other.

Advertising: making the familiar strange

In *Gender Advertisements*, Goffman applies institutional reflexivity of gender difference to billboard and magazine advertising. At the core of this materially vast book is his conceptualisation of gender display(s) that appear in all forms of advertising where there are 'actors' (male/female) present. Gender display is the subtle ways in which advertisers choreograph gender difference in advertisements. The subconscious displaying of gender tricks the consumer—or, as Goffman states, the audience are not even aware of it—into believing that this is a true display of gender. Moreover, once the gender display has been (de)coded, adverts featuring men and women together will appear bizarre to the audience. These taken-for-granted and accepted ways in which the advertiser conducts gender are mere representations; they are the 'hyper-reality' (Baudrillard, 1988) of gender difference that exists in the everyday. Through pictorial analysis, the scrutiny moves beyond broad gender-stereotypical themes of adverts to the subtler compositions within the 'frame'. Four dominant codes will be used in this chapter and Chapter 5: feminine touch, licenced withdrawal, ritualisation of subordination and family. There are two further codes that aid these dominant typologies: function ranking (men are in an executive role and the woman merely in a functional position) and relative size (the woman is smaller or lower than the man), and these are used fleetingly in the next chapter.

Goffman's core typology, 'feminine touch', is often portrayed in adverts wherein the woman is lightly touching herself or the product or 'using their fingers and hands to trace the outlines of an object . . . to cradle it or to caress its surface' (1976: 29). The light touch of the woman's hands (in contrast to the firm, utilitarian grip and control of men's) can involve self-caressing or touching of the cheek, hair, shoulders or mouth. This positions the body as a soft 'precious thing' as well as delicate and fragile, all the while in contrast to the adverts displaying the masculine clenched fist, tight grip or pointing/waving finger. The woman is more often than not positioned as sexualised, lightly touching her mouth, hand, arm crotch or breast. This is not just to accentuate femininity but to display sexual availability, accessible and tempting for the consumer. Feminine touch remains a pervasive central typology. As Gill states, '[W]hile men's touch was functional and instrumental . . . women [were] light and caressing and often seemed to have no purpose at all' (2007: 79). For this typology, women are tenderly touching the product or lightly touching themselves (hands, legs or, most often, their face and lips) in an irregular way to exert the idea that women are gentle, soft and caring. This phenomenon is still visible and most prevalent throughout the data from participants in all three countries in Chapter 5.

The second code, licensed withdrawal, refers to the woman as withdrawn from the situation, in a dreamlike ethereal state, looking away into the distance, down at the ground, bashful or perhaps covering her face with her hands. The code also alludes to notions of infantilisation, how adverts portray the woman as childlike in her approach to the world or quite simply psychologically removed, absent or dormant in the situation. Similar to feminine touch, it reveals undertones of vulnerability and fragility and upholds that women are often gripping on to the man, clutching their arm, looking for physical support, whereas, in contrast, he is confident in his stance and position within the frame. Goffman notes the man often holds his 'hands in his pockets' or is looking directly at the audience, always in control, always anchored, either gripping someone or something. Goffman's coding often speaks to a lack of agency; the woman is often found in a dreamlike state, suggests that the portrayal promotes indecisiveness or the will to act independently. In the licensed withdrawal typology, the woman is in need of reassurance or encouragement from the male counterpart to command or physically manipulate her. 'Licensed withdrawal' refers to women in advertisements who appear disoriented, psychologically removed from a social situation. Goffman states that:

> Women more than men, it seems, are pictured engaged in involvements which remove them psychologically from the social situation at large, leaving them unoriented in it and to it, and presumably, therefore, dependent on the protectiveness and goodwill of others who are (or might come to be) present.
>
> (Goffman, 1976: 270)

This category includes adverts in which women appear to be lost, confused, in a state of surprise, shock or dumbfounded. The code alludes to notions of infantilisation, portraying women as childlike in approach, often hands over mouth giggling, laughing and hiding a smile from the viewer beneath a product, object or hand (i.e. peek-a-boo). There is somewhat of an overlap with the 'feminine touch' code; however, this category is unique in that it taps into the stereotypical myths about women not in control and men as alert, aggressors or superior. This category speaks to notions of vulnerability, fragility and infantilism which are in stark contrast to the dominant self-aware male counterpart in the shot. Goffman notes the man often holds his 'hands in his pockets' or is looking 'directly at the viewer', always in control, always anchored—either gripping someone or something as a mode of announcing authority. Goffman's coding in *Gender Advertisements* does not speak of lack of agency; however, the way in which the woman is often found in a dreamlike state suggests that the portrayal promotes indecisiveness or the inability to act independently. In licensed withdrawal–coded advertisements, the woman is in need of constant reassurance from the male counterpart to command or physically manipulate her.

The third code, ritualisation of subordination, is the representation of the woman as physically lower in the frame in terms of position than her male counterpart(s). This code will—more often than not—include a woman lying passive on the ground, on one knee or kneeling down on all fours. She may also be standing on one leg with a bended knee or tilting her head to one side as if to look into the distance (a slight overlap with 'licenced withdrawal'). Once again, there are sexual undertones present in this categorisation of the woman's sexual availability or subservient or promiscuous positioning. Moreover, locating the woman lower demotes her as weaker, in terms of strength but also in terms of symbolic power and position in society (Bourdieu, 1991). Ritualisation of subordination appears when women adopt postures such as 'bashful' with arms or knees bent or lying down in order to indicate submission to men's authority.[1] Goffman noted that in advertisements that featured someone sitting or lying on a bed or a floor, that person was frequently a woman, a child or a woman in a childlike position or playful mood. Women are often found lying on some type of surface, whether a bed, floor or chair, in an unnatural fashion or an unnatural setting. The face (if shown) is perhaps confused or—utilising another code—'withdrawn'. It could also manifest as a dismembered body: the audience views just the legs, torso or breasts with the head cut off/out of shot.

The fourth typology, family, incorporates portrayals of everyday domestic life and the symmetrical illusions of the traditional nuclear family. For example, the mother and daughter will look or dress similar (or indeed the *exactly* same), irrespective of age, when they are participating in a similar activity, such as cooking, cleaning or applying make-up. In these hyper-reality adverts, there are 'devices [that] are employed to exhibit the presumed special bond between the girl and the mother and the boy and the father, sometimes in the same picture' (1991: 37). The same code applies to father and son, who are often participating in a highly gendered activity or game. Within the 'family' coding, Goffman observes, there is often an overlap with 'relative size': the father will always be taller or in a powerful position in comparison with his son, whereas mother and daughter will be of equal size (unless the daughter is much younger). 'Family' is a portrayal of domestic symmetry in the traditional nuclear family: a mother/daughter or father/son coupling will look similar (or, indeed, the same) or be participating in a similar activity, such as cooking, cleaning or applying make-up. In these hyper-reality mocked images or films, there are 'devices [that] are employed to exhibit the presumed special bond between the girl and the mother and the boy and the father, sometimes in the same picture' (Goffman, 1976: 37). In an advert for Patek Phillippe, the father and son strike a similar pose, the son emulating the father, the same confident look exhibiting a presumed 'special bond' over the object (the watch). The relative size is also noticeable; the father is taller.

1 A 2006 Dolce and Gabbana advert that depicted pseudo gang rape resurfaced on Twitter in February 2015. In 2006, the Advertising Standards Agency received 160 complaints claiming that it breached the ASA code, in that it condoned 'violence or anti-social behaviour'. See: http://www.huffingtonpost.co.uk/2015/03/18/dolce-and-gabbana0gang-rape-advert_n_6893044.html.

Similarly, in a Nivea advertisement, the mother and daughter are exhibiting a 'special bond' over the desired product. This is common in beauty advertisements in which the daughter is learning from the mother. Here, 'relative size' is the same; however, the mother is positioned in a subordinate position, crouched on the floor—there are also signs of 'feminine touch'—the fingertips of the mother delicately placing the cream on the child.

The auxiliary codes, function ranking and relative size, overlap somewhat, the former function ranking positions the woman lower within the advert or social structure (family, the workplace or any other social arrangement). Goffman proposes that when an advertisement involves a type of instruction, men are always the active agent, instructing or teaching women as if they were children (lower in the composition or actively listening). In a D&G advert, there is a mixture of two of Goffman's typologies. There is the 'function ranking': the man instructing (pointing) whilst the woman is slightly subordinate (arm turned inwards), but there is also the code 'relative size': the man is looming over the woman and has his arm around her gripping her, childlike, adding to the notion of instruction. Relative size (or sometimes 'social weight') portrays the phenomenon whereby the man is placed in a position above the woman or is seen to bigger in either height, size or sheer volume. He may not necessarily be above or bigger; he may be protruding or closer to the shot. This phenomenon is apparent when looking at the negative: it is rare to see the opposite, with the woman above, in control or instructing the man. Women are often shown to be smaller than men as a way to demonstrate their vulnerability and weaker emotional states. Goffman's analysis of this grouping centres on the height and girth of men: when compared to women, they are often taller or in control. This is a prevalent theme in adverts today: where at least one man and one woman will feature, the man is often taller and the woman shorter. This is particularly apparent when the man is displaying (or sometimes representing) power and strength. Goffman continues that, conversely, in advertisements in which women are meant to be socially superior to men, the women are frequently taller than the men, which powerfully demonstrates the value that society places on height as a symbol of influence and control. There may also be an added blankness or vacuity to the face. In the Gillette Venus razor advert, the woman is in a subordinate position with the man above her in control of the situation, his right hand on her leg, his legs wrapped around her, cocooning her body.

As discussed, gender display(s) in advertisements is not a consequence of evolution between the sexes, nor is it inextricably linked to essentialist ideas that these displays are natural; instead, there are 'schedules' for gender in advertising. This is akin to Goffman's dramaturgical approach and performance: it is all an act. In *Gender Advertisements*, Goffman revisits dramaturgical approaches to social norms and cultural values and uses the example 'a family on holiday' and how they may follow the cues for 'having a nice time'. This act may well come from the self, but it may also come from external schedules of 'having a nice time' as seen in many adverts selling breakfast cereal, toothpaste or cars. This cyclic approach can also be applied to displays and schedules of gender. As Gornick states, '[M]en and women take their cues about "gender behaviour" from the image of that behaviour that advertising throws back at them, and they contrive to become the "people" in those ads' (Gornick, 1979: viii). The engineering of the self is the most relevant in Goffman's work, the cyclical nature of individual actors taking cues from advertisements and mirroring or replicating the act in their 'real life' performances.

This is connected to the dramaturgical theorisations of performance and identity or social constructionist ideas of performance in which advertising is one of the many institutions for the conditioning of gender. At the core of the book is the term 'depicted femininity' or the adult-child relation portrayed in adverts featuring men as dominant figures, paternalistic in stance, and the women as the maternal. Goffman states that one of the best ways to understand advertising is to compare the gender display to the parent-child relationship in which the man in the advert will almost always take on the role of the parent whilst the subjugated woman behaves (or appears to behave) like a child. This will be discussed towards the end of chapter, but two examples are worth noting: women's hands barely touching or grasping an object or touching their own bodies or faces. There are inevitable overlaps of the themes (e.g. feminine touch), but this strand of thought applies where there is a male/female composition in the advert. The woman will also be seen to be in a daze whilst under the control of the male gaze or clutch of hands. This may be shown by a finger to the lips or the woman cuddling into the man as if to require protection, just like a child. As Gornick adds, infantilism is a distinct feature of gender stereotypes in advertising:

> [Women posing as] children, acting like children, looking like children: utterly devoid of the natural sobriety which one associates with the adult men. Grown women are seen standing with the head cocked away over to the side parallel to the shoulder, face front, eyes and mouth: smiling; or the head tucked into the shoulder, face-front, eyes looking up from under lowered lids, seductive-gamin style; or hands twisted behind the back; or the toes of one foot standing on the toes of the others in a 'aw gosh gee' posture; or arms and legs flying off in all directions like a clown; or hands dug deep into the pockets, the facial expression 'wicked' or 'merry'; and on every last face that damned 'dazzling' smile'.
>
> (Gornick, 1979)

In the next chapter, I will discuss how post-feminist thought has sought to argue that a shift has occurred in contemporary advertising, moving away from Goffmanesque infantilism to active resistance and mockery where the gender display and its interpretation are more complex (Malson et al., 2011; Blloshmi, 2013; Rome et al., 2020). However, what remains true in Goffman's analysis of advertising is the intricate detail, the mundanity, the everyday, the overlooked features that are brought to the foreground: clutched hands, jagged posture, arm(s) to waist or hip, finger biting, bended knees, sucking of fingers and rolled eyes but also the inverse: over-aggressive men shaving, pointing, grabbing, looking directly at the camera, a reassuring smile, confident laughter, arms folded, bended knee on an object. Gender displays that advertisers tirelessly regurgitate should appear peculiar and strange, but instead, audiences merely take them for granted as innate truths about gender. What is also apparent is the choreography of the gender displays: men and women are depicted as opposites. For example, in both 'ritualisation of subordination' and 'licenced withdrawal', the woman is 'kept in her place', whereas the man is seen dominating the product, space or woman. Goffman is somewhat apolitical in his approach, yet it is clear what he sets out to achieve: debunking the essentialist narrative or at least portray it as a fallacy. Gender is socially produced, and advertising plays a significant part in manufacturing it through codes and displays of gender.

Observing themes in gendered advertising

Throughout this chapter, I have explored Goffman's work on gender display, social difference and the codes derived from *Gender Advertisements*. In this final section of the chapter, I further explore these advertisement gender codes, which will be revisited and used to map gender display in contemporary adverts in Chapter 6. Based on his coding system, Goffman acknowledges gendered phenomena that are prominent in adverts, and there are some that I wish to draw out further. As a review, it is important to note that Goffman argues that in these frames, the positioning of the bodies and displays are counter to innate biology and natural traits—they are culturally defined versions of 'gender display'. The overarching theme in this work is gendered subordination—the idea that men are superior to women and women are in the shadow of men, often looking for or yearning for them in the frames. Essentially, advertisements are a reflection of Western culture: the feminine is subordinate in relation to what is revered as masculine. As noted, before, the messages in advertising have become normal, accepted and established so much so that they no longer appear odd. Once we question these unnatural poses, we can see the subordination, infantilisation and vacancy of the feminine body.

First, overwhelmingly, the woman in the advert is hardly ever taller than—or positioned above—the man. Second, the woman's hands are always touching, holding or caressing the product; they are never clutching, grasping or manipulating it (unlike men, who appear to be in control or handling the product with vigour and force). Third, when depicting instruction, the image will show the woman being instructed by the man. This is true also if the advert involves children—the boy will almost certainly be instructing or controlling the girl. Fourth, if the advert requires someone to lie on the floor or the bed, it will be the woman who is positioned passively and horizontally whilst the man is active and standing. Fifth, women are frequently depicted as drifting—either mentally or physically. This can be either when the woman is alone or with a man. If with a man, the woman will be shown as 'dreamy' or confused. The man, in contrast, will be asymmetrically alert with the readiness to compensate for the vacuous stance of the woman. Sixth, and related to this, women are pictured as lost or removed from the situation, leaving them disorientated or passive. Finally, when the man's gaze or head is averted, it is always towards something he is superior to (whether an object, female or child), whereas when the female gaze is averted, it is towards whatever male (old, young, child) is beside her.

Conclusion

This chapter began with the theorisations of the social construction of gender through the prism of Butler's and Goffman's work on performance and performativity. I then discussed Goffman's formation of dramaturgical frameworks in understanding social life, the use of frame analysis, social difference, institutional reflexivity and how his later work on gender display and advertisements was informed by his earlier work. Focusing on gender display and gendered advertisements, I outlined how the social structure of advertising shapes gender and how Goffman's work informs my analysis of gendered discourse in advertising. I then looked towards the numerous 'gender display' typologies that Goffman carved out through a meticulous catalogue of billboards and newspaper cuttings and offered contemporary manifestations to fit each typology. The aim of this chapter is to lay the theoretical foundations of this thesis: to test the contemporaneity of Goffman's coding and pictorial analysis from *Gender Advertisements*, particularly in the context of how new modes of advertising are in emergence since his 'static' analysis was formulated. The chapter outlines the predominant typologies in *Gender Advertisements* as a foundation upon which I build in Chapter 6. I have sought to sketch a reimagining of Goffman's coding by introducing contemporary images and, by doing so, start the process of revisiting, updating and testing Goffman's typologies. The final sections of the chapter showcase the abundance of 'coding within the typology', which Goffman succinctly deploys throughout *Gender Advertisements*, and the richness of his 'thick description' will be utilised in the analysis of data in Chapter 6.

References

Baudrillard, J. (1988) *Simulacra and simulations*. University of Michigan Press.
Benhabib, S. (2017) *Feminist contentions: A philosophical exchange*. Routledge.
Berger, P. L. and Luckmann, T. (1966) *The social construction of reality: A treatise in the sociology of knowledge*. Garden City, NY: Anchor Books.
Blloshmi, A. (2013) 'Advertising in post-feminism: The return of sexism in visual culture?', *Journal of Promotional Communications*, 1(1).
Bourdieu, P. (1991) *Language and symbolic power*. Polity.
Brickell, C. (2003) 'Performativity or performance? Clarifications in the sociology of gender', *New Zealand Sociology*, 18(2), pp. 158–178.

Brickell, C. (2005) 'Masculinities, performativity, and subversion: A sociological reappraisal', *Men and Masculinities*, 8(1), pp. 24–25.
Butler, J. (1990) *Gender trouble*. Routledge.
Cohen, S. (1972) *Folk devils and moral panics: The creation of the mods and rockers*. London, England.
Fine, C. (2011) *Gender delusion*. ICON Books.
Frisoli, A. (2019) 'How commercial advertising enforces gender stereotypes among children and the ways this affects them psychologically', *Sacred Heart University Scholar*, 3(1).
Giddens, A. (1991) 'Structuration theory: Past, present and future'. In: Bryant, C.G.A. and Jary, D., Eds., *Giddens' theory of structuration: A critical appreciation*. London: Routledge, pp. 201–221.
Gill, R.M. (2007) *Gender and the media*. Polity Press.
Goffman, E. (1959) 'Goffman, Erving', *The presentation of self in everyday life*. Bantam Doubleday Dell Publishing Group.
Goffman, E. (1974) *Frame analysis: An essay on the organization of experience*. Cambridge, MA: Harvard University Press.
Goffman, E. (1976) *Gender advertisements*. New York: Harper.
Goffman, E. (1977) 'The arrangement between the sexes', *Theory and Society*, 4(3).
Gornick, V. (1979) *Introduction in Goffman, E (1976) gender advertiments*. New York Harper.
Husserl, E. (2013) *The idea of phenomenology: A translation of Die Idee Der Phänomenologie Husserliana II*. Vol. 8. Springer Science & Business Media.
Lorber, J. (1994) 'Night to his day', in Tracey, O. (ed.) *The social construction of gender. The social construction of difference: Race, class, gender and sexuality*. McGraw Hill Humanities.
Lorber, J. and Farrell, S.A. (eds.) (1991) *The social construction of gender*. Newbury Park, CA: Sage, pp. 309–321.
Malson, H., Halliwell, E., Tischner, I. and Rúdólfsdóttir, A. (2011) 'Post-feminist advertising laid bare: Young women's talk about the sexually agentic woman of "midriff" advertising', *Feminism & Psychology*, 21(1), p. 74.
Nussbaum, M. (1999) 'The professor of parody: The hip defeatism of Judith Butler', *The New Republic*. Available at: https://newrepublic.com/article/150687/professor-parody (Accessed: 21 June 2024).
Paoletti, J.B. (2012) *Pink and blue: Telling the boys from the girls in America*. Indiana University Press.
Parsons, T. and Bales, R.F. (1956) *Family socialization and interaction process*. Vol. 7. Psychology Press.
Rome, A.S., O'Donohoe, S. and Dunnett, S. (2020) 'Problematizing the postfeminist gaze: A critical exploration of young women's readings of gendered power relations in advertising', *Journal of Macromarketing*, 40(4), pp. 546–562.
Salih, S. (2002) *Judith Butler*. Routledge.
Schutz, A. (1970) *Alfred Schutz on phenomenology and social relations*. Vol. 360. University of Chicago Press.
Scott, S. (2009) *Making sense of everyday life*. Polity Press.
Scott, S. (2015) *Negotiating identity*. Polity Press.
Scott, S. (2017) 'Erving Goffman', in Stones, R. (ed.) *Key Sociology thinkers*. Bloombsury.
Smith, G. (2006) *Erving Goffman*. Routledge.
Wadsworth, B.J. (1996) 'Piaget's theory of cognitive and affective development: Foundations of constructivism'.
West, C. and Zimmerman, D.H. (1987) 'Doing gender', *Gender & Society*, 1(2).
Young, I.M. (1980) 'Throwing like a girl: A phenomenology of feminine body comportment motility and spatiality', *Human Studies*, 3(1), pp. 137–156.

Chapter 5

Teenage voices

Introduction

This chapter further develops Goffman's gender display codes by analysing contemporary adverts as well as adverts taken from the focus groups participants; 'visual diaries' across the three case studies in Sweden, Spain and the UK. Throughout this chapter, I disseminate the core themes from the discussions and visual diaries gleaned from the focus groups. By revisiting and reflecting on Goffman's codes, I contend that gender stereotypes in advertising are not only discriminatory and display undertones of sexism but they also have a negative impact on the audience's perception of gender identity, self, objectification and sexualisation. I argue that the data supports this hypothesis and conclude that advertising is an implicit factor in the broader context of gender inequalities and subordination.

Goffman's typologies have informed the selection of data and subsequent analysis; they also help frame the similarities and differences in contemporary gendered advertising. Throughout this chapter, Goffman's typologies are revived to compare and contrast the contemporality of his codes when juxtaposed with modern adverts. In *Gender Advertisements*, Goffman's apolitical analysis of advertising downplays the undertones of misogyny, sexualisation and objectification in his coding; therefore, this chapter revisits the codes from a more critical and politicised perspective and makes use of them with advertising regulation in mind. Therefore, in this chapter, I wish not only to apply Goffman's coding to move beyond highlighting the mere absurdities of gender displays in advertising but also to argue that they are are problematic, misogynistic and discriminatory. In *Gender Advertisements*, the array of advertisements stems from a more innocent age of advertising with different style and target markets and, indeed, legal regulation. A further intention here is not only to revisit but also to update and develop Goffman's coding categories in light shifts in advertising technique and culture.

Three broad thematic categories materialised from the focus groups with further nuanced subthemes. The first theme, women as mothers, is congruent to 'feminine touch' and 'licensed withdrawal': specifically, the woman's

DOI: 10.4324/9781003336037-5

hands are seen to be touching, holding or caressing the product. They will also be looking into the distance: i.e. away from the scene or out of the frame. The subcategory 'mother the multitasker' also reflects Goffman's category of the family: mirrored patterns between mother and daughter where the clothes, hair, act or actions are symmetrical. I also develop the subthemes of irony, mockery and resistance, where mother(hood) is deconstructed and mocked in the advert. The second theme of neuroticism or 'women on the verge' (of insanity or hysteria or 'bonkers') reflects Goffman's licensed withdrawal typology with notions of simultaneous emptiness and phrenzy; a lack of agency or effect. Thirdly, objectified self, centres on degradation and hyper-sexualisation of the body. This theme is influenced by a confluence of three of Goffman's codes: ritualisation of subordination, licensed withdrawal and feminine touch. Adverts featured in this section are connected to one or all three of the codes: women presented as passive (available) bodies or sexualised through the touch to face or anatomy (or product).

Mothers

> I think that these products . . . they are always related to kitchens, to cleaning and things like that . . . they are more to do with women . . . women always appear more than the man in adverts in Spain.
>
> (Aurelio, male, Spanish focus group)

Goffman's 'feminine touch' typology reflects an advertising trend wherein the woman is frequently portrayed as faintly touching the product or lightly touching (or caressing) themselves. For Goffman, this presentation of gender seems to suggest—in unnatural and absurd terms—that women are intrinsically gentle, clean, soft and caring. The original pictorial analysis focused on advertisements featured products such perfume, toiletries and jewellery—all of which provide the place and space in which to portray women in moments of private (back stage) rapturous enjoyment. When read through a motherhood lens, this phenomenon is prevalent in advertisements that feature private back stage roles and skills assumed to be 'innate', such as cooking, cleaning or caring for children or grandparents. Rather than women's inherent 'gentleness' becoming entangled with sexuality, feminine touch is linked to a 'natural' positioning of the mother. Equally, the family typology is a portrayal as domestic symmetry of the nuclear family, which often positions the mother and daughter in either traditional activities or reified intimate settings such as cooking, shopping or applying make-up. By extending Goffman's pictorial analysis of the feminine touch and family, this section of the chapter locates them both in the broader inequalities of domestic chores, caring responsibilities and invisible labour encapsulated in motherhood.

Participants from all three case studies were keen to discuss motherhood as a form of gender stereotyping focusing on outdated characterisations that advertisers routinely deploy. These discussions dominated the focus groups and felt more important to the participants, especially the boys, than what would later unravel around objectification and sexualisation. Aurelio's statement reveals eagerness to address the issue immediately, and keenness was apparent in all three case studies. In all the initial meetings, motherhood was communicated as a 'gut feeling' around the usage of stereotypes in advertising. Participants were clear that advertising peddled the same outdated notions; mothers clean, cook, look after children, organise home life and family, provide emotional support, overtly show love and affection and absorb catastrophe and dilemma. When challenged on this, most participants remained unwavering in their views. Although participants were willing to shift slightly on their initial thoughts, the majority stood by this belief before they had embarked on their visual diaries or conducted any of their own empirical research. When questioning if there had been a change in how advertisers convey this message, some agreed minor shifts had occurred, but change was seen as either minimal, tokenistic or in some cases shrewd, where adverts were part of the joke and aware of the consumer's irony and consciousness:

> No . . . but that is changing little by little in Spain. Now more men are appearing in cleaning.
>
> (Josu, male, Spain)

In the Spanish and UK sessions, a large part of the time was dedicated to discussing motherhood and the iconography that surrounds the label. In the UK, participants agreed that women in advertising are presented simultaneously as mothers, wives and cleaners. Yet this representation was not passively accepted, with UK participants critical of how women are used in adverts to sell cleaning products:

> It's all the time . . . like, Mum by the washing machine and smiling. It's so weird. Why haven't we moved on?
>
> (Carly, female, UK)

Despite consensus amongst the UK and Spanish participants, the frustration with the mother figure did not lead to further debate on how the stereotype was harmful or what specifically within the advert stirred debate. The striking element of the 'mother' data is the lack of resistance from the participants. Here, a Spanish participant talks about fatalistic feelings of acceptance towards the association between mothers, child rearing and cleaners:

> I used to get upset with those things, but I think that we have seen that [advert] so many times that we get used to it. And that's not ok.
>
> (Amaranta, female, Spain)

Resistance to advertising seemed difficult to sustain, and Amaranta emphasises the fatigue felt when responding to the constant use of the mother in advertising. In the following extract, the rest of the group laugh with Aurelio as he presents his visual diary to the group during the second session. As he presents the advert, he begins to laugh at absurdity of his diary image. The image is of a woman in lingerie selling electrical goods in a supermarket:

> Look! [laughs] This one is about the electric brush and it [laughs uncontrollably] it, it says 'the most original and useful present for your mum'! And look! Then there's a woman with this brush smiling. [Group laughs]
>
> (Aurelio, Spain)

Aureli communicates the undertones of feminine touch and licensed withdrawal codes. The photo depicts a woman barely touching a toothbrush, holding it to her face. The other image brought to the meeting was a vacuum cleaner held firmly, but the mother is looking away out of shot and into the distance. The absurdity is understood on two levels: primarily, the way the model displays an unrealistic happiness towards the mundanity of an everyday task. This disconnected emotional response to the product directly feeds into feminine touch (entwined with licenced withdrawal) as a bizarre display of gender, rendering the woman as both soft and gentle but also vacuous. Secondly, the toothbrush as an original present for a mother reinforces the notion of women (mothers) as clean and caring but ecstatic in private Goffmanesque 'back stage' moments. In the following exchange from the UK between Daniel, Rachel and Skye, resistance to advertising leads to a more defiant exchange that representations of mothers as cleaners have undertones of sexism:

Rachel: [pointing at someone else's diary] What's that Mother's Day one?
David: 'Get back to the job that really matters'.
Daniel: Yeah, that's clearly a joke. [laughter and groans/sighs] It's clearly just a joke!
Rachel: Oh, Daniel!
Daniel: You people are so serious!
Mr Graham: Daniel!
Daniel: Clearly, it's a joke! [groans from Daniel and girls' laughter continue]
Becky: It's obviously a joke, but some might take it seriously.
Mr Graham: Is it that . . . I dunno, with Mr Clean you can get back to the real job that matters . . . being a mum or is it get back to the job of cleaning?
Harvey: Either way, sir—it's sexist!
Daniel: No! [again, more uproar, more laughter]

Skye: It's lose-lose, sir! Yeah, you can't get it right.
Daniel: It's supposed to be Mr Clean! He's got—
Skye: No, Daniel! It's sexist!
Rachel: Come on, Daniel, you know that it's sexist.

In this exchange, Daniel claims that a cleaning product advert linked to Mother's Day is a joke. Rachel and Skye take the opposing view that the advert is, at best, ambiguous and, at worst, sexist. Reading irony into 'mother' adverts was not just limited to the British focus group. In Sweden, although the notion of motherhood was not so strongly felt, the subject was touched on but swiftly put to one side:

> In Sweden, these [types of adverts] are becoming funnier; the mums are like . . . ironic.
>
> (Eva, female, Sweden)

To counter this, Swedish participants were less concerned with the use of the stereotypical mother in advertising and felt Sweden had moved on. Eva's and Daniel's ironic reading of women as mothers, cleaners or carers enables these types of representations in adverts to continue but also leaves some space to provide a critique of such depictions. This is a move beyond the general frustration felt earlier by both Carly and Aurelio. However, in contrast to Eva's perceived ironic take on cleaning adverts, the British group have rallied against Daniel to resist and confront him on the two-fold and facetious meaning of the advert. The ability to read irony, sarcasm or humour in motherhood advertising will be discussed in the following section of the chapter.

What's for tea, love? Mother the multitasker

Representations of mothers as multitaskers in advertisements demonstrate the way in which 'mother' is recoded as activities and chores. Here, I look towards adverts that became apparent whilst discussing why the participants found depictions of motherhood sexist or out of date in advertising. Moreover, I explore Eva's idea of irony through Hall's encoding/decoding theory (Hall, 2007; Soar, 2000) to show whether adverts are deemed inoffensive when overt humour is deployed. In all three countries, the participants felt at ease when discussing overused conceptualisations of motherhood in advertising and the entrenched iconography related to the maternal position inside and outside domestic life. Participants were quick to respond to the notion of gender stereotypes in advertising, with visual diaries reflecting clichéd images of the mother cleaning, cooking, washing or changing baby's nappy, shopping, tending delicately to their toddler's bump and everything in between.

As part of the visual diary research, the UK focus group participants included a popular Christmas advert from shopping retailer Asda. The Asda advert is a montage of events during the buildup to Christmas (buying presents, food, cooking, laying the table etc.), with the mother figure as protagonist and the tagline 'Behind Every Great Christmas Is Mum'. The advert received the highest number of complaints to the UK advertising regulator (Advertising Standards Agency) that year.[1]

UK participants split between feeling the advert was an original and true depiction of family life and the advert being an outdated, sexist imagining of Christmas. One participant, Daniel, kept his hand up all the way through the playing of the advert and was bursting to say something:

Daniel: I think it's good advertising! For example, in my family . . . I mean it's related to my family, it's exactly what we're supposed to do, and it's supposed to relate to people. It's a good advert!

David: So, going back to your original point, it's a true reflection of family life?

Daniel: Yeah, my mum does all that!

Emilia: Um, I was gonna say that it may be a reflection of mum, but it's setting up in girls' heads and maybe women that that's what you got to do. I mean, my dad does everything at Christmas.

Skye: Yeah, I just think that you should have more of a selection of families cos everyone's Christmas Day is, like. different. Because there's single dads and mums and then there's, like, grandparents looking after their grandkids, and the parents aren't around, so if they were more, like, diverse and the kind of family then, yeah . . . like, reaches out to more audiences, and that's good advertising

Rachel: I think it's like unfair on men as well. If my dad watched that, he'd feel quite hard done by. Like Skye said, my parents do pretty much the same round the house and on Christmas, and, like, watching that you get that it's just giving it all to mums—that's bad for women cos like this feeling that you got all this pressure to . . . so men do nothing, and you're not gonna get any of the appreciation.

Views on the advert diverge markedly along gender lines. One participant complicates the advert by reading it as illustrative of family life and motherhood and reflecting a typical Christmas in the UK. The gendered performance(s) made throughout relate to his life and his mother's social

1 See https://www.asa.org.uk/rulings/asda-stores-ltd-a12-213056.html The ASA received 620 complaints about the advert made by leading advertising agency Saatchi and Saatchi Ltd. The complaints were put into three separate categories: 1. The complainants (majority) stated the advert was offensive and sexist because it reinforced outdated stereotypes of men and women in the home. 2. The advert was likely to cause serious offence to single fathers or to men who played a primary domestic role. 3. Complainants objected that the ad was offensive and distressing to children or families who had lost mothers.

position. Reflecting on the mundane and everyday, the advert reflects Daniel's life and confirms his mother's gendered role as the multitasker and also what is socially normative at Christmas. Daniel's traditional view of the family also mirrors Goffman's commercial realism (1976): the way adverts reflect the ritual yet, simultaneously, are highly edited and hyper-ritualised versions of reality. Equally, commercial realism is reflected in Emilia's, Sky's and Rachel's accounts when they posit conflicting personal experiences and see beyond ritualised gendered representations of multitasking. Emilia's view reflects discourse on 'doing gender': how the 'doing' is learned from a young age and performed and policed through interaction (Butler, 1990; Lorber, 1994) and how parents place different expectations on children based on gender (Parsons, 1956; Butler, 1990). In return, children learn 'gender appropriate behaviour' (West and Zimmerman, 1987: 143).

The mother in the Asda advert also corresponds to Goffman's 'family' coding wherein the daughter/son mirrors the mother/father, mimicking the adult task and reflecting 'real life' dramaturgy. Embedded in the advert is Goffman's claim that social norms and cultural values are expressed in adverts and performed as 'ceremonies', using the notion of 'a family on vacation' and how, in advertisements, there is a clear set of cues for 'having a nice time' or external schedules that indicate to the audience (and other actors) 'Look, we are having a nice time'. The advert works in a similar fashion: a family at Christmas performing a technicolour hyper-ritualistic 'nice time' whilst reflecting the everyday. Cues, schedules and expressions are socially learned and socially patterned, and, as Goffman notes, advertisements depict for us not necessarily how individuals behave as men and women but how we *think* men and women ought to behave. This depiction serves the social purpose of convincing viewers that this is how men and women are or want to be or should be, not only in relation to themselves but also in relation to each other. Beyond Goffman's 'family' code and anti-essentialist arguments about the role of women and girls in the home, this exchange is also consistent with Butler's concept of performativity, the 'doing' gender and gender display. Emilia's assertion chimes with performative understandings of gender: that it has, over the years, somehow 'congealed' or essentialised into a form that makes it appear as if it has been there all along (Butler, 1990: 33).

Like Emilia, Skye argues that the representation of multitasking embedded in the advert is a myth—modern families in the UK are more diverse than those of previous generations. Drawing on her own experiences, Skye unpicks the illustration of the nuclear family that is displayed in the Asda advert by listing other modes of post-structural family: single-parent families, extended grandparent families, intergenerational and reconstituted families. The advert's use of the static nuclear family, therefore, does not reflect 'fringe' modes of family or, indeed, reflect the everyday life of those families. Goffman's symmetrical 'family' typology fits less now than originally, particularly due to societal shifts in the make-up of the post-structural family, whether real or imagined. Rachel's contribution is two-fold; first, the idea of women multitasking is far too simplistic. There is greater equilibrium in the family unit, and, drawing on her own experiences, the myth of asymmetry with more emphasis on the mum is outdated. Beyond post-structuralist critiques of the family, contemporary modes of family have at least split the division of domestic labour equally. Secondly, the advert sets a double burden by peddling the myth of women performing most work at Christmas but also denying them any expectation of appreciation for that labour. During the discussion, the UK participants were keen to discuss whether gendered representations in advertising merely reflected the everyday or the adverts informed the audience about what was expected based on gender stereotypes. In this particular exchange, the group discuss the gendered representation of the multitasking mother (Behind Every Christmas There's Mum) and dad ('What's for tea, love?') was brought to light after watching the Asda advert. This theme echoes the essentialism discourse from Chapter 4, in which participants make claims about one's gender based on their sex but also negotiate what roles men and women play in society and what labour they undertake. Daniel is 'mapping gender' onto an individual's sex and making assumptions that the mother's gender is innate: the mother's role is based on her sex and her sex as destiny.

Motherhood and irony

In Sweden, participants were lucid when adverts depicted motherhood and multitasking, countering the concept as outdated or ironic or saying that adverts now portray a more balanced division of domestic labour. Contrasting the Asda advert, one of the participants, Eva, plays a popular online Fiat car advert that features a tongue-in-cheek song 'Motherhood'. For Eva, ironic or knowing depictions of motherhood appear inoffensive as the audience's agency allows for irony and self-deprecation. Resembling the UK Asda advert, the Fiat advert engages with awareness and relatability, reflecting the everyday and mundane, but is posited somewhat lower in the hierarchy of offence when encoded by audiences as irony. For context, the Fiat advert aired across Europe at roughly the same time as the Asda advert and is equally explicit in listing the lived experience of motherhood; at face value, the two adverts should receive equivalent complaints. As Eva states, the key differences between the two adverts are humour and irony, which is played through various visual and verbal indicators: the self-deprecation of the white middle-class mum (suburban social class markers: a detached house, leafy neighbourhood, garage, Ugg boots, designer sofa and the car itself) in juxtaposition with hip-hop rhymes and references to a gangsta lifestyle. The protagonist's lyrics reflect post-feminist advertising: the 'bitches' are the family dogs, the 'babes' are her kids and the 'hoe' is just a garden hose kept in the back seat. The Fiat advert received little negative media attention, and no complaints were registered to the UK or Swedish self-regulation agencies. The commentariat criticizing the Asda advert were simultaneously praising the Fiat advert despite the fact that the same multitasking stereotypes were found in both adverts.

Acknowledgement of the role irony has in advertising has increased in recent years, and rather than assuming audiences are passive agents, contemporary advertising require a consumer's reflexivity (Hall, 1973). Ironic advertising nonetheless (re)produces harmful gender stereotypes and sexism in advertising, or, as Blloshmi claims, the reimagining or 'retro' stereotypes have reemerged on the advertising landscape (2013: 13). Ironic adverts, on the one hand, depict pro-woman messaging and, on the other, reinforce negative stereotyping such as the representations in the Fiat advert: doing the school run, cleaning and cooking. Post-feminist advertising (Blloshmi, 2013). 'femvertsing' (Varghese and Kumar, 2022) and commodity feminism (Goldman et al., 1991) all posit similar dichotomies that are present in the Fiat advert and, indeed, show how contemporary advertising reproduces harmful stereotypes through light-hearted techniques. Varghese and Kumar (2022) suggest that femvertising promotes products through notions of activism, resistance and empowerment yet are also a reaction to tighter advertising regulatory organisations that prohibit sexism, misogyny, harm and offence. The ironic advert therefore avoids such critique and regulation as it promotes 'real life' and uses humour.

Other participants were aware of irony (or humour) at various moments as they engaged with their visual diaries and adverts in the group discussion. Comments such as 'This must be a joke' or 'this is a good advert' or general enjoyment from advertising reflects agentic reading of adverts as ironic, funny or 'real'. As Blloshmi indicates, the re-emergence of ironic gender stereotypes in advertising materialises in the guise of irony as women are often portrayed in positions of power or where they show agency, but only in an 'exaggerated or mocking way', rendering them absurd or unrealistic (2013: 13). Therefore, when the portrayal of gender or the gender stereotype is amplified in a certain 'knowing' way with irony, the audience is aware, yet the gender stereotype (or sexualisation) is nonetheless reproduced and remains unchallenged. This explains Eva's reading of irony and engagement in the motherhood advertisement but equally clarifies why the Asda advert produces a rather more negative reaction within the groups. The Asda advert provides little humour or exaggeration and merely reflects, as Daniel indicates, the mundanity of chores in real life. Stern's work has shown that irony is a key tool in advertising as it is used to deliver humour as a reward but only to elite consumers (1990). Therefore, the consumer must be conscious or reflexive to engage with the irony in the advert and possess the correct habitus, cultural capital or a 'knowing' of the cultural clues (Bourdieu, 2011). Audiences of the Fiat advert are required to possess knowledge of hip-hop terminology and iconography—cribs, bitches, house arrest (bullet holes in the chest) the West

Coast hand sign and prison bars—but also middle-class markers: wine drinking, blenders, yoga etc. If consumers are to comprehend the irony embedded in post-feminist advertising, then they must retain the wide-ranging depth of cultural capital with which to read the advert as 'knowing' to understand the humour in the product, branding or language. The ironic knowing tone must also be made explicit through popular comedic tropes to be seen a non-offensive. Ironic advertising requires reflexivity; audiences with agency and understanding of the capital will only possess the capacity to critique 'retro' stereotypes.

Reflecting on the data from the three case studies, ironic advertising reproduces old stereotypes of motherhood and multitasking in advertising by utilising comedic undertones as well as knowledge that the consumer will engage with the advert with humour yet simultaneously feel uncomfortable with the message. Post-feminist ironic advertising is playing with 'cynical humour that draws on audiences existing knowledge of popular culture to present visual puns: stereotypes, self-mocking forms of humour' (Blloshmi, 2013: 12) Therefore, irony is a core facet of post-modern advertising that should be perceived not as humour but as a post-modern backlash to feminism (McRobbie, 1994; Leiss and Botterill, 2005). Understanding irony or 'knowing' (Bourdieu, 2011) was apparent in all three focus groups, where participants either recognised the advert as a joke or picked up on the cultural references, innuendo, double entendre or hidden meanings embedded in it.

Women on the verge

Influenced by Goffman's typology of 'licensed withdrawal', this second theme from the data explores the portrayal of women in adverts as hysterical, neurotic, confused, 'unhinged' or psychologically removed from the social situation. Goffman's licensed withdrawal typology depicts the woman having the opportunity to withdraw from a situation due to her dependence on—and protection of—others (usually male) and presents it in numerous ways: tuning out or appearing lost, confused, in a state of surprise or shock or perhaps dumbfounded by the product itself. This code overlaps John Berger's notion of 'the dream' (1978), Les Back and Vibeke Quaade's 'utopian dreams' (1993) and Goffman's dramaturgical conceptualisation of 'the stare' (1963). Berger's 'dream' motif derives from female embodiment in fine art, which has seeped into contemporary advertising and other mass media communications. The dream manifests as sexual desire: for example, the object in a painting is often the desired woman. In advertising, the same applies; consumers are sold ideas about the product or a lifestyle by faceless, dreamlike models. Berger points to other narratives in advertising: to dream of wanting the desired object (product) or lifestyle, to dream of later tonight, to dream of a far-away place (or, as Goffman suggests, gazing into the distance, preoccupied by thought), to dream of romantic love, innocence or purity. Goffman's typology connects with Berger's notion of the dreamlike state but also alludes to notions of disorientation, emptiness and surprise. This theme is linked to dominant feminine representations in advertising that portray women not only as dreamlike or vacant but also as neurotic, crazy or mad. Similarly, Back and Quaad's 'dream utopias', wherein advertisements fetishise stereotypes, selling consumers lifestyles and utopias that are both objectified and fragmented. This theme also draws on embodiment and the body through Orbach (2009), Showalter (1985, 1998) and Busfield (1994) and the clear correlation between advertising and depicting women as neurotic subjects as in a state of confusion or hysteria or, as Goffman notes, 'tuning out'.

Despite claims that Freud and Breuer have 'cleared up' the misconception of female hysteria (Gilman et al., 1993), participants across the three case studies discussed how women are routinely depicted as neurotic, hysterical or mad in advertising. Busfield's work rejects the flimsy association between the 'hysteria epidemic' of the 19th century and the fact that the majority of patients were women due to lack of statistical data (1994). Her work provides gendered landscape of mental disorders, and the stereotypes of such disorders are still pervasive today (i.e. in advertising), just as they were in Victorian England. The androcentric voice of the medical profession at the time led to Victorian obsessions (Hoagland, 1980), from historical figures such as the suicidal Ophelia (Showalter, 2016) and the Salem witch trials to novelty inventions such as vibrators (Mainses, 2001). As G.S. Rousseau (2004) notes, there has been no male equivalent historically—save melancholy—to female hysteria. This has been reflected in the group discussions on the Asda advert, in which one participant framed the female protagonist as looking 'a bit unhinged'. Schutzman (1999) explores the link between the language and imagery of 19th-century hysteria and contemporary images in advertising in the 1990s. Schutzman highlights how the 19th-century medical language of the *Hysteria* is openly transferred to and performed in contemporary advertising.

During the UK focus groups, participants diarised a Persil advert they had seen on social media, with a tagline: 'Are You a Dual Action Mum?' The advert depicts a woman multitasking in the shower, shampoo still in her hair and a scourer in one hand, cleaning the bath. The group discussed the underlying connotations of sexism connecting it to motherhood and the multitasking myth. The targeted advert requested its audience to comment underneath by 'Sharing Bonkers and Brilliant Moments Like These', sharing their 'crazy moments' in the comments section. The Spanish focus group were—as with the Asda Christmas advert—shocked and amused by the language and how unashamedly the advert presented itself. There was a lot of awkward laughter before anyone spoke about the advert and its tagline. Aureliano, Amaranta and Ursula supported one another in stating that the advert was halfway between humorous and offensive. The group were quick to point out that the language, image and idea are excessive rather than offensive:

Aureliano: I don't know . . . It's asking mothers to share photos and that is . . .[asks Ursula in Spanish]. . . It's shameful.
Amaranta: For me it's like . . . whoa, this is too much. . . . [laughs] It's a joke, you know?
Ursula: Yeah, it's really bad; the message under [the image] is, like, basically saying you are crazy.
Aureliano: I say it's shameful because women are not doing this—and this word 'bonkers'? It means?
Ursula: It means you are crazy, mad.
Aureliano: So yeah, this is bad; it's shameful.

In this exchange, Amaranta's pause reflects the previous theme of irony and mockery in advertising. But as the group move beyond Amaranta's acceptance of irony in advertising, they begin to dissect the advert critically, engaging with its undertones of neuroticism and madness. The break in Amaranta's speech also reflects notions of reflexivity and consciousness rather than consumers as passive agents. The discussion could easily have remained innocuous in tone, but the group's cohesion and linguistic encouragement demonstrate that whilst they are knowing agents willing to accept the cultural cues, they are also willing to read the 'hidden' encoded meanings, decoding undertones of sexism at the root of the advert. Amaranta feels that the advert is 'too much'—it is perceived as excessive or overwhelming in its portrayal of women. Pausing for a moment, her initial earnest reaction gives way to the absurdity of the advert; a quick release of laughter and 'It's a joke' signifies that she can't take the advert seriously.

Looking at the image of the 'Dual Action Mum' advert and the participants' discussion confirms the contemporality of Goffman's licenced withdrawal in advertising. The advert positions the mother as lost, 'tuned out', withdrawn from the situation and alienated from the product and action, distinct from the sexualised 'feminine touch' typology. The advert's language and the participants' critique are reminiscent of the licenced withdrawal coding: bonkers, crazy, mad etc. The associative meaning of the advert speaks to the coding elsewhere: for example, the vacant gaze into the distance, which again repeats Berger's and Shutzman's notion of a dreamlike state that is depicted in contemporary advertisements. Specifically, Berger's reading of the concept of 'dream' in renaissance fine art, where bodies are viewed through the male gaze. Replicated in advertising, it is read as looking away, the desire to be elsewhere, 'to dream of later tonight', an unfulfilled life, perhaps, or, as Berger claims, 'a far-away place'. It is in stark contrast to the female gaze in which the artist glares back at the viewer, in control of the situation as opposed to 'tuned out'.

After a reflective break to collect work for their visual diaries, the Spanish focus group returned with more ideas and contributions for this theme and returned to the notion of women portrayed as neurotic in adverts. Amongst other adverts, the participants mentioned medicine, cereal and feminine hygiene adverts. According to the participants, these products used tools similar to those of the Persil advert, and when asked to evidence these ideas in their visual diaries, the students returned with a video link to a popular sanitary towel advert. The advert presented a simple 20-second 'before' and 'after' montage of a young woman carrying out some basic everyday tasks: riding the bus, going to work and the gym and eating food. The two participants explained and translated the advert to me:

Meliquiades: I think that they want [us to] feel bad or maybe unbalanced.
Amaranta: Yeah! The advert says they [women] are crazy; they are not balanced. Here, take this tampon and you will feel balanced.
Meliquiades: There's this other advert in Spain. . . . It says . . . eh, take these tablets when you have [your] period, and you will be well.
Amaranta: And the advert is showing a woman who is crazy . . . and now she is balanced on the bike.

This exchange provides a critique to the dominant essentialist discourses from Chapter 4. In this instance, the participants dispute that there is inherent biological truth about women whilst they are on their period. Essentialist discourse characterises women as 'unbalanced', wielding the stereotypical view of women as having failed biology that cannot cope with their innate bodily functions. Participants in this group often demonstrated agency, particularly whilst talking about women being portrayed as crazy. In this piece, they do not passively accept dominant discourses that a woman's temperament is entwined with the menstrual cycle. Both Meliquiades and Amaranta reveal discomfort with this representation of women in the advert as unbalanced or unhinged. Meliquiades clearly states that the use of this representation is solely to sell a product that can restore the feeling of balance: 'eh, take these tablets when you have [your] period and you will be well'. Meliquiades is therefore rejecting the stereotype that is embedded and perpetuated in this type of advert. Returning to Shutzman's work on the performance of hysteria in advertising, this exchange supports the idea that although advertising is no longer vulgar and direct in its links to hysteria, the gender display and performance of hysteria are still pervasive today. The advert is not directly labelling the woman as having a 'failed' biology; however the subtext is quickly seized on by the participants. There are other moments in the UK group discussion where neuroticism and women's experiences are considered. During another session, Aaron questions why women are always seen as carefree in feminine hygiene adverts:

> I think, like they're carefree and energetic, that's not like how it is when you're on your period though, right? They're not portraying it as it really is, right? You're making less than it really is.
>
> (Aaron, UK)

Aaron's comment is a little less polished or thought through than the previous Spanish dialogue. Here, Aaron is arguing with a fellow participant who feels that the advert undermines what she perceives to be women's experiences. The participants from the UK produced a much lengthier discussion on neuroticism when discussing the Persil advert but were not—at first—as surprised as the Spanish or Swedish participants. Once past the concepts of motherhood and multitasking, the group became more interested in the idea of 'bonkers or brilliant moments'. In comparison, the response in the UK led to confrontation between the participants as one of the participants, Daniel, asserted that it was merely reflecting home life, particularly his own. Rachel, Skye and Emilia dissented:

David: What does this advert say to you Lottie?
Lottie: You know like you're a good mum when you're like cleaning and another thing at the same time. You're multitasking and men can't multitask. . . . It's like mums get enjoyment out of it. They don't. My mum don't.
Daniel: Yeah, I think a lot of women relate to this. Like my mum, she works part time and has to do all the cleaning. And dad works full time so . . . so I say an advert like that maybe. . . . You know, it's trying to get into the minds of those women and relate to them. And that's a lot of women.
David: You think this is a lot of women?
Daniel: Yeah! My mum likes to think that she's always busy, always got to do something. She won't let you catch her sitting down. . . . So, like, cleaning in the shower whilst showering is an exaggerated example, and it appeals.
David: It appeals and is a reflection of mums?
Daniel: Yeah, definitely.
Rachel: Yeah, but, like, it's trying to say that women have got, like, nothing else better to do. . . . Like you're a dual action mum when you clean the shower or wash[] it. . . . It's like making out that's all mums have going for them . . . that all they do is wash.
David: So is the advert just tongue in cheek, Rachel?
Rachel: No, you wouldn't get a man in there. If he was . . . what . . . he'd be, like, mowing in the shower? [laughs]

Skye: I am bothered by it—I just think it's really old fashioned. It's not making me angry; it's just annoying. Cos I think from my household, it's very much divided; like, my dad does all the cleaning.

Daniel: I just think people should be a bit light hearted. Like, they haven't offended anyone. The fact is a lot of women do still do this. It's not saying, like, men can't clean.

Rachel: Yeah, but, like, as girls are growing up, they are told . . . they are, like, saying this is what you should be doing when you are older . . . cleaning, cooking. Whereas you get a lot of ads that are, like, saving people—so obviously, when we grow up, we lean more towards that.

Daniel: Yeah, but maybe that's just what you want to do!

Emilia: No, Daniel, not if you have been raised that way. Daniel's saying, like, 'Oh, it's an option', but it's not. If you've grown up with those toys and those things, you do it subconsciously.

Daniel: Well, maybe you do it cos you want to do it? Maybe my mum does decide[] to raise me that way.

Aaron: Isn't that the parents' choice—the toys and all that? . . . It's not the advertisers' fault.

This discussion centres on two core ideas. The first is how advertising enters the subconscious, sows seeds and reproduces stereotypes, and the second is that advertising is a social structure, and audiences often lack agency. This second concept challenges the former: advertising is a robust informant of gender, yet the audience is not passive—they possess the agency to subvert the gender stereotypes embedded in advertisements. Lottie continues with the notion that multitasking is an enduring belief that has come to be seen as an innate quality of the gendered experience. Lottie asserts that this myth both overestimates women and underestimates men. The unfair portrayal of the woman as the multitasker is therefore unfair to both women *and* men: there is no enjoyment gained from multitasking or the pressure to live up to this unreasonable expectation. It is equally unfair to suggest that men are incompetent, which consequently renders them undervalued or belittled. Moreover, Lottie suggests that there's a sadistic undertone amidst all this in the advert: gendered labour is fun.

Daniel echoes his previous interpretation of advertising as reflecting 'everyday life' and says the advert is worthy of praise: his mother would understand the ideas conveyed, and many women would recognise themselves in this form of imagery. In developing this idea, he uses his mother as a lens through which to view and to understand the advert but also to comprehend how imagined audiences might perceive and react to this advert. The process is therefore cyclical: the advert selects an overtly familiar scenario; the targeted audience recognise themselves within that scenario and feel engaged and committed. This pattern is evident as Daniel is willing to acknowledge that the advert is an augmented version of the familiar. This amplified version of the familiar in the advert resonates with Goffman's commercial realism and the schedule in advertising: of 'having a good time', how advertisements distort reality and simultaneously instil in audiences recognisable and relatable 'props', cues and 'front stage' presentations of life. Daniel's determination to argue that the advert is a true representation of the everyday does not marry up to Rachel's view of the advert. Daniel and Rachel's argument communicates Goffman's commercial realism adage: adverts should appear peculiar, odd or strange when, in fact, audiences perceive them to be familiar, reflecting the 'social difference' in gender. Moreover, advertising is a clear agent in 'making the familiar strange' and blends well into Goffman's institutional reflexivity, where 'environments are manipulated' to 'exaggerate sex differences in order to justify gender inequalities' (1977: 323). Equally, as Goffman argues, advertising peddles 'folk beliefs' based on biology, stereotypes based on temperament and physiology which simplifies difference. The stereotype or 'folk belief' that women like to clean, feel unbalanced or are 'bonkers' for multitasking provides for a self-fulfilling prophecy about the gendered experience.

By revisiting Daniel's early comment, 'It's trying to get into the minds of those women and relate to them', Rachel's argument is reinforced when viewed from a structure/agency perspective. Advertising as a social structure provides younger audiences with representations of gender that they ought to fulfil. Rachel provides Daniel with a counterargument—boys as 'saving people'—and shows that there are gendered structures which instil knowledge of what it is to be a man. Emilia strongly defends Rachel's point on the lack of agency and the socialisation of young girls, which both contribute to the way in which gendered advertising enters the subconscious. Daniel's counterargument asserts that audiences possess agency—not that young girls have a choice to subvert this dominant discourse in advertising—but admits that such actions are consensual and accepted.

The discussion in Sweden was similar to those in the UK and Spain, with the overwhelming response from participants moving away from 'outraged' towards the feeling that the advert must be, at the very best, a joke. One of the participants, Martin, began actively searching for the Persil advert and read out the Facebook comments: laughing, he believed that the responses must also be ironic. In the recording, there is lot of background chatter about this image, and the atmosphere is one of awkwardness and discomfort. The focus group participants showed signs that they wanted to move on from the hysterical elements of the advert, and Eva pointed out a more obvious element of the advert—the overt notions of sexualisation and objectification:

> *But we're not talking about the main thing—she is an object.*
>
> (Eva, female, Sweden)

The Swedish focus group discussion disagreed with the label of neurotic/mad/bonkers and argued that women are depicted as stupid. During the discussion, Erik mentioned a large non-descript advert that he had seen in the local shopping centre that 'watches over the customers'. I, too, immediately remembered the image due to its curious duality of hiding in plain sight—vast in size yet invisible as it loomed over the shoppers. The advert depicts a gigantic carefree young woman in a long, flowing dress, looking into the distance and surrealistically walking over and amongst the crowds. When discussing the image, Eva was unaware of its presence, but others in the group were quick to confirm its existence:

Erik and Martin: Yeah!
Erik: It's like four meters tall!
Eva: [inhale of breath] Yes! I know the one!
David: Yes, blink and you'll miss it. What do you think it says about women?
Eva: That women should be more cheerful—or should be.
Eva: Yeah, should be! We should be happy and love life! Like we are stupid or something.

This exchange again speaks to the notion of making the familiar strange and the omnipresence yet invisibility of advertising in large spaces. It also speaks to hysteria and licensed withdrawal as it is projected onto—and performed in—advertisements. Eva's assumption about the advert—'women should be more cheerful'—extends further to Butler's policing of gender and performativity, the normative gendered expression of communicating perpetual happiness, loving life and carefree. Eva recognises and excavates the hidden codes embedded in the advert, how it perpetuates the notions of femininity and how women ought to be cheerful and carefree. In a further exchange on how masculinity is presented in advertising, Eva quipped:

Eva: Yeah and women are just there, pretty . . . stupid . . . and men are more . . . maybe . . . I don't know really.
Goran: 'That men are more . . . aggressive in the way they stand, but the women are usually quite model-like and bored.
Eva: Yeah, we're just bored aren't we?

Corresponding with Goffman's typologies, the large silhouette looming over shoppers depicting a woman looking away from the camera and into the distance reflects licenced withdrawal. Goffman's 'tuned-out' or the participants comments 'stupid' and 'bored' manifest in the dreamlike advert—much like Berger's conceptualisation of adverts imitating art—is very much like a large, framed painting in a commercial gallery with unaware *flaneurs* passing underneath, dreaming of their own purchases and desires to be elsewhere. At the second session, the group return, stating they have recognised Goffman's codes in advertising (in particular licensed withdrawal and feminine touch) as a familiar and recurring pattern in clothing, hair and beauty adverts. Eva mentions a large L'Oreal advert that she noted in her visual diary, and Signe quickly searches for images on her phone. Whilst discussing the image, the group agree that the portrayal of men and women is different. When discussing feminine touch, men are 'doing', and women are 'vacant'; Eva and Signe continue their interpretation that women are constantly presented as 'stupid' or 'lost' in adverts.

David: I think it was interesting when you said that men are 'doing' something women are just—
Signe: It's always like that! Contrasting with her and . . . in a way . . . the way she's almost like vacant. She looks a bit stupid or lost.
Eva: Women are just looking at something . . . like, totally vacant . . . like, blank.
David: What does the product or brand or concept say about the gender?
Eva: I think it says something like women are concerned about how they are looking and appreciated for what they are. Like we're stupid.

This exchange continues the 'stupid' narrative of advertising with Eva from the previous session. Eva extends the 'stupid' narrative to encompass the vacant stare (this time, the gaze directed back to the viewer), absent appearance and mouth open to give the overall appearance of emptiness. This advert speaks to the licensed withdrawal code and is also entwined with 'feminine touch'; hand delicately touching the model's face, accentuating the sensation of femininity. Goffman calls this 'legitimised withdrawal': women portrayed as either helpless or 'mentally absent'. Once again, the L'Oreal vacant look evokes Berger's 'dream' of wanting the desired product but also the desired self as well as the dreamlike stare into the abyss.

The objectified self

This theme explores the notions of sexualisation and objectification of women in advertising by revisiting and developing Goffman's code of 'ritualisation of subordination'. This section of the chapter looks at how the participants consumed and decoded adverts as distasteful, objectifying and spaces of disgust. I reflect on this final notion and how forms of resistance towards objectification and sexualisation in advertising are present amongst the participants.

> Media Mart, years ago, was very aggressive with this advertising. They were saying . . . they were using women with hardly any clothes. They were provoking us. They put women almost without clothes to attract men.
>
> (Aureliano, male, Spain)

The topic of objectification (and sexualisation) arrived late in all three of the discussions, after a break between the focus group sessions when the participants had time to complete their visual diaries. Aureliano's enthusiasm on the subject came towards the final moments of the initial focus group as he approached me when everyone else was packing away; his delayed and slightly muted response conveyed a sensitivity to this particular type of advertising. The same pattern occurred in the UK and Sweden: once the participants had become more settled in their groups, they all felt more at ease talking about their more personal responses to sexualisation and objectification. Once the more obvious topics of motherhood and women as neurotic were surpassed, more critical themes emerged and became more apparent: men and women used as objects or props or portrayed as stupid, adverts featuring magnified body parts, headless models or bodies positioned with no relevance or accordance to the product. At times in the initial meeting, the participants' views were muffled or constrained; frustrated that the boundaries of the initial discussion must be settled (what are stereotypes? what is gender?), the group's initial polite discussion was marred by flashes of anger—either explicit or by sighs or moans—reflecting what would later unravel: anger, hostility and detachment. The slow ascent towards what they deemed an obvious problem seemed, at times, tiresome for the participants. It was interesting to listen to these off-the-record and unguarded discussions, and the data reflects only some of the dialogue that emanated from this research. Nonetheless, this theme produced the most data once the participants across all three case studies reached the topic.

Recent high-profile advertising campaigns such as Ryanair, H&M and Unilever (beach body ready) are all present in the data and seamlessly slot into Goffman's coding. As discussed in Chapter 4, Goffman distinguishes the typology ritualisation of subordination, which depicts women adopting 'bashful' positions predominantly subservient to men: arms or knees bent, lying down in order to indicate submission to men's authority. This category of advert often features a woman on a bed or on the floor, substantially inferior to the other bodies (often men) depicted. For Goffman, this typology indicates women's social identity and relationship to men as subordinate, submissive or inferior. Beyond the lowering to—or worshipping of—the male (dominant) body, other forms body language are incorporated in this category, including social expressions (e.g. caressing, kissing, touching) towards the product or the male body. These expressions can be seen to convey another code in the advert—that the woman is figuratively a doll, a supposed 'plaything' or toy that is synchronously vacant and available from the angle of the male gaze. There is overlap with licensed withdrawal and ritualisation of subordination, and in sum, the theme includes an array of adverts wherein women appear to be submissive or lower in 'function ranking' (women are being instructed in the advert) or 'relative size' (lower position when in the presence of a man). I have not touched on these codes, but they are relevant to the theme of objectification; women are often physically below the male body or in receipt of the male function, order or instruction. I use the words of the participants and politicise Goffman's typology to include women's positions as not merely submissive but objectified, sexualised, absent, detached, dissected or cut off from the advertisement, as well as instructed, trained or disciplined.

In the Spanish focus group, ritualisation of subordination dominated the participants' visual diaries as most participants collected images that fit into the typology. The diaries included images in which the woman's legs were bent or torso was in a childlike position; the diaries predominantly featured women in a subordinate position or lying down in a suggestive way. I divided these visual data into two categories with the language of the participants in mind: sexualisation and objectification. Aureliano was eager to talk more about an advert he saw when he was younger and spoke of how the series of adverts had affected him as a young teenager feeling embarrassment and awkwardness, especially as the advert came on TV. Even after walking from the university building where the focus group took place to the bus stop where the students would be picked up, the conversation was maintained.

Aureliano was particularly focused on one advert that displayed a woman's legs with the tagline 'This way to heaven'. I begin with this image as the advertising had a real effect on not just Aureliano but the collective memories of the participants in Spain. Once the adverts were put up on the projector, the participants began to speak freely (in Spanish) about the advertising that they could remember from their youth. This advert set the tone for the remainder of the second focus group session, and although the Media Mart advert was eventually banned by the Spanish regulators, the discussion of similar adverts prevailed. When I asked Aureliano what it was about this particular advert that had troubled him, he reverted to the 'shameful' narrative. Ursula pointed out that in all the adverts, the women were 'not happy to be doing that job' and looked 'a bit stupid'. Overall, the atmosphere in the room had shifted from light-hearted discussions on the use of mothers (their mothers) to anger towards adverts that portrayed women as objects. Later on in the discussion, Aureliano was more direct about his thoughts on the Media Mart advert:

Aureliano: They [the advertisers] are just using the woman's body. . . . They just want to use the body to get the attention . . . these stupid men . . . look!

Lola: I think they use the girls with no clothes to attract people's attention.

Alvaro: They are also using some type of girls—you don't see fat girls or small girls; they are all one size.

This above dialogue moves away from Goffman's code and the theme of subordination and moves it closer to objectification and sexualisation—Alvaro's assertion that the advert is using a certain type of woman to bring about that attraction. This is closer to Goffman's 'commercial realism' claims and how messages have become naturalized through repetition in advertisements—unnatural poses where the woman is positioned as weak, powerless or in a position of lack when compared to her male counterpart. Whilst Goffman's code of subordination speaks to both concepts, I wish to unpack the ideas a little further and apply more contemporary adverts and the voices of the participants to highlight how advertisements are more explicit. Advertisements in this category are demonstrably portraying coded hyper-feminized (or unnatural) images to audiences to attract attention, and although this advertiser's trick is no new feat, the participants' decoding shows a disgust towards the advertiser's intention. Objectification and sexualisation will be discussed from a legal perspective in the upcoming chapters; however, I argue that participants are aware of such terms across the three cases studies and resist such forms of adverts.

In Spain, most of the group's discussion revolved around notions of ideal/perfect body type, allowing the audience to make connections with the particular body type to sell the product. This theme was repeated in the discussion, particularly using the woman as an object. Here, Ursula talked about cereal advert that was based on the premise of looking 15 years younger and how she thought the use of a model in a bikini and her fully clothed partner seemed to be for manipulative means:

Ursula: Cereal is a daily product . . . in the morning, but the woman is very thin; she is only with a bikini. And if you eat, you will become thinner, and that . . . 'you are what you eat' comes to my mind.

Aureliano: No, it's more than this. I think that she . . . [is] there to like attract people to buy but also that women think they will consume it, [and] they will look like her. Yes. But this is attracting men to the body too. She's a beautiful woman . . . so I don't know. I think she is there to attract. For those reasons.

Ursula: Yes, and she gets the guy at the end!

The advert resonates with the subordination code in that the woman appears to be under the control of the man and weak both physically and symbolically when positioned against the male equivalent. Goffman argues that advertisements never produce such performances in which the male is in a position of subordination and thus that the arrangement between the sexes is strange.

A similar discussion took place whilst discussing a separate advert promoting perfume:

Amaya: 'You should be like this and you will be delicious'. So the apple is delicious, you are delicious and the perfume is delicious. It's like that.

Ursula: She looks strange in the first picture—her mouth is strange.

There are multiple codes at play in this DKNY advert in addition to the undertones of eating 'healthily'. The woman is in a lower ranking position and a smaller 'relative size' than the male equivalent. There is an element of control—the male pushed up against the woman with his arms wrapped around her—but also the feminine touch of the apple. This speaks to the genesis of Goffman's *Gender Advertisements*: the notion of advertisements representing parent-child compositions, in which the male will often play the parent and female the child. In Goffman's interpretation of adverts replicating infantilisation, he notes that women will be depicted not only as controlled by the parent figure but also with her fingers in or close to her mouth, perhaps sucking or biting, reflecting 'innate' feelings of anxiety or feeling lost—or, as he claims in licenced withdrawal, removed from the situation and thinking of nothing at all (1976). In the DKNY advert, the body is contorted, subordinated to the parent's arms and unaware of the surroundings, comforted by the security of not just the male grip but also his gaze.

In the following data, taken from a wider discussion about a well-known Ryanair case, the participants talk about the objectification of the cabin crew in a calendar published by the company.

Amaranta: Yes, maybe violence. I am a woman, and when I saw that, I feel like [in] these calendars, those women are treated like an object.

Ursula: Flying on that plane will . . . will get you these women . . . in no clothes. It's, it's silly.

There is a clear absence of the controlling male body in the Ryanair advert; however, I argue that Goffman's attention to the minutiae moves beyond the obvious objectification and sexualisation of the half-naked body. Instead, as with the Ryanair adverts, Goffman's attention is towards the body as passive, limp or lying on the ground, on one knee or kneeling down. Highlighting such bashfulness and the bended knee alongside a head tilted to one side speaks to connotations of infantilisation and yet, paradoxically, availability. The advert presents the undertones of the women's sexual availability (as noted in the data) as well as subservient or promiscuous positioning.

Highlighting these subtleties is making the familiar strange; it is to shine a light on the unnatural poses that would seem absurd if the male were to replicate them. Or, as Goffman claims, '[A]lthough [the advertisements] cannot be taken as representative of gender behaviour in real life . . . one can probably make a significant negative statement about them, namely, that as pictures they are not perceived as peculiar and unnatural' (1976: iv).

Resistance and mockery

Over the last decade, the UK Advertising Standards Agency have seen a sharp rise in 'sexist' and '[poor] taste and decency' complaints. This, paired with ongoing activism, mockery and resistance towards high-profile ad campaigns (e.g. the Ryanair calendar, H&M's bikini bus stop adverts and Unilever's 'Love your Body') has produced a space for sexist advertising to be debated not just within the advertising industry but in public spaces. This is no more evident than Protein World's 'Are You Beach Body Ready?' advert campaign. So vitriolic was the response that it became commonplace not just to reject the advert but to openly mock it via social media and graffiti on billboards.

Inspired forms of resistance came through the channel of social media, and individual acts of resistance morphed into collective reactions as the advert became a symbol of mockery. The social media platform Twitter (X) and the climax of the #EverydaySexism campaign (Bates, 2014) meant that the advert gained press attention and, inevitably, became a parody across Europe, America and Australia. Although the Advertising Standards Agency found that the advert had not breached any of its public decency or sexualisation grounds,[2] it was banned on public health concerns due to its promotion of an unrealistic extreme weight-loss programme. The advert's mockery came at the time of my first focus group in the UK and featured heavily in the discussions in both sessions.

In the UK focus group session, the participants brought up the advert towards the end of the discussion and were willing to engage with it in numerous ways. Initially, Skye was critical of how advertisers manipulate audiences with unrealistic body image and what is 'perfect':

> I just think if a woman wants a body like that, then she can have it. . . . [I]f she doesn't want it, then she doesn't have to. But it's kind of ironic, though, how billboards and magazines and bus stops, like, promote confidence but at the same time put stuff like this out saying we're not perfect.

2 Advertising Standards Agency Report on Protein World 1 July 2015, available online: https://www.asa.org.uk/rulings/protein-world-ltd-a15-300099.html accessed 21 February 2018.

Rachel and James were of a similar gauge when asked how the advert made them feel:

Rachel: Yeah, I'm fine with it. I mean, yeah, she looks lovely . . . but I don't really mind.

James: You see it all the time; not many people have that kind of body. So, like, they're trying to get to people. I mean, they're not gonna get someone in that is, like, bigger. You know what I mean?

It was only when Daniel interrupted that the rest of the group retaliated:

Daniel: You know, they're just saying work out, and you can have a nice body like this if you aren't happy with your own body or you can have a more sought-after body. Yeah?

Rachel: [who has been hitting the her ruler against the table] It's just really unrealistic, Daniel! Not all girls have naturally big hips or big boobs! That's not in the protein; that's surgery! There's not much you can do about that.

The discussion between Daniel and Rachel was representative of the focus group discussion on objectification and sexualisation of the female body. There were similar instances in Sweden and Spain when the participants vented anger towards unrealistic body types, fat-shaming adverts (e.g. the 'Take Courage' advert) and anorexic models (the Yves Saint Laurent advert).

What this data and image reflect is the need to update Goffman's typology on subordination in line with feelings of disgust towards advertisers that objectify and sexualise the body. Goffman's code is not entirely repeated in these examples. This is clear in the 'Beach Body Ready' advert as the representation is almost silhouette—no bended knees, bashfulness, function or size ranking. There is also little reference to other codes: feminine touch, licensed withdrawal. The advert does, however, speak to Goffman's framing of being 'doll-like' or a 'play toy', and thus, through the male gaze, the body is positioned almost as a Barbie doll framed in a box of yellow. Through this understanding of the coding scheme, Goffman's typology has limited space to manoeuvre on contemporary 'empowerment' advertising, which contradicts notions of submission by producing adverts in which the body is bolt upright, erect, face to the camera, in control of the situation and not 'tuned out'. Moreover, the advert lacks any 'setting', scene or 'stage'. There is little context and few props or performances taking place as there are no other 'actors' in the composition—just a blank canvas. Questioning the reasons behind the modes of resistance and mockery towards advertising in both the focus group and in public spaces shows there is a clear lack in Goffman's work. Focusing on mere subtleties of advertising as Goffman does demonstrates a problem with his analysis, rendering it impracticable, particularly when mobilising resistance. However, I argue that by reading Goffman's subordination code in the wider context of his work and claims of how adverts appear 'unnatural' or distorted, his typology is relevant. Because the 'Beach Body' pose is decontextualised, because there are no other actors or props, the pose itself seems unnatural: a doll on the shelf ready to be plucked and played with. Decoding the advert through lack of context renders it absurd. Indeed, the stance of the model *is* unnatural or, as Goffman claims, the absurdity of 'the degree to which advertisements embody an artificial pose reflecting on perhaps yet another artificial pose—that is, the process by which we come to think of what we call our 'natural' selves'.

Conclusion

In this chapter, I revisited and evaluated Erving Goffman's gender display coding schema through contemporary advertisements taken from the visual diaries of the participants and my own collation of adverts that have helped inform the focus groups of the research topic. At the beginning of the chapter, I touched on the key codes that have informed my own themes for the research, feminine touch, licensed withdrawal and ritualisation of subordination. In addition to these three codes, I reintroduced some of the underlying concepts from Goffman's work in *Gender Advertisements* such as the parent-child complex and infantilisation but also 'commercial realism' and 'making the familiar strange'. Together, the codes and concepts have helped inform my analysis of the data as well reimagining of the codes to construct my own themes in the data.

'The mother' merges some fundamental stereotypes that are found in contemporary advertising, and the participants picked up on categorisations such as the cook, the cleaner, the carer and 'the multitasker'. Drawing on Goffman's codes, I argued that the depiction of the mother is a multifaceted stereotype in advertising: caressing and fetishizing the product whilst at the same time feeling withdrawn and removed from the chore. In this theme, I focused on the Asda and Fiat adverts which centred on the same ideas of domestic labour, arguing, however, that decoding one as sexist and the other as ironic required agentic understanding from the participants. 'Women on the verge' reimagined Goffman's licenced withdrawal code and explored the stereotype of women in adverts portrayed as neurotic or mad. In addition to Goffman's codes, I have drawn upon the concepts of embodiment and hysteria. I have argued that advertisers frequently portray women as either manic, neurotic or vacant and empty. Goffman's coding, relevant to this theme, highlights the ways in which women are often depicted in a dreamlike state, 'tuned out' or removed from the situation. The Persil and L'Oreal adverts provided the source for these discussions and reflected the participants' feelings of surprise that adverts contained the language of hysteria or imagery of vacancy. The third theme, 'objectified bodies', revisited Goffman's ritualisation of subordination and the ways in which the female body is objectified, sexualised and put into unnatural and absurd subservient positions. Goffman's typology works with contemporary advertising and most of the visual diaries and, indeed, discussions contained the participants' desire to hold this theme in advertising as problematic. I argue that, despite appearing outdated, Goffman's coding scheme maps onto contemporary forms of advertising such as the controversial 'Beach Body Ready' advert—an advert that, on first impressions, does not reveal the obvious coded messages of subordination.

In the next three chapters, I discuss how each of the case studies—Sweden, Spain and UK—has sought to tackle gender stereotypes in advertising. Throughout these chapters, I analyse the legislative and regulatory codes each state has assembled and critique some of the current and past case law that has helped develop the tackling of gender stereotypes in advertising.

References

Back, L. and Quaade, V. (1993) 'Dream utopias, nightmare realities: Imaging race and culture within the world of Benetton advertising', *Third Text*, 7(22), pp. 65–66.

Bates, L. (2014) 'Everyday sexism', see also Everyday Sexism Project. Available at: https://everydaysexism.com/ (Accessed: 21 June 2024).

Berger, J. (1978) *Ways of seeing*. Vol. 1. Penguin UK.

Blloshmi, A. (2013) 'Advertising in post-feminism: The return of sexism in visual culture?', *Journal of Promotional Communications*, 1(1).

Bourdieu, P. (2011) 'The forms of capital', *Cultural Theory: An Anthology*, 1.

Busfield, J. (1994) 'The female malady? Men, women and madness in nineteenth century Britain', *Sociology*, 28(1), pp. 259–277.

Butler, J. (1990) *Gender trouble*. Routledge.

Gilman, S.L., Gilman, S.L., King, H., Porter, R., Rousseau, G.S. and Showalter, E. (1993) *Hysteria beyond Freud*. University of California Press.

Goffman, E. (1963) 'Embarrassment and social organization', *American Journal of Sociology*, 62(3).

Goffman, E. (1976) *Gender advertisements*. New York: Harper.

Goffman, E. (1977) 'The arrangement between the sexes', *Theory and Society*, 4(3).

Goldman, R., Heath, D. and Smith, S.L. (1991) 'Commodity feminism', *Critical Studies in Media Communication*, 8(3), pp. 333–351.

Hall, S. (2007) 'Encoding and decoding in the television discourse', in *CCCS selected working papers*. Routledge, pp. 402–414.

Hoagland, S.L. (1980) 'Androcentric rhetoric in sociobiology', *Women's Studies International Quarterly*, 3(2–3), pp. 285–293.

Leiss, W. and Botterill, J. (2005) *Social communication in advertising: Consumption in the mediated marketplace*. Psychology Press.

Lorber, J. (1994) '"Night to his day": The social construction of gender'. *Paradoxes of gender*, 1, pp. 1–8.

Maines, R.P. (2001) *The technology of orgasm: "Hysteria", the vibrator, and women's sexual satisfaction*. JHU Press.

McRobbie, A. (1994) *Postmodernism and popular culture*. Psychology Press.

Orbach, S. (2009) *Bodies*. Picador.

Parsons, T. (1956) 'Suggestions for a Sociological Approach to the Theory of Organizations-I'. *Administrative science quarterly*, pp. 63–85.

Rousseau, G. (2004) *Nervous acts: Essays on literature, culture and sensibility*. Springer.
Schutzman, M. (1999) *The real thing: Performance, hysteria, & advertising*. Wesleyan University Press.
Showalter, E. (1985) *Female malady*. Penguin Books.
Showalter, E. (1998) *Hystories: Hysterical epidemics and modern media*. Vol. 2. Columbia University Press.
Showalter, E. (2016) 'Ophelia, gender and madness article'. Available at the British Library Website: https://www.bl.uk/shakespeare/articles/ophelia-gender-and-madness.
Soar, M. (2000) 'Encoding advertisements: Ideology and meaning in advertising production', *Mass Communication & Society*, 3(4), pp. 415–437.
Stern, B. (1990) 'Pleasure and persuasion in advertising: Rhetorical irony as a humor technique', *Current Issues and Research in Advertising*, 12(1–2), pp. 25–42.
Varghese, N. and Kumar, N. (2022) 'Feminism in advertising: Irony or revolution? A critical review of femvertising', *Feminist Media Studies*, 22(2), pp. 441–459.
West, C. and Zimmerman, D.H. (1987) 'Doing gender', *Gender & Society*, 1(2).

Chapter 6

Sweden

Introduction

This is the first of three chapters exploring national perspectives on legislation and regulation of gender stereotypes in advertising. The objective of these three chapters is to capture the different practices across Europe and how divergent legal frameworks operate in tackling harmful content and gender stereotypes in advertising. From these national perspectives, I glean examples of good practice from legislation, self-regulation and soft law to imagine what might a pan-European regulatory code could look like and what harmful gendered content and gender stereotypes the code could regulate. Each of the three countries has navigated conflicting legal principles such as freedom of expression, freedom of information, principles of gender equality and non-discrimination. Considering these clashes in legal principles, I unravel the dissimilar cultural, legal and political structures of the three countries to reveal how they have legislated and regulated the issue. By identifying the current legal, political and social issues that intersect the regulation of gender stereotypes in advertising, I observe distinctive frictions in the member states that impede such legislative or regulative aims. For example, Sweden's legal, political and societal interest in freedom of the press and extensive (market-driven) freedom of expression rights which have thus far thwarted legislation on sexist advertising.[1] I then provide some observations on future developments in each of the member states and look towards what the European regulatory code might look like. Developing a report of each of the three case studies' legal traditions, norms and histories falls outside the limits of this book, so instead, I provide an account of historical, political and social issues that have helped shape pathways that have brought about law and policy on combatting sexist advertising. The focus of the three chapters will specifically be the legislation, regulation and case law that have developed concepts such as objectification, sexualisation, reification and gender

1 In 2018, the city council of Stockholm banned sexist advertising from billboards. Similar action has been taken in other European capitals such as Glasgow and London.

DOI: 10.4324/9781003336037-6

stereotypes in advertising. Finally, the chapters scrutinise the self-regulators and their ethical codes in each country, the methodologies they employ and how they interact with non-state actors.

Normative legal instruments

If an amateur rambler is off walking, there comes a time when they may come close to the edge of a cliff or a dubious ridge. The question for the organisation that maintains health and safety for the hiker is perhaps how to keep them safe without infringing on their experience as a walker. The options are either a fence at the top of the cliff edge, perhaps a warning sign for good measure, or an ambulance at the bottom to ensure those who are injured get to the hospital in time. This allegory is fundamentally how legislation and self-regulation of advertising works: legislation—or pre-screening by the regulator—can catch a problematic advert before it reaches its desired audience or wait for it to cause offence on billboards, TV screens or smartphones. The latter is what most European countries have decided works best (EASA, 2024). As this chapter provides an overview of the different approaches to combatting sexist advertising, it will become apparent that there are different methods and tools available when regulating advertising, and they are more complex than the rambler analogy. It is therefore necessary to categorise some of these methods and provide a brief outline of their merits and drawbacks. As discussed in Chapter 3, there has been a considerable amount of work by EU institutions and non-state actors such as the EASA on the best option for combatting gender stereotypes and sexist advertising. These soft law and self-regulation approaches have always produced the same conclusions: legislation is far too a blunt instrument, each member state ought to be allowed to regulate (or legislate) as they see fit depending on cultural differences, and, more importantly, the classification of irony, taste and good humour is not universal (Earle, 2016: 58). At a national level, tackling sexist advertising ranges from stringent legislation (see, for example, Spain's Organic Act 2004) that can prohibit certain forms of advertising to merely 'naming and shaming' certain adverts that are considered unacceptable (Antoniou and Akrivos, 2020). Across Europe, there are four ways to prevent advertisers from broadcasting sexist content. Along this scale, the most recognisable is legislation, which seeks to act as the fence at the top of cliff edge, with clear concepts such as prohibition of objectification, sexualisation or gender stereotypes in advertisements. Numerous EU member states such as Spain (Organic Law protection measures against gender violence 2004) and Finland (Consumer Protection Act 1978) have produced legal instruments which prohibit sexist advertising. Legislation prohibiting gender stereotypes in advertising comes in many forms; some countries have sought to enact legislation through marketing and consumer protection laws (Finland, Norway and Denmark) while others have pursued legislation through gender equality laws (Spain).

EU member states tend to sidestep legislation by including ambiguous terms in self-regulatory codes and avoiding explicit terminology in the legislation, such as providing definitions for 'sexualisation' or 'gender stereotypes'. A further common route has been through governmental regulatory bodies. These state-aided regulators are a dying breed and are slowly being replaced by industry-led self-regulation organisations (SROs), such as the UK's Advertising Standards Authority, which is funded by—and made up of—private industry. SROs follow the International Chamber of Commerce (ICC) code of conduct on inappropriate advertising,[2] with various penalties and sanctions but typically a ban or fine. State-funded regulation is increasingly rare since the introduction of 'third way' self-regulation in the mid-1990s and the impetus for a *laissez-faire* approach to the market. As outlined in Chapter 3, the timing of this approach is linked to the availability of satellite and cable TV and the hundreds of new TV channels across the EU, which consumers began to sponsor through watching advertisements. The expansion of SROs became a better way to regulate an ever-expanding market, giving the consumer the 'power' to regulate their own intake of advertising. SROs commonly consist of both traditional governmental regulation (i.e. trained staff but not necessarily lawyers) and engagement with the industry stakeholders (predominantly advertising agencies). Since the introduction of the EASA in 1991, SROs are increasingly in vogue across Europe, and despite criticism for being too weak in certain areas, such as food and alcohol (Hastings et al., 2010), they have dominated the landscape of advertising regulation. In the realm of sexist content, the SRO is often seen as taking the pressure off governments that lack consensus to legislate on such a complex topic. The SRO is not as blunt as legislation; it characteristically takes a much softer approach, encouraging best practices by engaging with advertisers, providing services such as training or the pre-screening of adverts before they reach their audiences. Through the introduction of the EASA, the European SROs of the early 1990s have all faced significant changes, and most are dynamic enough to react to moral or cultural shifts. The final mode of curbing sexist content in advertising is through the use of non-state actors such as watchdogs, lobbyists, NGOs, campaigners and activists. Across the EU, there are numerous organisations that fit within this bracket, with most working alongside the industry. Their work tends to coincide with the work of the SROs, as well as activism campaigns, bridging the gap between petitioners and formal legitimate avenues of complaint. This final grouping of non-state actors is gaining prominence across the EU and will be discussed in subsequent chapters.

2 A consolidated version of the ICC code can be found on its website: https://iccwbo.org/publication/advertising-and-marketing-communication-practice-consolidated-icc-code/ (accessed 21 June 2024).

Conflicting legal principles

Attempts to restrict sexist advertising—whether enshrined in legislation or regulation—has led to a theoretical debate with two opposing positions. On one side of the division, there are countries reluctant to encourage legislation that sanctions advertisers as they perceive (or at least their constitutions do) that legislative control of gender stereotypes in advertising would constrain freedom of expression. Svensson and Edström (2015) use the term 'market-driven freedom of expression' to explain the widespread use of self-regulatory bodies or co-regulation (including specific industry regulation, such as for beer and spirits) as the preferred option to tackle sexist content in advertising. On the other side of the argument are some EU member states that have taken pre-emptive steps in ratifying Article 5(a) of CEDAW, which seeks to remove all cultural stereotypes in society or have set aside the exclusions from article 3(3) of the Goods and Services Directive 2004/113/EC. By legislating on sexist advertising, these states are willing to position the protection of fundamental human rights, such as gender equality, above freedom of expression. This is conceptualised as 'democracy-driven' freedom of expression—curtailing sexist advertising by prohibiting sexual content and stereotypes, regardless of the advertisers' claims that legislation is a restriction of free press. This side of the debate represents two forms of logic:

> The rationality of democracy-driven freedom of expression is committed to safeguarding free and independent information and expressions as a prerequisite for democracy. The rationality of the market-driven freedom of expression is committed to safeguarding all information and expressions regardless of their interests and purposes.
>
> (Svensson and Edström, 2015: 499)

Both freedom of expression and gender equality are democratic values that legislators wish to commit to, and as there is an inherent tension between these two fundamental rights, the question is whether or not seeking to legislate on gender stereotypes is a restriction on freedom of expression. The remaining chapters therefore contemplate divergent perspectives on this debate.

In this first chapter, I discuss the first national perspective, Sweden, a country that has so far remained reluctant to legislate on gender stereotypes in advertising, unlike its Nordic neighbours (Kosunen et al., 2017; Svensson and Edström, 2015; Swedish Women's, 2015, 2020). Sweden's constitution and history are entangled with the Free Press Act (1776)—the earliest recorded act on free speech—and is consistently over-cautious when opting for a democracy-driven freedom of expression. This freedom has been interpreted as a market-driven right, which seeks to appease the functioning of the media rather than the foundations of democracy-driven freedom of expression.

Tampering with the Swedish constitution to incorporate legislation on advertising would symbolically be perceived as interfering with the wider mass media and, critically, an affront to the Free Press Act. Although there have been numerous attempts in Sweden to shift towards a ban on gender stereotypes, the state has yet to opt for legislation. Since 2014, the Social Democrat governments Lovfen and Andersson have continued to pledge to curb gender stereotypes in advertising (and media) in their manifestos, but this has not come into fruition. Chapter 7 looks at Spain, on the polar opposite end of the theoretical debate by passing legislation from a democracy-driven perspective Martin-Llaguno, 2016; López Jiménez, Dittmar and Portillo, 2021). Since it came into effect in 2004, there have been numerous criticisms of the legislation; however, the positioning of gender equality above the advertising industry is emblematic. The UK's position on gender stereotypes is somewhat similar to Sweden, in that there is no current legislation that prohibits the use of gender stereotypes in advertising. However, the recent amendment to the Advertising Standards Authority's ethical code reflects a more proactive approach to catching harmful forms of gender stereotypes before they reach audiences.

Legislation on sexist content in advertising has proven problematic for Sweden and is often criticised by its neighbours for not living up to its Scandinavian feminist image (Svensson and Edström, 2015; Edström, 2022). Sweden is often held up as the nation-state that has helped define the 'Nordic legal family' or 'Scandinavian law',[3] yet it simultaneously falls victim to this classification. The Scandinavian categorisation often renders its members as homogenous, particularly in gender-related legislation and policy. There are, of course, numerous similarities and overlap amongst the Nordic countries, and comparisons within this 'family' of nations can often be overlooked by lawyers and policy makers wishing to neatly group the countries together. For example, the 'Nordic welfare model' is as universally recognised (Kvist, 2012) as the Nordic model on sex workers (Skilbrei and Holmström, 2011). The legal grouping of the countries is often deemed similar from a comparative law perspective (Zweigert et al., 1998), and their political, economic and cultural binding is measured with the same yardstick. It is therefore unsurprising that deeper analysis of the Nordic Legal family[4] has been analysed

3 From a *legal culture* perspective, the Scandinavian legal 'family' can be split into east and west Scandinavia. The west includes Norway and Denmark, the latter of which has been more influential, with monarch rule from Copenhagen up until 1814. Sweden is often cited as the most influential state in the family; however, it has only influenced Finland's constitution as both were part of the same country until Finland came under Russian rule in 1809. For further discussion on legal family traditions and 'Scandinavian' law, see Bernitz, U. (2007). What is Scandinavian law? Concept, characteristics, future. *Scandinavian studies in law*, *50*, pp. 15–16.

4 'Nordic' incorporates the nation states of Sweden, Norway, Finland, Denmark and Iceland, as opposed to 'Scandinavian', which would merely include Sweden, Norway and perhaps Arctic

sparingly in comparative law (Bernitz, 2007). Similarities within this family include but are not limited to their legal theory foundations, formation of their basic legal concepts and principles and kinship in their methodology, as well as codification, precedent and sources of law. Therefore, one would assume—from a distance—that the 'Nordic family' are wholly similar, if not the same. However, say this (as I have) to a Swedish constitutional lawyer, and you will be hastily scolded with raised eyebrows; it is akin to suggesting to a British constitutional lawyer that English law is no different from French law. Nordic comparative law academics such as Malmstrom (1969) and Husa (2000) have concluded that the members of the Nordic family, although distinctive, slot nicely into the four Western Europe legal groupings: continental, common law, Latin American and Nordic. Moreover, Bogdan (2009) aligns the Nordic family with the continental model, distancing it from the common law (e.g. UK) or Latin (e.g. Spanish) approach. This view has been shared by comparative lawyers (Zweigert and Kötz, 1998) over the years, but surprisingly, little comparative law has focused on how the Nordic countries diverge, particularly in their methods and attitudes towards gender equality. Jumbling these nations together as homogeneous neglects scrutiny of divergence amongst them, particularly when it comes to legislation on gender stereotypes and sexist content in advertising. I raise this as that not only is the notion of the 'Nordic model' to be contested but also because the Swedish legal system and its constitution is different from the rest of her sisters within the family, it therefore at times, hinders the state in legislating on prohibiting sexist advertising. This difference becomes more apparent when considering specific elements of the legal system, particularly the history of and attitude towards freedom of expression and the press, advertising regulation and the use of self-regulatory bodies. I do not aim to chart the history and development of the Swedish political and legal system within this chapter. However, to illustrate how Sweden contrasts with its fellow Nordic countries, I will unfurl some of the key characteristics of Sweden's political, historical and constitutional details before analysing the Swedish legal system and its approach to freedom of expression and advertising regulation.

The Swedish system of government

Sweden is typical of any modern European representative democracy in that it follows a constitutional parliamentary democracy, a written 'constitution' and a metamorphosing civil code (Ortwein, 2002). The addition is the 'weak' monarch, who serves as the head of state. The monarch's residual

Finland. For further discussion on the Nordic/Scandinavian debate, there are countless pieces of literature within law, politics and geography. I have used the most common term developed in legal literature; however I am aware of the debate put forward by academics such as Ulf Bernitz (*What Is Scandinavian Law?*) from the Stockholm Institute for Scandinavian Law.

power is not too dissimilar to the British monarch, and at the end of the Second World War, the head of state's powers gradually diminished until the coronation of King Carl XVI and *Regeringsformen* (The Instrument of Government Act 1974). *Regeringsformen* is one of four fundamental 'basic' laws that make up the Swedish constitution and is the key piece of legislation that reduced the monarch's already dwindling powers to produce the modern-day mode of Swedish government. The introduction of *Regeringsformen* to the constitution shifted the monarch's symbolic position to provide the *Riksdag* (Parliament) with concrete powers it had already assumed. This constitutional shift provided numerous changes, most significantly a single chamber and a shift of powers from the head of state to the prime minister and Parliament. *Regeringsformen* provides a template and rules on how to form a government and a catalogue of basic freedoms, rights and regulations, as well as the basic rules for the day-to-day running of the Parliamentary institutions. This limits the monarch position to a ceremonial figure for state functions and state visits. In recent years, two important pieces of 'European' law—the European Convention of Human Rights and accession to the European Union—have considerably reshaped the Swedish constitution, with both international agreements receiving acts of Parliament in the 1990s. In 2009, the *Riksdag* amended the *Regeringsformen* section of the constitution to encompass and reflect the modern changes in Swedish society, principally sexual orientation rights, rights of minorities (particularly Roma Gypsies and indigenous Sami people), and children's rights, but, most importantly, to strike down new laws that contravene the EU Charter of Fundamental Rights. *Regeringsformen* is one quarter of the Swedish constitution. The remaining three are *Successionsordningen* (the Act of Succession 1810), which provides rules on monarch accession, *Tryckfrihetsförordningen* (the Freedom of Press Act 1945) and *Yttrandefrihetsgrundlagen* (the Freedom of Expression Act 1991).

Freedom of expression

The constitutional and legal principles of gender equality and freedom of expression are held up as important foundations in Swedish culture. Gender equality is found first and foremost in the Discrimination Act (2008), which prohibits discrimination (direct and indirect) based on gender and guarantees equal rights for all, regardless of race, religion, sexual orientation and transgender identity. Advertising does not fall within the scope of the act, and therefore, the Swedish Equality Ombudsman is limited in tackling gender stereotypes and sexist advertising. Unlike its neighbours, Sweden is the only Nordic country that is yet to explicitly legislate on gender stereotypes in advertising (Svennson, 2014). Throughout the Nordic countries, gender equality is positioned above freedom of expression rights, and gender stereotypes and sexist advertising are regulated in advertising via legislation and self-regulatory codes and ombudsmen. Despite Sweden leading the way for pushing the anti-discrimination agenda and legalisation in the early 1970s, Swedish law lacks legislative instruments that explicitly prohibit gender stereotypes and sexist advertising. The Swedish Marketing Act (2008) protects consumers against unfair or misleading adverts, but the Swedish Market Court ruled that the purpose of the act was not to cover sexist advertising or advertising that might cause harm or offence (Nordic Council of Ministers Regulation of Gender Discrimination Advertising in the Nordic Countries 2017). The Marketing Court found that any measures in the act that sought to regulate the media would breach the constitution's *Yttrandefrihetsgrundlagen* (the Freedom of Expression Act 1991). This stems from an earlier version of the act and a ruling from the Marketing Court in 1976. The court ruled that the scope of the act did not include gender discrimination in advertising. This precedent has made it nearly impossible to bring any action on the basis of the act and reduced the likelihood of future legislation on gender stereotypes in advertising. The reasoning behind the decision is that the role of the act is to protect the consumer and not specific characteristics such as gender (Kosunen et al., 2017). It is worth noting that freedom of expression has not hindered any of the other Nordic countries' attempts to legislate or been seen as a barrier to regulating gender stereotypes. Where all the Nordic countries have both legislation and self-regulation to tackle the problem, Sweden is heavily reliant on its self-regulatory body, *Reklamombudsmannen*. Freedom of expression is so entwined with the constitutional make-up of Sweden that it has been an obstacle for campaigners and governments over the last 30 years.

This next section of the chapter is a discussion of how and why Sweden has failed to legislate on gender stereotypes in advertising, including analysis of the political landscape and the historical anchoring of freedom of expression in the Swedish constitution. I will begin by broadly discussing the government's political will to legislate on gender policy issues and then move to specific attempts to prohibit gender stereotypes in advertising by charting political discourse and legislative attempts over the last two decades. I will then discuss the potential re-emergence of a ban on gender stereotypes in advertising under the current left-wing alliance under Prime Minister Stefan Löfven (2014–2021).

The 'golden child' of Europe for gender equality

Sweden has, until recent years, been celebrated as one of the more progressive, egalitarian and gender-equal countries in Europe (Martinsson et al., 2016). This label is based on various factors, such as an egalitarian welfare system with ample parental leave provisions (Kvist and Greve, 2011) and high levels of social assistance and well-being, particularly if you are a woman (OECD, Better Life Index). It is also one of the best places to grow up as a young girl (PISA, Kids Rights Index, 2024). Female representation is high across different occupational fields, and despite a dip in the number of parliamentary seats held by women, Sweden has been seen as the most feminist states in the world. Politically, this arguably true. Sweden has historically had the most female members of parliament, currently 46.7% (UNWomen, 2024), and has led the way in terms of female representation since the 1950s (Dahlerup, 2011). In 2014, the SDP-led coalition declared itself the first 'feminist government in the world', but, in recent years, the varnish has begun to peel away from Sweden's global reputation as a liberal feminist country (Martinsson et al., 2016). The problems are few but centre around the rise of the radical right (Off, 2023) and the post-pandemic crisis, both of which contradict the older international image of progressive Swedish exceptionalism (Rydgren and Van der Meiden, 2019). Despite these events, Sweden retains its feminist and 'woman-friendly' appearance (Jezierska and Towns, 2018; Edström, 2022), and its sympathy and dedication to feminist issues knows no bounds: intervention policies on pornography, sex work, equal pay and, most recently, safeguarding of trans issues with gender recognition laws are just a handful of areas in which the country is deemed objectively progressive.

Despite this, Sweden has yet to completely fulfil its international obligations in safeguarding gender equality issues. For example, it has yet to ratify CEDAW and BPfA (1995) obligations by providing legislating on gender stereotypes in advertising and tis he only Nordic country that relies solely on self-regulation (Svensson and Edström, 2015; Kosunen et al., 2017; Edström, 2022). It is incongruent that the state can legislate on numerous normative gender-based issues yet is unable or reluctant to tackle systemic sexism such as gender stereotypes in advertising. This is particularly unusual as other forms of gender stereotypes have been tackled through legislation and policy. For example, the removal of gender stereotypes in Swedish culture is by no means a modern concept: gender-neutral schools, pronouns and toys are just some of the few legislative 'victories' of the two decades. Indeed, Sweden was held up as spearheading the regulation of advertising—particularly advertising aimed at children. Legislation in this area has moved towards the removal of gender stereotypes in advertising: for example, a blanket ban on televised advertising to children existed up until its repeal 2010. The Court of Justice in the EU's decision in the *De Agostini* case not only maintained that Sweden's ban on advertising to preteens did not in breach of free movement provisions, but the Advocate General's opinion also seemed to actively promote such a ban. The most recent example of tackling gender stereotypes is the gender-neutral pronoun 'hen', which was added to the Swedish dictionary.

The proposal to provide legislation on gender stereotypes in advertising began in 1996 under Göran Persson's SDP government, which sought to turn feminist principles into legislation. During his second term, Persson offered his concern with any such legislation: 'I'm a feminist, but I don't want to push these issues so hard that I create hostilities in society'. This sentiment reflects the SDP's gender policy throughout his two terms of office as banning sexist advertising was discussed and shelved numerous times due to the party's fears that such a ban would infringe on the state's protection of freedom of expression and, more importantly, reignite old battles on free press between the traditional print media and government. Over the years, the language of the draft legislation loosened from 'ban' on 'sexist imagery' to prohibiting all advertising that could be 'considered sexist', incorporating terms such as 'gender stereotypes' and 'commodifying' women's bodies. The shift in language at the draft stage further provided Parliament with sufficient reason to freely critique such a ban as unworkable and a step too far. The legislation was eventually deferred, and pressure to deliver on the SDP's feminist manifesto dwindled. A decade later, the government gave the draft legislation one final opportunity, and in the summer of 2006, an official government report on gender-discriminatory advertising and sex and gender discrimination was commissioned and passed to a team of legal experts led by Eva-Maria Svensson (SOU, 2008: 5). The report outlined a simple argument: it would be possible to legislate on gender discrimination in advertising without infringing on the strong freedom of expression status of the constitution. Svensson Edström outlined the report's argument:

> [D]iscriminatory commercial messages should not be protected from intervention, because they are discriminatory and discrimination is prohibited in other areas of society. Thus, commercial messages do not have the same protection as other messages (because the main purpose is to sell something, not primarily to disseminate some opinion), and the issue of considering something to be discriminatory or not is too important to leave to self-regulation by the industry.
>
> (Svensson and Edström, 2015: 499)

The report was put before the national parliament but abandoned in 2008, partly due to a change of government—the SDP had lost vast numbers of seats in the election to Fredrik Reinfeldt, the newcomer and moderniser of the Moderate Party. The Minister for Gender Equality, Nyamko Sabuni, stated at the time that the crux of Sweden's problem with legislating on gender stereotypes in advertising was obvious:

> I don't think legislation is the most effective means to use, and in this case, I would rather protect the freedom of speech than legislate against gender discriminatory advertising.
>
> (Dagens Industri, 24 April 2008)

Almost a decade later, the issue was reignited with the return of the SDP and left coalition partners, who cited gender stereotypes in advertising as a public health issue, particularly for women and young girls in Sweden. Understanding why Sweden has consistently rejected legislation (and perhaps why it will reject it again) requires some consideration of the constitution. The final two sections of the Swedish constitution (freedom of expression and of the press) reflect Sweden's determination and historical ties to safeguarding freedom of expression. The Swedish legal system ensures that legislators (and the judiciary) have limited influence on the limits on the principle (Bull, 2009; Kenyon and Svensson, 2017). This commitment is influenced by Montesquieu's theorisation of separation of powers (Bull, 2009) which was influential at the time of Sweden's Free Press Act (1776). Svensson and Edström (2015) argue that a market-driven freedom of expression is both an inherent Swedish common good and the most easily recognisable part of the Swedish constitution. Sweden is equally committed to gender equality through its Fundamental Law (Constitutional Law) Instrument of Government Law (1974), as well as the legal obligations in EU law (Article 11 of the Charter of Fundamental Rights, Article 2 and 49 TEU) and the ECHR (Article 10). At first glance, these two values embedded in the constitution seem relatively dormant, but according to Svensson and Edström (2015), the strong principle of freedom of expression in the constitution is the biggest obstacle to achieving gender equality in terms of banning gender stereotypes in advertising. The purpose of the Freedom of Press Act (1776) and Fundamental Law (1974) chimes with the EU's Copenhagen Criteria: that all members shall have a free press and uphold fundamental human rights. The two arms of the constitution have two broad principles: first, to ensure free exchange of opinions and pluralism of information, and second, to ensure the proper functioning of a free press and a media that is able to provide such information and opinions. Implicit in these acts is the notion of ensuring that a free press and freedom of expression are paramount for a functioning democracy, where citizens are well informed and the media are free to critique all notions of government.

The two pieces of freedom of expression legislation provide some basic guidance on advertising categories and whom it is addressed to (e.g. children) but generally provides for regulation of media and press and not sexist content or gender stereotypes in advertising. Misleading or 'unfair' advertising is covered by separate pieces of legislation across numerous acts of parliament in Sweden: the Marketing Act (2008), based on unfair business-to-consumer commercial practices (Directive 2005/29/EC), and the Radio and Television Act (2010) based on the AVMS Directive 2010/13/EU. Neither of the acts contains any specific provisions on gender portrayal or taste and decency.[5]

5 There have been attempts to use s.5 of the Marketing Act to curtail discriminatory advertising. S.5 of the act states that all marketing must be in line with 'good practice'. Whilst drafting

Self-regulation in Sweden: from prohibition to pillory

As both the Marketing Act (2008) and the Radio and Television Act (2010) fail to catch advertising as a form of sex discrimination, Sweden is heavily reliant on its self-regulatory body, *Stiftelsen Reklamombudsmannen* (RO), to tackle gender stereotypes in advertising. Prior to the RO, the Swedish Consumer Agency (state administered) had traditionally dealt with sexist advertising, but its role gradually diminished during the 1990s until it was formally passed on to ERK, a government-led self-regulatory body which has also since expired. Although ERK ran as a self-regulatory body, the government oversaw most of its activities, and its members were trained and distinguished market lawyers or advertising specialists. With state backing, ERK possessed numerous powers: namely, the pre-screening tests and the right to strike down adverts that contravened its regulatory code before they were televised. The ERK's criteria for sex discriminatory advertising was three-fold and congruent with Article 4(1) of the International Chamber of Commerce's Code on Advertising and Marking Practice, which broadly prohibits sex discrimination in advertising.

Under the ERK's criteria, an advert can be banned from all forms of media if it positions a woman as a sexual object, reproduces out-of-touch gender roles that position women (and men) in a degrading way or is in any other way 'degrading' to women or men. From 1989 until its closure 2009, ERK issued 377 bans (9.4% of the 3,990 complaints received). During the organisation's existence, advertising agencies became more influential in how ERK operated, with increasing numbers of industry representatives working alongside its legally trained regulators to hear cases involving sexist content. The dilution of legal practitioners with advertising agency representatives became more popular across all EU member state regulators with the push towards the use of more self-regulatory organisations. In Sweden's case, banning an advert became less popular due to this market-driven change. One of the final 'public' exchanges between the ERK and an advertiser is a good example of this shift from banning to 'naming and shaming' an advertisement. The Black and Decker advert (2008) embodies the diminishing power of ERK as the company behind the advert had clearly contravened the regulatory code by reproducing gender stereotypes through its advert promising customers a 'pleased wife guarantee'. The advert offered customers' wives a 'beauty makeover' worth 350 Swedish kroner when they spent over 1,500 kroner on tools. ERK deemed the advert to be degrading to both men and women due to its use of archaic gender stereotypes and Black and Decker removed the advert

the act, 'good practice' meant using the ICC code for guidance; however, due to an earlier case concerning advertising regulation in 1976 in the Marketing Court, it was held that gender discrimination does not fall within the scope of the act. Therefore, regulation of gender stereotypes falls outside the Marketing Act.

immediately. This form of arrangement between the regulator and advertiser became commonplace as the powers shifted from ERK to the self-regulatory body and paved the way for ERK's complete replacement, Stiftelsen Reklamombudsmannen (RO) and the Reklamombudsmannen Jury (RON).

The Reklamombudsmannen

Sweden's current regulator appears similar to the ERK in name, field of enquiry and regulatory powers. However, the key difference is that the regulator is not a public body; it relinquished its sanctioning powers and is therefore only able to 'name and shame' adverts through public notices and campaigns. RO follows the ICC's code on sexist advertising and reflects the ERK's original criteria to define what constitutes discriminating advertising. Unlike the ERK, its staff are not advertising or market lawyers—most staff work in the advertising industry itself, and the body is funded by the industry and 'volunteers'. At the time of writing, the RO's website does not provide a comprehensive list of financiers but identifies some of its 'sponsors', which are primarily from the beer and spirits industry. Although the RO does not provide for sanctions, it publishes its considerations and decisions online and is generally considered accessible and transparent (Svensson, 2014; Svensson and Edström, 2015). The term 'Reklamombudsmannen' denotes a professional-sounding body that is accessible, providing information and links to the ICC's code, and the tone of the language is quasi-legal—'trials' are 'held', and 'cases' are 'upheld'—and the complaint form is simple to use with mobile screenshots as one of the suggested modes of complaint. The shrewd use of 'ombudsman' is not a coincidence; the term originates from and is known across the Nordic countries to mean 'representative', and therefore, its connotations and symbolism loom larger than the actual day-to-day operations of the body. The term indeed renders connotations with the Swedish Parliamentary Ombudsman, a body that was set up in 1809 (33 years after the Free Press Act of 1776) as part of the Montesquieu-esque separation-of-powers overhaul of the Swedish constitution. The Swedish Parliamentary Ombudsman receives complaints about public authorities from citizens with issues ranging from complaints against the civil service to infringement of local by-laws. The use of the term instils confidence that consumers' complaints will result in some form of inquiry and sanction, just as with the parliamentary ombudsman. The RO (like many of the other self-regulatory bodies) is therefore merely symbolically powerful, at least in an etymological sense, but also appears noble: the term is historically linked to lawyers and advocates, which may leave the consumer under the illusion that the body has some kind of legal underpinning. The reality is quite different as the RO not only lacks effective legal sanctions, but it is also heavily entangled with the industry it purports to regulate. Sanctions are replaced by training programmes for advertisers, 'naming and shaming' via press releases, public campaigns (adverts) and engagement with the media. Complaints about sexist advertising are relatively frequent in Sweden (Kosunen et al., 2017).

Over the years, both the CEDAW committee[6] and Beijing Platform for Action monitor[7] have been critical of Sweden's lack of legislation. The Swedish Women's Lobby (SWL) cites the failure to implement the 2008 report and the RO's ineffectiveness as a regulator as contributory factors in the upsurge in sexist advertising in Sweden. This is criticism is three-fold: the RO lacks economic sanctions, it doesn't have the power to withdraw advertising campaigns, and since the introduction of the RO, there is no indication that the use gender stereotypes or sexist content has been reduced. On the contrary, there has been an increase in cases of sexualisation and objectification in advertising (Swedish Women's Lobby, 2015).

This criticism is amplified when considering that the other Nordic countries use an amalgamation of legislation and self-regulation (Kosunen et al., 2017), particularly Finland's joint SRO and legislative approach, which has been held up as a leading light in self-regulation. However, some academics have argued that the RO of Sweden operations is highly effective as a 'third way' of naming and shaming bad or distasteful advertisements (Kosunen et al). The 'third way' of the naming and shaming companies is apparent in almost all SROs across Europe and has left a void for the final form of regulation to develop: non-state actors. NGOs, campaigners and grassroots activists have blossomed in Sweden due to lack of government intervention. Extending the pillory strategy through public campaigning, this grouping has carved out a space in which to actively hound advertisers that fall foul of their arbitrary rules through social media. Digital campaigns in conjunction with other digital feminist groups have coerced the RO to take a tougher stance in removing gender stereotypes in advertisements. Since 1997, the SWL have been one of the strongest consortiums in this grouping and have been involved in lobbying government to legislate on the issue and for the RO to toughen their stance on regulating sexist advertising. Made up of 47 members, the SWL have set up their own alternative to the RO; Reklamera encourages consumers to report any form of sexist advertisement to the organisation. The organisation has been very successful in its approach to the issue by attracting younger consumers to report sexist adverts through social media sites and adding the hashtag #reklamera in the comments. As well as pressuring advertisers and brands, the campaign advocates for the revival of legislation on sexist advertising and gender stereotypes in Sweden. At the time of writing, #reklamera has dissolved into the ether of other social media

6 See CEDAW, 'Concluding observations of the Committee on the Elimination of Discrimination against Women: Sweden' (3 08–29866 CEDAW/C/SWE/CO/7) (8 April 2008) para 23.

7 Sweden's follow-up to the Platform for Action from the UN's Fourth World Conference on Women in Beijing (1995), covering the period between 2009 and 2014. (U2014/240/JÄM).

hashtags in Sweden, but campaigns such as #reklamera demonstrate some of the issues with online movements. Whilst online campaigns are good at directing audiences to engage and critique advertising, the consumer traffic is ultimately moved away from a formal complaints procedure that might have at least some impact. Adverts are often criticised online, and social media websites provide easy access to express such critiques; however, angry comments underneath an advert on Facebook do not amount to an official complaint. Secondly, online campaigns often reach their peak and fade out. This problem is common across most anti-sexist movements: for example, the UK's 'Everyday Sexism' campaign has similarly decreased over time, acting as a community rather than a campaign (Golbeck et al., 2017). Finally, online campaigns do not always result in state intervention or legislation. Instead, the campaign acts a rouse—an online debate—but with little sanctioning in place. This will be discussed in the final case study, the 'Beach Body' campaign, in Chapter 8.

Conclusion

In the absence of legislation, Sweden, relies solely on self-regulation to curb the use of gender stereotypes and sexism in advertising. This is largely linked to the conflicting principles of gender equality and freedom of expression enshrined in both the constitution and legislation. It is also related to a lack of political will in both the SDP and moderate governments of the last 20 years. As advertising is not within the scope of either the Marketing Act (2008) or the Sex Discrimination Act (1976), the state has relied on the self-regulatory organisation the Reklamombudsman (RO) to fill the void left by a lack of legislation. Despite an increase in complaints from consumers regarding sexist advertising, the RO lacks sanctioning powers, both in economic terms (fines) and in regulation (withdrawing the advert) and instead relies on pillory. A culture of self-regulation and a pseudo-ombudsman appears to be the 'safest' option in Sweden as legislation is out of kilter with the constitution, which places emphasis on (market-based) freedom of expression and free speech. Since the demise of its previous and more powerful SRO, the current regulator appears an attractive 'third way' of avoiding legislation.

References

Advertising Standards Authority (2017) 'Depictions, perceptions and harm'. Available at: https://www.asa.org.uk/static/uploaded/e06425f9-2f9f-44c3-ae6ebd5902686d44.pdf (Accessed: 21 June 2024).

Antoniou, A. and Akrivos, D. (2020) 'Gender portrayals in advertising: Stereotypes, inclusive marketing and regulation', *Journal of Media Law*, 12(1), pp. 78–115.

Bernitz, U. (2007) 'What is Scandinavian law? Concept, characteristics, future', *Scandinavian Studies in Law*, 50, pp. 13–30.

Bogdan, M. (2009) 'Private international law aspects of the introduction of same-sex marriages in Sweden', *Nordic Journal of International Law*, 78, p. 253.
Bull, T. (2009) 'Freedom of expression in Sweden: The rule of formalism', in Kierulf, A. and Ronning, H. (eds.) *Freedom of speech: Abridged*. Nordicom.
Dahlerup, D. (2011) 'Women in Nordic politics – A continuing success story?', *Gender and Power in the Nordic Countries*. Available at: http://kvinfo.org/history/women-nordic-politics-continuing-success-story (Accessed: 21 September 2017).
Earle, R. (2016) 'The self-regulatory system', in Lindsay, R. (ed.) *Ad law: The essential guide to advertising law and regulation*. Kogan.
Edström, M. (2022) *Gender equality and media regulation study: Sweden*. Fojo: Media Institute.
European Equality Law Network (2021) 'Directive 2004/113/EC on Gender Equality, in search of the forgotten directive'. Available at: https://www.equalitylaw.eu/downloads/5614-directive-2004-113-ec-on-gender-equality-in-goods-and-services-in-search-of-the-potential-of-a-forgotten-directive-1-38-mb (Accessed: 21 June 2024).
European Advertising Standards Alliance (2024) https://www.easa-alliance.org/about-ad-standards/the-benefits/
Golbeck, J., Ash, S. and Cabrera, N. (2017) 'Hashtags as online communities with social support: A study of anti-sexism-in-science hashtag movements', *First Monday*, 22(9).
Hastings, G., Brooks, O., Stead, M., Angus, K., Anker, T. and Farrell, T. (2010) 'Failure of self-regulation of UK alcohol advertising', *British Medical Journal*, 340, p. b5650.
Husa, J. (2000) 'Guarding the constitutionality of laws in the Nordic countries: A comparative perspective', *The American Journal of Comparative Law*, 48(3), pp. 345–381.
Jezierska, K. and Towns, A. (2018) 'Taming feminism? The place of gender equality in the "Progressive Sweden" brand', *Place Branding and Public Diplomacy*, 14, pp. 55–63.
Kosunen, N., Asikainen, A.R., Gústafsdóttir, G., Haggrén, H. and Lång, K. (2017) *Regulation of gender-discriminatory advertising in the Nordic countries*. Nordic Council of Ministers.
Kvist, J. (ed.) (2012) *Changing social equality: The Nordic welfare model in the 21st century*. Policy Press.
Kvist, J. and Greve, B. (2011) 'Has the Nordic welfare model been transformed?', *Social Policy & Administration*, 45(2), pp. 146–160.
López Jiménez, D., Dittmar, E.C. and Vargas Portillo, J.P. (2021) 'Self-regulation of sexist digital advertising: From ethics to law', *Journal of Business Ethics*, 171(4), pp. 709–718.
Malmstrom, A. (1969) 'System of legal systems', *The Scandinavian Stud in Law*, 13, p. 127.
Martin-Llaguno, M. (2016) 'Regulating sexist advertising in Spain', in Edström, M., Kenyon, A.T. and Svensson, E.M. (eds.) *Blurring the lines: Market driven and democracy driven freedom of expression*. Nordicom.
Martinsson, L., Griffin, G. and Nygren, K.G. (2016) 'Introduction: Challenging the myth of gender equality in Sweden', in *Challenging the myth of gender equality in Sweden*. Policy Press, pp. 1–22.
Off, G. (2023) 'Gender equality salience, backlash and radical right voting in the gender-equal context of Sweden', *West European Politics*, 46(3), pp. 451–476.
Ortwein, B.M.I. (2002) 'The Swedish legal system: An introduction', *The Indiana International & Comparative Law Review*, 13, p. 405.
Rydgren, J. and Van der Meiden, S. (2019) 'The radical right and the end of Swedish exceptionalism', *European Political Science*, 18(3), pp. 439–455.

Skilbrei, M.L. and Holmström, C. (2011) 'Is there a Nordic prostitution regime?', *Crime and Justice*, 40(1), pp. 479–517.

Svennson, E.M. (2014) 'Nordic regulation of gender discriminatory advertisements', in Edström, M. and Mølster, R. (eds.) *Making change: Nordic examples of working towards gender equality in the media*. Nordicom.

Svensson, E.M. and Edström, M. (2015) 'Freedom of expression vs. gender equality', *Tidsskrift for Rettsvitenskap*, 127(5), pp. 479–511.

Swedish Government Official Report SOU (2008) Könsdiskriminerande reklam – kränkande utformning av kommersiellameddelanden. http://www.regeringen.se/49b70e/contentassets/6a83d9be02594fe3a2877dfd986b79e2/konsdiskriminerande-reklam---krankande-utformning-av-kommersiella-meddelanden-sou-20085

Swedish Women's Lobby (2020) 'Sexist advertising in Nordic countries'. Available at: https://sverigeskvinnoorganisationer.se/wp-content/uploads/2020/05/Sexist-advertisement-in-the-Nordic-countries.pdf (Accessed: 21 June 2024).

Swedish Women's Lobby Paper (2015) 'Living up to CEDAW– What does Sweden need to do?' (Accessed: 21 June 2024).

UNWomen (2024) https://www.unwomen.org/en/what-we-do/leadership-and-political-participation/facts-and-figures

Zweigert, K. and Kötz, H. (1998) Comparative law. Oxford University Press.

Zweigert, K., Kötz, H., Weir, T., Kötz, H. and Weir, T. (1998) *Introduction to comparative law*. Vol. 3. Oxford: Clarendon Press.

Chapter 7

Spain

Introduction

In contrast to Sweden, Spain has provided legislation prohibiting the use of gender stereotypes and sexist content in advertising. The tackling of gender stereotypes in Spain operates under the guise of wider measures aimed at reducing domestic and gender-based violence. Comparatively, this is a somewhat unusual approach, and this chapter provides a detailed discussion of how Spain equates gender stereotypes and sexist advertising to violence against women. Since the introduction of the Organic Act on Integrated Protection Measures against Gender Violence (2004) ('The Gender Violence Act') and subsequent egalitarian laws of the Zapatero era, Spain is often held up as a pioneer in combatting violence against women (Cubells and Calsamiglia, 2018; Lopez-Zafra and Garcia-Retamero, 2021). The Gender Violence Act helped shape Spain's policy and legislation on proactively protecting women's rights, and one overlooked tributary of the act is the explicit inclusion of prohibiting gender stereotypes, misogyny and sexism in advertising. Rather than relying on Sweden's approach of self-regulation of advertising (Svensson and Edström, 2016), the legislation perceives gender stereotypes and misogyny in advertising as contributory factors in gender-based violence and thus an unlawful practice (Martin-Llaguno, 2016). The ramifications of this act are finally beginning to blossom in Spain, with fewer complaints regarding misogynistic or sexist content in adverts and a broader reduction of gender stereotypes in advertising (Lopez-Zafra and Garcia-Retamero, 2021). Amongst the EU27, where most states opt for self-regulation, providing legislation linked to gender-based violence is a somewhat unorthodox approach. This chapter provides a detailed discussion of how, using feminist perspectives, legislation on prohibiting gender stereotypes in advertising can complement the use of self-regulation. Furthermore, as Spain equates sexist advertising to violence against the woman, I posit why this approach might be a lesson for other states that are looking to legislate on gender stereotypes and sexism in advertising. I begin this chapter by providing a brief historical backdrop of

DOI: 10.4324/9781003336037-7

Spain's shift from dictatorship under General Franco to the modern European democracy of the 1970s onwards, contextualising Spain's tackling of gender-based violence as well as the 'radical centre' (Giddens, 1994) politics of *la nueva via* (the new way) that led to the adoption of the Gender Violence Act in 2004. I then provide analysis of the Gender Violence Act and the test cases of Ryanair and Cillit Bang, which have derived from both the legislation and Spain's SRO, Autocontrol.

From dictatorship to democracy

The blueprint of the unlawful use of gender stereotypes in advertising can be found in the original constitution, *La Pepa*, of 1812. It is worth briefly highlighting that the original liberal democracy-driven freedom of expression that underpinned *La Pepa* is regarded by Spanish constitutional lawyers (Villiers, 1999) and comparative lawyers (Roberts and Sharman, 2013) as a liberal use of free press and expression principles. The relatively modern Spanish legal system and constitution evolvesd after the death of General Francisco Franco Bahamonde in 1975. After Franco's death and the end of dictatorship, the constitution rapidly took shape with an election in 1977 and establishment of the Constituent Cortes (National Parliament). On 6 December 1978, the Spanish Constitution was ratified. These swift three years of change were shaped by numerous actors, but the most important were the *padres de la constitucion* (fathers of the constitution), representing the different autonomous regions of Spain. This is an important feature, as will become apparent in the test case of Ryanair in the regional Malaga Court. The fathers supposedly represent—at least symbolically—the political spectrum as well as autonomous regions of Spain, and therefore, the constitution is also the result of consensus building amongst political parties and autonomies of the time. The constitution, amongst other principles, ensures equality between citizens and thus has secured the sex discrimination agenda of the early 2000s set by President Zapatero's government. The Spanish constitution replaced Franco's complex *leyes fundamentales* with a simpler version based on popular notions of sovereignty, separation of powers and the creation of bicameralist parliament: that is, a congress and senate. The constitution is influenced by Western European constitutions, predominantly West Germany's and Italy's (Villiers, 1999), due in part to the reunification similarities but also to Spain's distinct efforts to respect its own quasi-independent regions. The constitution is in stark contrast to the four decades of Franco's regime that preceded it, and the constitutional character reflects the nation's shift to a more feminist and, indeed, human rights–based approach. The principles that emanate from the constitution, such as gender equality, freedom of expression and political freedoms such as the right to form a political party and freedom of assembly echo the bad times of the past. Political freedoms, such as the right to form political parties and freedom of assembly rights, have led to some problems: for example, the Basque region was not represented in the constitutional negotiations, and this ultimately led to separatist disputes, the resurgence of ETA and the deadliest period of killings from 1976 to 1980. This consensus-building regionalist approach to the constitution has also led to division within the legal system, which will be addressed later in the chapter. The structure of the constitution is complex; therefore, I will summarise only those elements that are important for the creation of legislation in the field of sex discrimination in advertising.

As a starting point, it was clear from 1976 that Spain wished to join the European Economic Community (EEC) (Wallace, 1976; Barbé, 2000) and therefore wished to aim for—and present itself as—a liberal democracy with a legal system that protects fundamental human rights, in particular the rights of women. Balfour and Quiroga (2007: 123) have argued that the rewriting of the Spanish constitution was an opportunity—as with reunified Germany—to start afresh and provide a constitution that could potentially heal old wounds and protect all citizens. This is certainly true on the surface; from the constitution's preamble, there are principles on the protection of rule of law, human rights, rights of minorities and equality between men and women.[1] However, it was during the early years of Spain's accession to the EEC that the development of the Spanish discrimination policy fully emerged. Since joining in 1986, Spain was fraught with EU supremacy issues due to the its promise to protect and respect its autonomous regions (Juste and Sío-López, 2016). Therefore, the autonomous regions and communities in Spain are important elements of the constitution and a quirk of the Spanish legal system. This is a significant factor as the Ryanair test case for sex discrimination and the reification of women and their bodies in advertising took place in the regional court in Malaga, which receives semi-autonomous protection. The autonomous regions and courts of Spain are the most intriguing and important factors of the country's constitution and political make-up (Villiers, 1999). Prior to the civil war in 1936, Spain recognised just three regions that had developed comprehensive forms of autonomy: the Basque, Cataluña and Galicia. Although Spain had operated as a unitary state for the previous 150 years, these regions were important post-Franco and received special attention due to the fact that the regime had crushed all notions of autonomy through suppression of cultural difference. Moreover, these regions suffered the most in terms of torture, murders and political persecution. The efforts by the founding fathers resulted in the creation of *estado de las autonomías* (state of autonomies), which is found in Article 2 of the constitution. This article seeks to balance unitary state *centralismo* and self-governance. As Villiers states, Spain is 'a form of

1 Section 14 provides for equality between men and women, and Section 35 provides for non-discrimination in the workplace and Section

federalism characterised more by interdependence, concurrence or cooperation than by independence' (1999: 81). There are numerous problems with the autonomous states, but chiefly, it has been the (in)flexibility that has led to confusion and uncertainty over legal precedence. This is significant for the Ryanair test case, in which the conflict hinged on whether or not federal legislation could be interpreted by a regional (or autonomous) court. From a technical angle, the constitution does not provide a definition of what 'autonomy' means or what powers a region does and does not have. The decentralised structure is also complex and often confusing: there are now 19 *autonomías* (including the autonomous cities), which provide for less cohesion but, more importantly, provides for political diversity. Article 137 of the constitution goes some way in explaining the principle of the co-existence of legal systems and how the duality of state and region can operate. Since 1978, the legal system(s) have developed a parallel body of law: the regions and state co-exist, with the constitution acting as a bond between the two. The *autonomías* can be considered 'mini states' (Villiers, 1999) with their own presidents, governments, administrations and legal personalities.

Therefore, considering all this, one might perceive that the *autonomías* have their own legislative powers and character. However, the *autonomías* can be limited or even modified by *ley organicas* (substantive or fundamental laws) if a regional law is seen to be *ultra vires* or falling below the standard of national legislation. *Ley organicas* are central to the state powers held in the constitution and usually relate to laws surrounding fundamental rights or civil liberties. *Ley organicas* can be separated from *ley ordinaras* in that the former requiresan absolute majority from congress members, whereas the latter require just one-third of the vote.

Towards gender equality and the politics of *la nueva via*

As with Sweden in the previous chapter, Spain under the Socialist Party (PSOE) progressed dramatically during the early 2000s, particularly with gender equality legislation and egalitarian issues (for example, same-sex marriage, adoption rights and gender equality laws to improve gender equality in political representation). President Rodriguez Zapatero's government adopted a position (*la nueva via*) similar to Tony Blair and Bill Clinton's third way and ran the Socialist Party's election campaign on the promise to tackle the wider social justice issues of the day in exchange for a neoliberal economic agenda (Giddens, 1994). Three main legislative aims were made clear in the party's manifesto: sex discrimination, gender-based violence and same-sex marriage. Zapatero's premiership (2004–2011) saw Spain enter a further stage of political integration into the EU or, as Kennedy states, the Socialist Party were keen to embrace the political 'modernization' and 'Europeanization' of Spain (Kennedy, 2001). Zapatero was also keen to symbolically heal the wounds of the past by removing the surviving Franco statues and establishing a memorialisation commission to resolve the horrors of the 'white terror' (Franco's mass killings and the disappearance of thousands of women). The eradication of gender stereotypes in advertising is therefore merely part of the wider picture of legislation that was adopted under gender equality reforms. Laws on employment rights, political and economic representation, and gender mainstreaming; same-sex marriage law, including adoption rights; childcare and paternal leave law; gender identity and transgender rights were all enacted in the first parliamentary term.

The Gender Violence Act

On 7 October 2004, Zapatero's Socialist Party had secured a strong majority of votes from members across the political divide in the Spanish Congress to ensure his first piece of legislation as prime minister of Spain would enter the constitution. The full title of the legislation, 'Integrated Protection Measure against Gender Violence' (Ley Organica 1/2004 BOE-A-2004–21760), gives some indication of what the legislation entails; however, as the list of measures is vast, I will concentrate on providing analysis of significant elements. First, contextualising this legislation is necessary to understand how the act became Zapatero's first constitutional change and to paint a picture of the magnitude of the task. There are numerous problems when discussing historical gender-based violence in a Spanish context. First, due to the dictatorship, there is very little data or literature on the subject, and, secondly, due to censorship and cultural control, some of the stories that have been told since are either misunderstood or deemed political propaganda (Heras, 2006). It is certain that women's position under the regime was one of persecution, forced labour, sexual violence and a time of mass femicide (*las mujeres desaparecidas*) (Mendiola Gonzalo, 2013). The civil war had brought feminism to Spain, but life for women under Franco reverted to pre–civil war conditions: legislation influenced by Napoleon's Civil Code positioned women as minors and prohibited contraception and divorce, and gender segregation in school and work was enforced (Davidson, 2011). Domestic violence was treated strictly a private sphere or a family matter; hence, post-Franco, this traditional view remained despite early legislative attempts in the 1980s to combat gender-based violence. Due to this enduring traditional view and the 40 years of a dictatorship that followed, there have been very few government policies, regulations or legislative measures to tackle the problem. According to the United Nations,[2] prior to accession to the EEC in 1986, Spain had

2 United Nations Global Database on Violence against Women (Spain) http://evaw-global-database.unwomen.org/en/countries/europe/spain.

adopted just one preventive measure: the constitutional amendment of 1983 on equal opportunities in the workplace. Various pieces of legislation had been passed in Spain but were limited to outside the private sphere. Segregated education under the Franco regime and the state educational programme *Formacion del Espiritu Nacional* (formation of the national spirit) produced essentialist binary norms: men were trained for either the military, politics or hard labour and women for home life and motherhood. Therefore, the history of state-induced violence against women and the educational impetus to segregate the sexes in Spain influenced and shaped the political agenda of this period. Zapatero and the PSOE government's motivation to combat gender-based violence and (re)define the representation of women (e.g. in advertising) as a form of gender-based violence came as part of this raft of measures. In addition to the stigma from the Franco era, the second influence for legislation was a spike in the number of victims of gender-based violence in Spain during the 1990s and early 2000s. One particular case, that of Ana Orantes, caused a public outcry when the 60-year-old was thrown off her balcony and set alight by her husband.

The Gender Violence Act is a reaction to escalating intimate partner violence but also increased public discourse and the PSOE's engagement with women's groups in Spain (Martin-Llaguno, 2016). The act covers numerous provisions that seek to tackle gender-based violence in Spain and establishes a new court, *Juzgados de Violencia Sobre la Mujer* (Violence against Women Court). Despite being initially established as a criminal court to hear victims of violence cases, it has slowly evolved and now deals with civil and family law cases. The act diverges from Spain's previous positioning of gender-based violence as a public problem that all institutions must address through prevention, protection and sanctions (Alberdi and Matas, 2002). As part of wider gender mainstreaming programme and drive to responsiblise state institutions, the act places specific obligations on advertisers and prohibits specific adverts in two broad ways: (a) the use of a woman's body (or part of it) that is detached from the advertised object ('reification') and (b) adverts that use an image that portrays women in stereotyped behaviours. Within the act's preamble, this provision falls under the educational sphere; however, the main provision, Article 10, positions the prohibition of sexist advertising as a human dignity facet. The main provision is an amendment of Article 3(a) of the Advertising Act 34/1988, which now prohibits advertisements which 'act against the dignity of persons or are contrary to the values and rights enshrined in the Constitution'. Such adverts depict 'women in a degrading manner, either by directly using their bodies or parts of the same as a mere object unrelated to the product being promoted' or 'associate[e] their image to stereotyped roles antithetical to the principles of our law'. The most significant and important element of the act is that it depicts sexist advertising as contributory to the violence referred to in the legislation.

As the Gender Violence Act is positioned as a fundamental right embedded in the constitution, the Spanish prohibition of sexist and harmful gender stereotypes in advertising diverges from most EU member states' notions of market-driven freedom of expression (e.g. self-regulation agencies, authorities and watchdogs) as it endorses the ban as a constitutional human right to dignity. The act also provides more powers to *Observatorio de la Imagen de las Mujeres* (Women's Image Observatory) (OIM). The observatory was established in 1994, six years after the initial Advertising Act (34/1988) was implemented. The new powers from the legislation provided that the OIM can advocate on behalf of the complainant. The act also included the launch of the National Advertising Plan, whereby all public authorities must produce and promote information and awareness campaigns on how to raise a complaint under the legislation. Awareness programmes have been the most effective element in the implementation of the act. Through the work of women's groups and NGOs, protests and sit-ins have become regular occurrences in Spain. This dualistic approach—targeting the general public as well as the regulators—has led to foregrounding gender-based violence in public debate and partial blame on sexist content and gender stereotypes in advertisements. Women's groups, along with NGOs, were quick to identify particular sexist advertising, co-ordinate small protests and, most importantly, film the sit-ins and share them on social media platforms. The Ryanair calendar case in 2014 was one of the first to be tested in the courts and has provided legal principles and tests.

Ryanair case

Despite the Ryanair calendar case being heard in the regional Malaga Court in Spain, the origins case were in the UK. The original calendar advertising campaign had previously run across Europe in various guises since 2008 and had caused controversy, particularly in the UK and Ireland. The Ryanair calendar adverts were a series of commercials—both on billboards and online—that depicted female airhostesses in lingerie representing different countries for each calendar month. Some of the adverts that ran simultaneously with the campaign also featured airhostesses or models in lingerie, and one advert depicted an calendar model in a school uniform. The adverts prompted three responses in the UK: an online petition initiated by a Ryanair hostess, which received 11,000 signatures; an inquiry from the UK's Advertising Standards Authority (ASA), based on ten complaints from consumer organisations; and an investigation by the UK's Office of Fair Trading (OFT). The advert campaign continued to run over four years until it was investigated by the ASA and OFT.

All advertisements linked to the calendar were banned in the UK by ASA in 2012. The case received attention from Spanish NGOs, which subsequently ignited public debate on misogynistic advertising in Spain, the relationship advertising has with domestic violence and how Ryanair should be sanctioned. At the time of the UK ban, there was a spike in the number of general complaints about sexist content to the Spanish advertising observatory (OIM), and further complaints escalated the issue. In November 2012, the Ryanair calendar was released and advertised across most EU member states both online and in print. In Spain, a women's group, Tyrius, and consumer group Adecua issued a joint formal complaint to OIM and requested a test case at the new Violence Against Women Court employing the Gender Violence Act. The joint complainant's argument maintained that the advert contravened Article 3 of the act, which prohibits the 'reification' of women, arguing that the women are positioned as 'mere objects' with 'no connection' between the image and product/service (air fare prices). The advert featured the slogan '*¡Tarifas al rojo vivo! ¡Y la tripulación!*' ('The tariffs are red hot, and so are the crew!'), which the complainant argued was misogynistic and carried clear sexual connotations.

In the judgement, the court agreed that the advert reified women by positioning the stewardesses in 'clear sexual invitation'. The court also agreed with the juxtaposition argument made by the complainant that the model stewardesses had 'absolutely no connection whatsoever' with the product, service or message. The use of a female body was deemed artificial, and the calendar was used as a tool to increase website traffic. Most importantly, the court indicated that although it was apparent that the average citizen would not be offended by women in bikinis, they might be dismayed to see the reification, juxtaposition and the dignity of women under attack. As the Ryanair advert used sexualisation and objectification to attract attention, regardless of its content, the court condemned the airline and called for the removal of the advert from the website, online advertising and analogue advertising such as billboards and newspapers. The significance of the complainant's 'reification' argument is important when compared to the earlier decision made in the UK by the ASA and shows how the significance of the term is anchored in the Gender Violence Act. Comparatively, the ASA sanctioned Ryanair with a pause in sales of the calendar and banned the advert for being 'offensive' and the 'stance and gaze' of the models sexually suggestive.

Self-regulation: autocontrol

Autocontrol, the self-regulatory organisation of Spain, supplements the Gender Violence Act in tackling sexist content and eradicating gender stereotypes (Marín, 2011). Autocontrol operates in a similar way to most European SROs—an industry regulating itself. It emerged at a time of satellite TV, cross-border broadcasting and the Court of Justice of the European Union's attempt to regulate the market as well as freedom of expression case law in the European Court of Human Rights. Autocontrol is a product of the Advertising Act of 1988; it was established in 1995 as an independent organisation that loosely follows both the International Chamber of Commerce's ethical standards of advertising and European Advertising Standards Alliance[3] but was set up to fill in the gaps left by the Advertising Act of 1988. Article 10 of the SRO code provides specific remedies for the sexualisation of women and adverts that use outdated gender stereotypes to sell a product. Autocontrol is bolstered by the Gender Violence Act and, consequently, has numerous ongoing cases on the reification of women and gender stereotypes in advertising. Autocontrol's jury is independent of the SRO and is made up of experts from across different areas from law to economics to sociology (López Jiménez et al., 2021). The jury reaches a decision based on the SRO's ethical framework, but it may also wish further consult industry-based regulators such as the beer and spirits advertising regulatory bodies. Although there are numerous individual advertising agencies attached to various industries, the current trend indicates that the majority of complainants are passed over to Autocontrol. If an advert is deemed to have breached the either the SRO code or the Advertising Act, the advertiser is asked to modify or terminate the advert. The Ryanair case highlights the involvement of NGOs and outsider organisations in this process, in particular OIM, one of the larger organisations running parallel to Autocontrol, but also smaller watchdogs such as Siamura.[4]

The most significant facet of Autocontrol is the non-binding pre-screening provision, Copy Advice, that assesses an advert's suitability prior to its production and distribution. Unlike many other SROs, Copy Advice acts as a quasi-guarantee that adverts will at least not fall foul of the legislation or regulatory code. At the time of the Ryanair case, Copy Advice published its first women's report, with 0.24% of consultations resulting in a breach of the ethical code or what might be deemed reification of women. Of these, 43% were related to the 'dignity' of women and 37% to the juxtaposition of women's body, and 20% involved outdated gender stereotypes. Despite this pre-screening advice centre, their actions are limited to an advisory role, and numerous companies proceed with their advertising campaigns irrespective of the advice. Moreover, the advice can be deployed cynically by advertisers as a defence when an advert receives complaints.[5] The Autocontrol division

3 The ICC, along with the EASA, provides basic principles and guidance for regulators. Articles 2 and 3 of the ICC code cover social responsibility and decency. https://iccwbo.org/ (accessed 21 June 2024). The EASA code ensures that advertising is 'legal decent, honest and truthful [and] prepared with a due sense of social responsibility'. https://www.easaalliance.org/ (accessed 21st June 2024).

4 Siamura is primarily a Spanish advertising observatory collating evidence and complaints against advertising with sexist content. See http://siamura.eu (accessed 21 April 2021).

5 Ryanair sought advice from Copy Advice prior to their campaign. As the company had a history of complaints, the Spanish SRO asked them to seek advice prior to the campaign. The advice was later used as a defence in the Ryanair calendar case.

of the Spanish regulatory system has, in recent years, come under fire for failing to raise awareness of its powers as an SRO. Autocontrol also has a public image and legitimacy problem with frequent relaunches; in particular, in 2010, the SRO received heavy criticism from the European Commission as it failed to meet the expected targets of the Roadmap to Equality Programme.

Austerity and the re-emergence of sexual violence and femicide

Since the Gender Violence Act, Spain has witnessed radical economic, political and social change, which unfortunately placed gender equality concerns firmly on the back burner. The fallout of the Madrid terrorist attacks in 2004 followed by the 2007 economic crisis pushed Zapatero's government's wider raft of social reform to the side, replaced by tighter security measures, austerity and cuts to public services. In 2008, conservative opposition leader Mariano Rajoy enjoyed the support of Nicolas Sarkozy and Angela Merkel, and by the end of the decade, the PSOE were all but replaced by Spanish conservativism. In 2011, Spain had one of the highest unemployment rates in the EU, and the general election was won by Rajoy's promise to decrease the deficit, increase employment rates and deliver educational reform. Gender equality reform switched to regression, particularly abortion rights and cuts to women's key services. Although there is no clear correlation between austerity and femicide in Spain, there has been a sharp rise in deaths and a general increase in the number of reported domestic violence cases. Arroyo and Coronas (2017) highlighted that, in certain autonomous regions, femicide and domestic violence have fallen. However, the Pamplona gang rape case in 2019 reignited the call from campaigners and NGOs to increase budgets and secure changes to the Gender Violence Act. Amendments to the Gender Violence Act do affect the advertising section, and irrespective of the Ryanair calendar test case, there appears to be little progress in tackling sexist advertising in Spain. The core problem lies in the foundations of the act—namely, the legal ambiguity of the terms 'reification' and 'gender stereotypes, which has hampered attempts to bring action as well as the application of law (Martin-Llaguno, 2016). Despite numerous training programmes and public awareness campaigns set up by Autocontrol, there has been little guidance on what is meant by the terms covered in the act—'reification', 'sexualisation' and 'gender stereotypes'. Beltrá and Martin-Llaguno (2012) argue that precedent has been set on the definition of objectification and sexualisation in advertising by the work of Autocontrol and its decisions since 2010. The Spanish Congress have not reformed the Gender Violence Act, and Autocontrol have been reluctant to provide separate explicit and unequivocal guidance on how the terms in advertising should be interpreted by the courts (González, 2008; Martin-Llaguno, 2016). According to Martin-Llaguno, the act's application is inadequate: if applied broadly, it will inevitably catch all forms of gender stereotypes that may or may not appear sexist. If applied narrowly, then advertisers are at liberty to breach both the act and the Autoctontrol's ethical code. The same criticisms of the Gender Violence Act therefore apply to Autocontrol. The lax and vague definitions of 'reification', 'sexualisation' and 'gender stereotypes' are problematic, and the case law of Autocontrol rarely develops these terms. The monitoring of the case law by Autocontrol has shown that the jury often overcomplicate definitions such as 'reification', leading to confusion in the decisions. The most problematic definition with Autocontrol and the Ryanair case seems to be the broader term 'gender stereotypes'. Tato Plazo (2006) argues that the SRO code should strike down gender stereotypes if the gender representation is found to be playing a role traditionally associated with women such as cooking, caring and cleaning; however, as will be discussed in the next chapter, the term is more multidimensional. The definition of 'gender stereotype' is slowly untangling through the case law of Autocontrol, and the Cillit Bang case is a good example of the problems with the act and Autocontrol's lack of guidance on sexist content, lack of scope for online content and issues surrounding the pre-screening legal team in Copy Advice.

In 2016, the cleaning brand Cillit Bang produced an advertising campaign depicting 32 women discussing their cleaning experiences via the use of 'vlogging'. Of the 32 vlogs, not one featured a man using the cleaning products. Using the Gender Violence Act in conjunction with the Autocontrol code, a consumer protection organisation, Consumidores en Red, challenged the advertiser based on the following: (a) the adverts' exclusion of men performing cleaning chores and using the product and (b) using outdated stereotypes that portray women as cleaners and carers. ('With the new thicker foam, you wipe the washcloth and see how clean and shiny. And it lasts for days and days. With Cillit Bang, I can spend more time with the kids'.) In its ruling, Autocontrol agreed with the claimant and stated that the lack of men in the advertisement provided a clear breach of Autocontrol code, and the advert featured outdated 'stereotypical behaviours with a clear allocation of role by gender'. Autocontrol specifically highlighted two elements that had led to the breach of the code: first, the campaign (of three separate adverts) featured exclusively women, and secondly, all the advertisements had common characteristics: a collage of photographs of the alleged product users (all of them women) and a voice-over of one of the users explaining how to use the product. Finally, during the closing of the advert, a woman's voice says, 'Try it and tell us yourself!' The advertiser's defence to the complaint was that despite the advert featuring only women, it did not position women as inferior, and cleaning products are mainly bought by women. This last factor is quantified by multiple online surveys, questionnaires and focus groups collated by the advertising company. Cillit Bang also gained the clearance of Autocontrol's pre-screening service, Copy Advice. Cillit Bang's argument was rejected and the advert subsequently banned.

The significance of this case is partly in Cillit Bang's marketing research and its defence that the advertisement was a reflection of Spanish society. Cillit Bang's argument was that it neither reified nor objectified women, and because it reflected Spanish women's everyday lived experience of cleaning and caring, there was no harm or offence caused as the portrayal of women in the advert emulated a housewife's daily routine and was therefore not an outdated stereotype.

Autocontrol is somewhat akin to the Swedish SRO Reklamombudsmannen (RO) as it operates as an independent body with quasi-independent juries. The key difference here is Autocontrol's jury, which consists of experts in certain fields such as sociology and law (López Jiménez et al., 2021), as opposed to RO's jury, which is made up advertising 'insiders'. Autocontrol is also sponsored by the same industry insiders and follows a 'weak' reactive code that responds to complaints rather than a proactive code that seeks to pre-empt sexist advertising. However, there are some distinctive elements of the Spanish approach which place it in a better position. Autocontrol's sanctioning powers are substantially tougher and convey the right to ban (or ask the advertiser to amend) the advert, as opposed to the mere pillory powers of Sweden's SRO. Whilst there is no unconditional pre-emptive tool, the Copy Advice appears prepared to restrict adverts that breach the code or act, unlike RO. The fundamental difference is the symbolic role the Gender Violence Act has in shaping the Spanish perspective on tackling gender stereotypes. By including sexist advertising in the act, developing a precedent in the courts, the Spanish model purports that there is a clear relationship between advertising and gender violence discourses, particularly towards women, irrespective of whether the advertisement perpetuates gender stereotypes or the reification/sexualisation of women. The UK's SRO, Advertising Standards Authority, which is assessed in next chapter, possesses a very similar set-up and ethical code; however it has not gone as far as Autocontrol or the judicial review in sanctioning sexualisation/objectification in advertising.

Conclusion

This chapter has set out the ways in which Spain regulates gender stereotypes and misogyny in advertising and does so through the prism of violence against women legislation. The Gender Violence Act (2004) identifies the correlation between stereotypes and violence by including a section specifically on prohibiting sexist content in advertising. Unlike most EU member states that rely on predominantly on SROs and regulatory codes, the Gender Violence Act provides statutory definitions of gender stereotypes by prohibiting adverts that use a woman's body when it is detached from the advertised product (reification) and those in which an image of a woman is used in relation to stereotypical behaviour. The statutory inclusion of reification attempts to reduce legal ambiguity and provide Spain's SRO Autocontrol with extra scope to extend its reach. The two test cases have provided some much-needed indication as to how the definition might be interpreted by the SRO jury in future cases. The Ryanair case provided substance to the reification test whereby women were portrayed as detached 'objects' with 'little or no connection' to the product and service offered. Similarly, the Cillit Bang case highlights how women are represented as being exclusively in charge of housework chores and cleaning, thus perpetuating gender stereotypes and role assignments. To obtain material gender equality, the Gender Violence Act has sought to show the links between media representations of women and gender-based violence. The inclusion of sexist advertising in the act is a symbolic one, and the subsequent precedents set by the two test cases indicate how the Spanish approach substantiates the links between representation and violence against women. The inclusion also has a symbolic role in guiding Autocontrol and the ways in which the SRO tackles gender stereotypes in advertising, moving beyond the language from 'soft' regulatory codes towards a more substantive approach.

References

Alberdi, I. and Matas, N. (2002) *La violencia doméstica: informe sobre los malos tratos a mujeres en España*. Fundación La Caixa.

Arroyo, A. and Coronas, C. (2017) 'Intimate partner violence in Spain: Medical and legal aspects', *GSL Journal of Forensic Research*, 1, p. 103.

Balfour, S. and Quiroga, A. (2007) *The reinvention of Spain: Nation and identity since democracy*. Oxford University Press.

Barbé, E. (2000) 'Spain and CFSP: The emergence of a 'major player'?', *Mediterranean Politics*, 5(2), pp. 44–63.

Cubells, J. and Calsamiglia, A. (2018) 'Do we see victims' agency? Criminal justice and gender violence in Spain', *Critical Criminology*, 26(1), pp. 107–127.

Davidson, J. (2011) 'Women, fascism and work in Francoist Spain: The law for political, professional and labour rights', *Gender & History*, 23(2), pp. 401–414.

Giddens, A. (1994) *Beyond left and right: The future of radical politics*. Stanford University Press.

González, R. (2008) 'Aportaciones de la Ley de medidas contra la violencia de género a la prohibición de publicidad discriminatoria', *Revista de derecho de la competencia y la distribución*, 2, pp. 145–160.

Gonzalo, F.M. (2013) 'Forced labor, public policies, and business strategies during Franco's dictatorship: An interim report', *Enterprise & Society*, 14(1), pp. 182–213.

Heras, M.O. (2006) 'Mujer y dictadura franquista', *Aposta. Revista de Ciencias Sociales*, 28, pp. 1–26.

Juste, A.M. and Sío-López, C.B. (2016, 8 July) 'Spain and the European integration process'. Available at: https://www.cvce.eu/content/publication/2010/5/11/bf91b328-fbed-4a65–9a3b-eadc21a7e831/publishable_en.pdf.

Kennedy, P. (2001) 'Spain's 'third way'? The Spanish socialist party's utilization of European integration', *Journal of Southern Europe and the Balkans*, 3(1), pp. 49–59.

López Jiménez, D., Dittmar, E.C. and Vargas Portillo, J.P. (2021) 'Self-regulation of sexist digital advertising: From ethics to law', *Journal of Business Ethics*, 171(4), pp. 709–718.

Lopez-Zafra, E. and Garcia-Retamero, R. (2021) 'Are gender stereotypes changing over time? A cross-temporal analysis of perceptions about gender stereotypes in Spain', *International Journal of Social Psychology*, 36(2), pp. 330–354.
Marín, I.P. (2011) 'Autorregulación: análisis de las resoluciones del jurado de autocontrol de la publicidad discriminatoria de la mujer', in *El levantamiento del velo: las mujeres en el derecho privado*, pp. 983–1016.
Martin-Llaguno, M. (2016) 'Regulating sexist advertising in Spain', in Edström, M., Kenyon, A.T. and Svensson, E. (eds.) *Blurring the lines: Market driven and democracy driven freedom of expression*. Nordicom.
Navarro-Beltrá, M. and Martin-Llaguno, M.M. (2012) 'A systematic review of gender and advertising studies', *Catalan Journal of Communication & Cultural Studies*, 4(2), pp. 171–183.
Roberts, S.G. and Sharman, A. (2013) *Echoes: The Cadiz constitution in Hispanic history, culture and politics*. Cambridge Scholars Publishing, p. 394.
Svensson, E.M. and Edström, M. (2016) 'Market-driven challenges to freedom of expression and the interaction between the state, the market, and the media', *Nordicom Review*, 37(2).
Tato Plazo, A. (2006) 'Violencia de género y publicidad (Gender violence and advertising)', *Revista Autocontrol*, 107, pp. 1–6.
Villiers, C. (1999) *The Spanish legal tradition: An introduction to the Spanish law and legal system*. Dartmouth Publishing, pp. 8–9.
Wallace, W. (1976) 'Wider but weaker: The continued enlargement of the EEC', *The World Today*, 32(3), pp. 104–111.

Chapter 8

The UK

Introduction

This chapter provides analysis of the UK's advertising regulatory framework, including a discussion of the SRO Advertising Standards Authority (ASA), its ethical codes and ASA cases form the last decade: American Apparel, Protein World (Beach Body Ready) and the Asda Christmas advert. These cases have been controversial, garnering the most complaints and testing ASA codes (harm and offence, protection of children) and subsequently led to the overhaul of the ASA ethical code and guidance in 2019 to include the term 'harmful gender stereotypes'. The chapter explores some of the ASA rulings since the new rule was added to the codes, indicating how sexualisation, objectification and gender stereotypes ought to configured together to catch the essence of harmful gender stereotypes and sexist content in advertising. To contextualise the sole reliance on the national SRO, the chapter begins with a brief overview of the current legislative framework, covering gender equality and the lack of legislation on gender stereotypes in advertising.

Gender equality

Over the last 50 years, the UK has developed a progressive yet hesitant gender equality programme. Prior to joining the Common Market, the ad hoc, piecemeal approach was one of ant-discrimination laws, but it has slowly transitioned to mainstreaming gender equality (Verdin and O'Reilly, 2020). Gender equality law and policy in the UK have undoubtedly been influenced by membership of the EU; however, some of the victories of the early 1970s, such as the Equal Pay Act (1970), came from unions and grassroots movements. Since the Equal Pay Act, it would appear the UK has been on a ceaseless struggle to end gender-based inequality: the recognition of marital rape, various domestic violence legislations and policies, maternity and paternity laws and transgender recognition are just some of the few areas the judiciary and legislature have sought to develop. The Equality Acts of 2006 and 2010

DOI: 10.4324/9781003336037-8

were fuelled by New Labour ideology aim to curb the remaining loopholes that remained in gender equality laws. The Equality Act has unfortunately been dismantled by the previous Liberal-Conservative coalition and current Conservative government(s) (Conley, 2012). Despite a market-oriented neoliberal approach limiting the transformative possibilities of the Gender Equality Act (Burton, 2014), it has proven fairly successful in addressing some of the shortcomings from the previous decades (Fredman, 2022).

Beyond the legislative framework, gender equality has a long way to go in the UK. Over the last decade, both NGOs and academics have purported that legislation has systematically failed women in the UK. For example, a recent Fawcett Society report 'Double Trouble' (2024) takes an intersectional perspective highlighting how the gender pay gap is increasing, particularly for black, minoritised and low-skilled women. This year, a consortium of women's groups have claimed that the combination of austerity, Brexit, the COVID-19 pandemic and the 'cost of living' crisis has put gender equality 'into reverse' ('Impact of the rising cost of living on women' TUC Report 2023). Moreover, whilst political representation has generally improved since the 1970s, the UK still ranks fairly low compared to other European countries (EIGE, 2023). Of the four most recent crises, austerity has had the biggest effect on women and girls. Since the financial crash of 2008 and the subsequent response from the coalition government, austerity measures have been disproportionately inflicted on women (Greer Murphy, 2017; Evans, 2015), such as the freezing of welfare benefits, and cuts to key services such as shelters and legal aid have disproportionately affected women (McNeil, 2019). Austerity policies have tended to harm women more than men in society, irrespective of age, class or race (Ginn, 2013), and as Conley (2012) claims, the coalition government's austerity measures have fundamentally failed to recognise how men and women live their lives or how the cuts will disproportionately impact poor and vulnerable women (Conley, 2012).

The various assaults on women's rights have inevitably kicked peripheral issues in the UK—such as legislation on gender stereotypes and sexist advertising—into the long grass. There have been tenuous attempts to incorporate sexist advertising into legislation; for example, the Equality Act (2010) does not explicitly address the advertising industry; however, advertisers should ensure they comply with the duties set out in the act: namely, that they do not discriminate when offering goods and services. The UK government's guidance on this states that, as a matter of good practice and business, when accessing 'goods, facilities or services fairly, regardless of their age, gender, race, sexual orientation, disability, gender reassignment, religion or belief, and guard against making assumptions about the characteristics of individuals'. More recently, the Online Safety Act (2023) includes additional enforcement powers to the communications regulator Ofcom; however, this is limited to monitoring and regulating advertising target adverts at children for alcohol and tobacco, subliminal messaging and fraudulent ads.

Self-regulation: Advertising Standards Authority

The UK has very few legislative instruments that cover sexist advertising or gender stereotypes in advertising. Those that do cover direct discrimination (e.g. advertising jobs only to men), such as the Sex Discrimination Act (1975), which prohibits certain forms of advertising aimed at women or men (Crown et al., 2024). As a result of this lack, the main arm of advertising regulation derives from the self-regulation organisation the Advertising Standards Authority (ASA). The sections of regulatory code that covers sexist advertising are 'taste and decency' and 'social responsibility'. According to Earle (2016), these two classifications of advertising are flexible and require constant attention as moral and cultural standards shift in the UK. Revisions to the code take place every five years, and, in a report published in the summer of 2017, the ASA signalled for clearer regulation of advertising that feature stereotypical gender roles or characteristics which might be harmful to people, including advertisements that mock people for not conforming to traditional gender stereotypes. Advertising and marketing regulation in the UK is somewhat similar to Sweden in that it predominantly relies on industry-led self-regulation rather than governmental-influenced regulation. However, the ASA is significantly different in its approach to regulation, such as its quasi-state-run locus and its appeal system but also in its complex organisational design. The ASA is a far more complicated organisation than the Swedish RO or Spanish Autocontrol as it is somewhat confusingly made up of various bodies, ethical codes and appeal organisations. By and large, the organisation can be divided in to two distinct bodies: CAP and BCAP.

The Committee of Advertising Practice (CAP) is the main arm of the ASA that produces and reviews the advertising code (CAP code) and regulates non-broadcast (or passive) advertising: for example, online advertising and traditional forms such as newspapers and magazines. The broadcast content (i.e. active or live), such as television and radio, is covered by the Broadcast Advertising Code (BCAP). Since the Communications Act (2003), BCAP exercises the duties of the UK Office for Communication (Ofcom). As discussed in Chapter 2, such duties include logistical responsibilities such as advertising time limits and scheduling requirements. Other duties include the regulation of misleading content and 'harmful or offensive' advertising, which are also covered by the CAP code rules. The Advertising Standards (Broadcast) mirrors the ASA in its approach to regulating active advertisements. Despite this division within the organisation, the CAP and BCAP are fundamentally the same when it comes to defining, regulating and sanctioning sexist content in advertising. Similar to Spain's Autocontrol, a 'copy advice' (Clearcast) is also available for pre-screening advertisers consent and, at present, is free of charge. The endorsement of the codes is straightforward, a jury of 12 (made up of industry and non-industry adjudicators) will review the advert in question, but it can also be reviewed by an independent panel and subsequently sent for judicial review if necessary. The ASA then asks the advertiser to remove the content (or promise it won't be shown again) or amend the advert. Certain advertisers with a history of controversy may be routinely asked to send their advertising campaigns to copy advice for pre-screening, although this is rarely requested. In the section of the chapter, I will discuss the two codes (CAP and BCAP), provide analysis on some of the recent rulings and scrutinise the future outlook of advertising regulation in post-Brexit UK.

The Advertising Standard Authority's ethical codes

The Committee of Advertising Practice (CAP) was established in 1961 and has ever since been made up of industry representatives. At present, it consists of 12 members, two thirds of whom are independent of the industry. This is significantly similar to the Swedish RO and, indeed, across all members of the EASA, where the tendency has been to rely on the advertising industry rather than independent adjudicators or lawyers. The CAP code covers traditional forms of advertising such as newspapers, magazines and billboards as well as adverts in printed material, on posters, in the cinema, DVD and online adverts (e.g. banners, pop-ups and videos) and any other non-active adverts that include contractual conditions that they must comply with the code. The ASA's application of the code is two-fold: first, when considering complaints about an advert that breaches the code, and secondly, through extensive training and regulatory projects. BCAP, on the other hand, covers broadcasting content and is determined by the Communications Act (2003). It covers all advertising from licenced television, radio, teleshopping and interactive TV. As discussed in Chapter 3, this type of advertising falls under the AVMS Directive and is subsequently extensively reviewed by the EU institutions. Television has traditionally been the medium which receives the most complaints, which highlights the power of traditional modes of advertising (Earle, 2016). However, over the last decade, complaints, specifically from the codes on harm and offence, are garnered from online platforms (Auxtova et al., 2021), where ads are 'camouflaged' to the content (Tokeley, 2021).

The ASA received 39,000 complaints in 2024 (up 13% from the previous year), split roughly evenly between broadcast and non-broadcast, with around 80% of cases not requiring further investigation (ASA, 2023). Although the complaint procedure is straightforward, the registration of a complaint is not. In recent years, attempts have been made to improve access. The ASA website now offers a step-by-step guide, and users are guided with multiple questions and drop-down options (e.g. online behaviour advertisements). The complaints are assessed against the two codes and usually result in an ASA executive decision that there is no need for an investigation. An advert may be withdrawn by the advertiser due to negative media coverage or the sheer number of complaints received from the general public. With the increase in use of social media, controversial adverts are often picked up by campaigners, activists and NGOs and dispelled within in days, rendering the ASA's proactive component void. Some complaints are dealt with informally and are listed online; however there is no mention of what the original complaint was. As with most self-regulatory bodies, the ASA lacks transparency (Boddewyn, 1992; Auxtova et al., 2021), especially around the nature of complaints.

The guiding principle of the CAP code is that advertising should always be 'legal, decent, honest and truthful'. For the BCAP code, a similar tone is promoted: 'advertisements should not cause . . . widespread harm or offence'. In addition to these two guiding principles, both codes assert that advertisers must prepare their adverts with a sense of responsibility to their audiences and society in general. In sum, adverts must be decent, not cause harm or offence and generally be prepared responsibly. The code's main regulatory remit for gender stereotypes and sexist content now falls under three main areas: 'social responsibility' (Rule 1.3: responsibility to consumers and to society), sanctioning the causing of 'harm and offence' (Rule 4.1: harm and offence on the grounds of gender), sanctioning the encouragement of violence (Rule 4.4: 'condone or encourage violence') and protection of children (Rule 5.1; ads featuring children must contain nothing that is likely to result in their physical, mental or moral harm). Following an ASA report 'Depictions, Perceptions and Harm' (2017), a new section was added to 'harm and offence' that explicitly covers the use of gender stereotypes in advertising. In June 2019, the additional rule provides much clearer guidance on harm and offence and states that advertisements 'must not include gender stereotypes that are likely to cause harm, or serious or widespread offence'. The ASA's new rule is supported by guidance from their website and includes five sections: gender stereotypical roles and characteristics, sexualisation and objectification, using humour, taking care with depicting contrasting stereotypes and other stereotypical depictions (ASA, 2019). This new rule will be discussed further later in the chapter.

If a complaint 'matches' any of the rules or is seen to breach the spirit of the code, then the CAP/BCAP have some powers at their dispersal. As with the Swedish RO, these regulatory powers are limited when it comes to passive adverts. The ASA has no power to financially sanction the advertiser; however, it can rely on other 'softer' approaches, such as asking that the advert be modified or removing the advert. Prohibition is often a last resort; as chief executive Guy Parker noted in 2016, the adverts that attract the highest number of complaints 'are often not the ones that need banning' (ASA, 2016). Upheld decisions that include sexualisation, objectification or outdated gender stereotypes tend to receive a considerable amount of media attention, and there is increasing evidence of this in the last five years. The ASA relies on a customary and conventional practice with media outlets whereby the carrier will agree not to publish an advert that has had a case upheld. The final 'sanction' is the option to refer the advertiser to the 'copy centre' for vetting and training. This sanction is reserved for serial offenders and is seen as symbolic pillory rather than regulation. The 'copy centre' is similar to Spain's SRO Autocontrol in its approach to advertising regulation as it offers free legal advice for would-be advertisers, ensuring they are not in breach of the CAP code. The copy clearance is required for all TV broadcast advertisements by all licensees and is run by Clearcast. Clearcast is mandatory for channels that require a licence, and the process is straightforward. A script is provided, feedback is provided against the existing CAP code, and approval is granted when a timed version of the advert is seen. Clearcast is not required by non-broadcast ads and is only available to adverts that may be widely distributed to high-risk audiences (e.g. children) or concern sensitive areas (e.g. mental health charity adverts).

The next section is a discussion of some of the ASA cases that have led to the ASA's report 'Depictions, Perceptions and Harm' and the new harm and offence rule covering gender stereotypes, sexualisation and objectification. The following adverts are also from the participants' visual diaries and the focus group discussions from Chapter 5. The first advert is from an American Apparel online campaign that features the sexualisation and pornification of young girls. The second case is the Protein World adverts of 2015–16 ('Beach Body Ready'), which were initially investigated for misstatement but were also scrutinised for various issues, including the sexualisation and objectification of women, links to body dysmorphia and eating disorders. Finally, the Asda 'Mum' advert of 2013, which received the most ASA complaints of that year and was investigated for the use of outdated gender stereotypes. These cases reflect the complexity of self-regulation and how 'harm and offence' and 'social responsibility' are too wide to catch problematic advertising that features gender stereotypes, sexualisation and objectification. This section also reflects a felt and often visible backlash in the UK that is garnered through new modes of online communications well as traditional 'analogue' modes: graffiti and 'subvertising'.

The American Apparel ruling

According to Crown et al. (2024), there is a clear precedent in the ASA decisions when it comes to sexualisation and objectification and when the advert features a child in an adult context. These decisions are tinged with the over-arching 'social responsibility' clause of the code. The upheld American Apparel decision in 2014 was a result of two public complaints about an advert appearing on the company's Instagram account that voyeuristically depicted a schoolgirl leaning over a car bonnet with the taglines 'Back to School' and 'School Days'. The advert was both featured on the company's website and sponsored on Instagram. The complainants felt the advert was irresponsible, sexualised young girls and objectified women. American Apparel's defence was that the advertising would only be available to followers of the company on the platform. American Apparel also relied on its renowned and intentionally provocative branding, which customers were fully aware of prior to following them on the platform. Moreover, they argued that the model featured in the advert was 30 years old, the advert was not part of the 'Back to School' campaign, that the image was posted by an inexperienced member of their junior social media team. In their ruling, ASA claimed that the advert had breached several rules in the code: social responsibility (1.3), harm and offence (4.1) and children (5.1). Action was duly taken to remove the adverts from social media platforms, as it was argued that besides breaching the code, the advertiser owed the consumer and wider society a sense of social responsibility, particularly through using children.

The ASA ruling considered how the advertiser 'dissected' the model in the framing of the advert and whether the advert's intention was to focus on the skirt (product) or crotch. The ASA made particular reference to how the legs were detached from the body and how the image was gratuitous and objectified women whilst simultaneously imitating the rise of 'up-skirting' photographs (images that are taken without permission). The ASA also considered how the advert targeted young women and potentially school children. With this, the regulator stated the advert 'had the potential to normalise a predatory sexual behaviour' as the image was clearly linked to the 'School Days' and #BTS (Back to School) campaigns, and, due to this linkage, it would be impossible for the consumer to differentiate between the adult model and teenage schoolgirls. Finally, with regards to ASA's defence of the consumer's agency to opt in/out of the advertising, the adverts would feature on social media regardless as sponsored content and therefore inevitably appear on consumers' news feeds. The advert was found to be objectifying women and sexualising adolescent girls. The ruling reflects the effectiveness of applying the CAP code; however, the underlying problem with this ruling (and others) is the lack of preventative action by the ASA as it later transpired that an intern had placed the advert on the Instagram account. A further ruling mirrored the American Apparel decision on the issue of the pornification of teenagers. In 2017, two TV adverts and a poster campaign for clothing retailer PrettyLittleThing were deemed to have breached the same rules, despite obtaining approval from the Clearcast pre-screening. The campaign featured sexualisation and objectification, despite the 'children' being 23- and 24-year-old models.

Objectification and sexualisation in the context of children are clearly well established and safeguarded by the ASA; however, the ASA's approach to the sexualisation and objectification of adults in adverts remains unclear. By comparison to American Apparel and PrettyLittleThing, the decision by ASA on a campaign produced by Protein World reflects this lack of will to sanction or rebuke an advert that sexualises women.

The Protein World ruling

Protein World billboard campaigns received widespread criticism across major cities around the world and, in particular, stirred debate on advertising regulation in London, Paris and Berlin. There were two particular poster campaigns, the first in 2015 and the second in 2017. The first Protein World advert is an interesting case due to the ASA's ruling that the advert contained numerous misstatements (nine in total) of weight loss claims, despite receiving clearance from the copy advice, Clearcast. The advert is also of note due to the amount of attention, hostility and resistance it received on social media, on the London underground and on street billboards. During the spring of 2015, the first advert depicted a toned woman in a bikini with the question 'Are you beach body ready?' The advert was regarded as controversial due to the use of a model whose body was unrealistic and unattainable. The physicality and omnipresent nature of the billboard version of the advert provided space for debate and subvertising on the London underground and bus stop billboards, allowing audiences to interact with the poster by adding graffiti. The campaign also received criticism from women's groups due to its objectification, sexualisation, body shaming and encouraging eating disorders. The campaign also received a lot of attention through Twitter (X) users, who began to tweet pictures of the defaced advert with comments etched on the posters. The campaign also instigated 70,000 e-signatures from an online petition, and social media users left 'comments as complaints' underneath the online version of the advert. The advert formally received a relatively high number of public complaints (378) through the ASA, all of which cited harm, offence and social responsibility. It is also worth noting that it was the most easily identified and discussed advert in my focus groups from Chapter 5.

Due to the amount of coverage the advert received, the ASA launched a separate investigation unrelated to the misstatement ruling. The investigation was based on two types of public complaint: first, that the advert appeared to promote an idealised body shape, and other body types were deemed inferior. The use of the idealised body type amounted to body shaming and was therefore offensive (breaching the 'harm and offence' part of the code). Secondly, the advert was seen to be socially irresponsible due to the juxtaposition of the image of a slim, toned body with the tagline question 'Are You Beach Body Ready?' The ASA refused to agree with the complainants' 'harm and offence' objections due to Clearcast's pre-screening of the advert and also the meaning of the 'Beach Body Ready' tagline. The CAP argued that the term has a broader meaning beyond undertones of fat shaming and, therefore, would not cause audiences harm or offence. They said that the meaning of the term included feeling:

> comfortable and confident with one's physical appearance to wear swimwear in a public environment. . . . [W]e did not consider that the accompanying image implied that a different body shape to that shown was not good enough or was inferior.
>
> (ASA ruling, Protein World, 2015)

The ASA also claimed that the advert did not amount to body shaming as it did not promote a particular body shape but rather probed readers to 'think about their figures'. Rule 4.1 (harm and offence) was therefore not breached. Rule 1.3 on social responsibility was considered, but the ASA could not find a breach. No response or reasoning was provided in the final ruling. Protein World's second poster campaign produced the same reaction from campaigners and the general public. The advert featured Khloe Kardashian dressed in a leotard with the tagline question: 'Can You Keep Up with a Kardashian?' The advert received 14 official ASA complaints citing social responsibility but not harm and offence and received social media response similar to the previous campaign of 2015. On the surface, the ASA's rulings appear identical: the body image promoted in the advert was 'desirable and aspirational' and did not 'appear to be out of proportion or unhealthy'. The tagline question was a double entendre; viewers, having viewed the TV show, would understand the context of the question, and although the language had undertones of 'competitive quality', it did not encourage extreme weight loss. Protein World's defence was also similar to that in the 2015 case: Clearcast cleared the poster, internal research had been conducted, and, in addition, the advert satisfied Transport for London's criteria. The key difference is that 'harm and offence' were not investigated due to the nature of the complaints.

The two ASA rulings and the wider social and traditional media discourse provide a number of conclusions and recommendations. First, the ASA appear to have responded to the wider public's disapproval stemming from social media rather than the official complaints through the ASA. Within this, the ASA also fail to use pre-emptive measures to vet the billboard posters (which have the ability to reach a wider audience) for potential offensiveness. This measure dates back to 1998 when CAP code's response to campaign posters produced a special measure to pre-screen 'shocking' or 'offensive' posters. This was the case when United Colours of Benetton produced a poster campaign that included shocking images and was subsequently banned (Crown et al., 2024). The use of the pre-screening for content that may be deemed shocking or offensive has set a fairly new precedent. The rulings from the computer game Mortal Combat equally featured stabbing and decapitation, which were intended to be ironic and humorous; a nasal spray advert which featured the tagline 'Want Longer Lasting Sex?' was deemed offensive and subsequently banned. The ASA did not follow this precedent but rather investigated the claims retrospectively. The CAP special procedure on posters must therefore be applied across all adverts that may actually or potentially cause offence to the wider public. Moreover, it is not certain what caused the ASA to investigate the advert. This is an important question for future claims against sexist content in understanding what mode of complaint is required to engage the ASA. It is probable that the ASA buckled due to the vast attention both the adverts received—both illegitimate means, such as the graffiti/social media response, and legitimate discourse, such as the Change.org petition, social media and mass media debates that the organisation ought to be seen to be reacting to the campaign. Secondly, in conjunction with the CAP special procedure on poster vetting, the ASA relied on the use of Clearcast clearance as a defence. The use of the pre-screening argument renders their investigation and its decision irrevocable. In Spain, the case law from SRO suggests that Autocontrol are content in admitting they were initially wrong with their pre-screening, as in the case of Ryanair. This notion should be applied in the UK; irrespective of the pre-screening advice, the ASA should be able to refute the advice of Clearcast and sanction an advert. Thirdly, the CAP code provides that advertisements that cause 'harm' or 'offence' or are 'socially irresponsible', generally and, in this context, specifically on the grounds of sex shall be prohibited (Earle, 2016). Thus, the CAP code definitions are far too narrow as the two cases highlight how the code falls below a basic human rights approach in not including a section on discrimination. Prior to the additional new harm and offence rules imposed in 2019, it proved difficult to sanction adverts that sexualised or objectified specific groups—such as women. The ASA avoid scrutiny in their decision-making process as an advertiser—for example, Protein World—is quite able to prove that no one was offended or no harm was caused when the advertiser can cite its own market research focus groups or surveys as part of their own clearance research. The onus therefore must be shifted to the ASA and Clearcast to provide more vetting and ensure that adverts are fully pre-screened. With this in mind, Sections 1 and 4 of the CAP required rewriting with a human-rights based approach underpinning the terms. For example, with 'harm', there must be an enhanced identification of the capacity that the media has to cause harm towards specific groups: for example, women and young girls. Children (as discussed with the American Apparel case) provide a much higher threshold, safeguarding the protection of the child's right not to be sexualised or objectified.

The Asda ruling

The 2013 Asda Christmas advert received a similar reaction from the general public, campaigners and the ASA. The Christmas advert was aimed at a wide market, with identical adverts featuring on TV, video on demand (catch-up TV) and online platforms. The content of the advert depicted a mother carrying out numerous tasks in the build-up to Christmas with the voice-over tagline: 'It doesn't just happen by magic; behind every great Christmas, there's Mum, and behind Mum, there's Asda'. The ASA received 620 complaints about the advert with the majority indicating that the advert was offensive and sexist as it reinforced outdated gender stereotypes of both men (hopeless, lazy dad) and women (exhausted, chore-ridden mum). Asda's defence of the advert hinged on the argument that the depiction of motherhood at Christmas was accurate rather than sexist, and although the depiction of motherhood was not universal, extensive market research, including feedback and focus groups,[1] indicated that their customers identified with the advert's representation of the average family at Christmas. As discussed in Chapter 5, the advert arguably reflected common experience and not the alleged outdated stereotypes.

As the advert was broadcast live, it was scrutinised by Clearcast. Clearcast considered the portrayal to be understood by the majority of viewers as an honest representation of Christmas in the UK, that the father was active in helping with the chores and that the advert 'celebrated the mother in a positive way'. Asda's defence was bolstered by licensed broadcasters such as ITV and YouTube, which believed the advert was suitable as it would appear on TV when a 'housewives' audience would be watching, and the advert relied on truisms and painted a positive picture of motherhood at Christmas. The ASA decided that no action was necessary, and, in the assessment of the advert, the ASA agreed with Asda's own research on the experiences of mothers at Christmas. Moreover, the ASA claimed that the advert was a relatively realistic representation of motherhood and would not breach the 'harm or offence' element of the code:

> We considered viewers were likely to understand the ad was not prescriptive of the experience of all at Christmas; rather it reflected Asda's view of the Christmas experience for a significant number of their customers. We therefore considered the ad was not likely to be seen as condoning or encouraging harmful discriminatory behaviour, or reinforcing negative stereotypes of men or women in general, and, for those reasons, considered it was unlikely to cause serious or widespread offence.
>
> (ASA Press Statement, 2013)

This is the only mention of gender stereotypes in the ASA's ruling, and looking at its precedent, the regulation of the stereotypical mother is predictable in that stereotypical representations of motherhood rarely result in the breach of code's 'harm and offence' chapter. Of the 1,574 rulings that include the terms 'gender stereotype' and 'motherhood', there are just 6 upheld decisions, which

1 1,896 mothers who shopped at Asda were surveyed and 8 out of 10 claimed that they would be responsible for the chores represented in the advert. The chores included gift buying, wrapping, Christmas tree collection and decorating, food shopping, cooking, playing with the children and sitting on the odd chair at dinner.

usually requires an additional breach of the CAP/BCAP code, such as misleading information or the excessive sexualisation/objectification of women.

To conclude, prior to the new 'harm and offence' rule, the CAP/BCAP code was limited in tackling both the use of gender stereotypes and the sexualisation/objectification of women in advertising. The code's key sections, social responsibility and harm/offence, rarely rendered adverts as discriminatory. Despite instigating discussion and scrutiny of the ASA's regulatory code and sexism in advertising, the organisation (and Clearcast) have been reluctant to prohibit adverts that receive a high number of complaints.

New 'harm and offence' rule

The ASA came under considerable pressure after the two Protein World adverts. Both online and analogue responses reflect a fourth wave or digital feminist revolt (Retallack et al., 2016), in which women seek to secure change through social media platforms by subevertising and brandalism (Dekeyser, 2021; Smith-Anthony and Groom, 2015). As discussed previously, resistance to the adverts was widespread, whilst the reaction from the ASA was muted, citing a lacklustre precedent that failed to sanction adverts that sexualised or objectified adults. In light of this failure, it is also conceivable that the 'Depictions, Perceptions and Harm' report was born out of this failure to act on these adverts between 2015 and 2017.

In July 2017, the ASA released its report on the use or gender stereotypes in advertising, 'Depictions, Perceptions and Harm'. The report identified six categories of gender stereotypes: gendered roles and occupations, gendered characteristics or behaviours, mocking non-conformity, sexualisation of girls and women, focus on a particular body or body parts (objectification) and promoting unhealthy body types. The report states that although the ASA already has a 'harm and offence' framework and precedent in its rulings that prohibit adverts which objectify or sexualise women, there is need in the industry to tackle advertisements that fall outside this framework and feature the aforementioned list of gender stereotypes. The report states that the ASA aims to 'strengthen' the regulatory codes with emphasis on gender stereotypes, 'new standards' will be developed to tackle the problem, and further training and advice will be made available to clients. The evidence from the report is comprehensive: an in-depth review of the CAP/BCAP codes, public opinion reports, stakeholder suggestions, academic and NGO responses and a list of divisive rulings. The adverts that have informed the report seem to be on the spectrum of what has been discussed so far in this book: sexualisation, objectification, reification, body image, irony, humour, motherhood and gender(ed) roles. It also highlights some of the problematic cases in which the ASA have lacked the regulatory teeth to intervene on gender roles and sexualisation/objectification: for example, the Protein World ruling, GAP (girl grows up to be a butterfly, the boy an academic) and KFC (man ridiculed over his anxiety). The report is critical of the ASA's recent decisions but, oddly, limits the parameters to the last three years of advertising. This criticism is particularly on body image, sexualisation and objectification; however, the report argues that the rulings are 'broadly in the right place', and the decisions concerning the depiction of gender roles 'have rarely been formally investigated by the ASA in the past'.

In 2019, the ASA added section 4.14 to the 'harm and offence' rule to include the use of gender stereotypes: 'advertisements must not include gender stereotypes that are likely to cause harm, or serious or widespread offence'. This new insertion to the code is, as Antoniou and Akrivos (2020) argue, a welcome decision as complaints can now be neatly housed in the gender stereotypes bracket, whereas, in the past, the ASA have struggled to 'fit' complaints to a specific rule in the code. The new addition to the harm and offence rule brings with it further ASA guidance on what constitutes a gender stereotype (ASA, 2019). The ASA guidance now provides some scope as to what are deemed to be problematic gender stereotypical characteristics—'attributes or behaviours that are usually associated to a specific gender'. The new rule does not ban all forms of gender stereotypes per se, only problematic characteristics and roles that are:

- always uniquely associated with one gender
- the only options available to one gender or
- never carried out or displayed by one gender

Some of the early test cases after the new gender stereotyping rule was added are worth noting. The first test case features the notion of an incompetent father and received 128 complaints. The advert for Philadelphia cheese depicts two new fathers who are distracted by food whilst in a sushi-style restaurant; both place their babies on a conveyor belt and continue eating. When they realise the babies have moved on, they rush over to collect them, adding, 'Don't tell Mum'. The ASA argued that the intentionally humorous 'Don't tell Mum' at the end of the advert amounted to a harmful stereotype and found that the portrayal of new fathers infringed the new rule. The second advert from People Per Hour in 2020 is in the form of a poster portraying a women and the text: 'You do the girl boss thing. We'll do the CEO thing'. The complainants claimed that the poster depicted a harmful gender stereotype as it portrayed women in the tech industry in a patronising and belittling way. Moreover, the 'girl boss' adage:

> suggested that a person's gender was relevant to their job performance; that a female boss might be out of the ordinary; and used a well-established stereotype that men were more suited to senior business positions than women.
>
> (ASA ruling, People Per Hour, 2020)

The ASA agreed with the complainants, stating that the advert plays on an outdated trope that women inherently lack IT skills and that the term 'girl' infantilises and patronises women, and upheld the complaints. The third case is an advert by Volkswagen in 2019, which received three complaints. The advert features four scenarios: a man and woman camping on a cliff edge, two male astronauts in a floating in a rocket and male para-athlete doing the long jump. The fourth scenario features a woman reading a book on a bench with a pram nearby. A car passes, and she looks into the distance. The ASA agreed with the complainants that the advert feature dmen in active, adventurous roles and the woman, contrastingly, in a more risk-averse care-giving role. The final case by advertiser Gorilla Glue (2023) features a father and his two sons playing in the living room; they all fall over, breaking a candlestick and a toy plane. A gorilla appears, glues the objects back together and walks off. The father is then tackled by his two sons; the tagline is 'Uh-oh, someone's in trouble. Or perhaps not. You see, Gorilla Super Glue fixes all kinds of breaks quickly. And Mum stays none the wiser. For the toughest jobs on planet Earth'. The complainants argued that the advert portrays fathers as fun and carefree and responsivities mothers, rendering them as more serious, concerned and tidy. Gorilla Glue argued that the advert was a light-hearted approach to household problems, and the advert did not indicate that the mother had to clear the mess up. Clearcast argued the advert did not perpetuate gender stereotypes as the mother is not depicted, and the items broken might be of sentimental value, rather than fathers being more carefree. They also added that being carefree and playful is not specific to one gender and could be reversed. The ASA chose not to uphold the complaints and said that the representation(s) in the advert did not amount to harmful gender stereotypes. The first three of these four cases provide some clarity on the guidelines and depth of the new 'harm and offence' rule on gender stereotypes. Taken together, they appear logical, providing clear precedent as to what a harmful gender stereotype is and a clear message to advertisers who believe a gender stereotype will pass if there is an element of knowing, humour or irony. The final advert does play into gender stereotypes: mother more concerned with sentimental value, prone to cleaning, less 'fun' or risk averse (as with the Volkswagen ruling) and, therefore, diverges from the earlier precedent set by the ASA around 2019. As Antoniou and Akrivos (2020) have highlighted, whilst the amended harm and offence rule is to be welcomed, it provides a one-dimensional and rather 'flat' understanding of gender that further ossifies a reductive masculine-feminine binary. Moreover, the new rule reverts to a somewhat heteronormative understanding of gender characteristics and roles again, reducing the concept to traditional male-female binary, ignoring both the complexities of contemporary forms of masculinity/femininity and non-binary identities.

In addition to the insertion of gender stereotypes into the BCAP/CAP codes, the ASA have provided further guidance on sexualisation and objectification as well as test cases. The ASA has clear precedent on these two concepts and, as has been discussed so far in this chapter, the cases on the concepts have led to divergent rulings. Whilst the new harm and offence rule on gender stereotypes does not cover these terms, the ASA guidance provides clarification as to what is deemed harmful or offensive when it comes to sexualisation and the objectification of women and men. Both terms have previously been assessed through the lens of offensiveness, rather than as a harm (Antoniou and Akrivos (2020); however, since 2021, the ASA has begun to consider sexualisation and objectification as a harm *and* an offence, recognising the complexity in how a gender stereotype may manifest: 'Ads should not stereotype women by presenting them as sexual objects, or depicting women in a sexual and objectified way for the purposes of titillating viewers' (ASA, 2022). The ASA now recognises the interplay between a harmful gender stereotype, sexualisation and objectification as was seen in an online Halloween-themed Bayyboo advert (2021) that featured women in lingerie and costumes. The tagline states, 'Halloween is the one night a year when a girl can dress like a total [bleep!] and no other girls can say anything about it. The hard-core girls just wear lingerie and some form of animal ears'. Objectively, the bleep could be perceived by viewers as the word 'slut', intended as a description of the women featured in the advert. The ASA agreed that the women were not overly sexualised/objectified but the

> linking . . . with the denigrating term 'slut', and implying women should aspire to being objectified, was problematic. Overall, we considered that the ad was likely to cause serious offence and included a gender stereotype in a way that was likely to cause harm.

Conclusion

In this chapter, I have provided an analysis of the UK's legislative and regulatory powers to curb gender stereotypes in advertising. As advertising regulation is a mere footnote in the Gender Equality Act (2010), the UK has relied heavily on an independent SRO that is operated by—and dependent on—an industry that it seeks to protect. This chapter has shown how the ASA has developed a robust regulatory framework by exploring specific previous of ASA 'harm and offence' rulings from the last decade. These rulings are excavated to highlight how the CAP/BCAP codes required updating to incorporate the regulation of gender stereotypes. At the time of writing, the Advertising Standards Authority had begun to develop its new rule through varied rulings that were discussed towards the end of the chapter. However, the inclusion of the term 'gender stereotypes' seems at odds with the foundation of any such reforms as the advertisements that caused the criticism featured complaints about overt sexualisation, objectification and 'body shaming'.

References

Advertising Standards Authority (2017) 'Depictions, perceptions and harm'. Available at: https://www.asa.org.uk/resource/depictions-perceptions-and-harm.html (Accessed: 21 June 2024).

ASA (2016) https://www.asa.org.uk/news/the-ads-that-attract-the-most-complaints-aren-t-always-the-ones-that-need-banning.html

ASA (2022) https://www.asa.org.uk/advice-online/offence-sexism.html

ASA (2023) https://www.asa.org.uk/news/annual-report-2023.html

ASA Press Statement (2013) https://www.asa.org.uk/news/may-your-ads-be-merry-and-right.html

Advertising Standards Authority Advertising Codes (2019) Available at: https://www.asa.org.uk/codes-and-rulings/advertising-codes.html (Accessed: 21 June 2024).

Antoniou, A. and Akrivos, D. (2020) 'Gender portrayals in advertising: Stereotypes, inclusive marketing and regulation', *Journal of Media Law*, 12(1), pp. 78–115.

Auxtova, K., Brennan, M. and Dunne, S. (2021) 'To be or not to be governed like that? Harmful and/or offensive advertising complaints in the United Kingdom's (self-) regulatory context', *Journal of Business Ethics*, 172, pp. 425–446.

Boddewyn, J.J. (1992) *Global perspectives on advertising self-regulation: Principles and practices in thirty-eight countries*. Westport, CT: Quorum Books.

Burton, B. (2014) 'Neoliberalism and the equality act 2010: A missed opportunity for gender justice?', *Industrial Law Journal*, 43(2), 122–148.

Conley, H. (2012) 'Economic crisis, austerity and gender equality: The UK case', *European Gender Equality Law Review*, 2, pp. 14–19.

Crown, G., Lloyd-Taylor, G. and Earle, R. (2024) *Advertising law and regulation*. A&C Black.

Dekeyser, T. (2021) 'Dismantling the advertising city: Subvertising and the urban commons to come', *Environment and Planning D: Society and Space*, 39(2), pp. 309–327.

Earle, R. (2016) 'The self-regulatory system', in Lindsay, R. (ed.) *Ad law: The essential guide to advertising law and regulation*. Kogan Page.

EIGE (2023) https://eige.europa.eu/publications-resources/publications/gender-balance-politics-november-2023

Evans, M. (2015) 'Feminism and the implications of austerity', *Feminist Review*, 109(1), pp. 146–155.

Fredman, S. (2022) *Discrimination law*. Oxford University Press.

Ginn, J. (2013) 'Austerity and inequality: Exploring the impact of cuts in the UK by gender and age', *Research on Ageing and Social Policy*, 1(1), p. 31.

Greer Murphy, A. (2017) 'Austerity in the United Kingdom: The intersections of spatial and gendered inequalities', *Area*, 49(1), pp. 122–124.

McNeil, A. (2019) 'Are we all in this together? Exploring the impact of austerity on access to justice for women', *The UCL Journal of Law and Jurisprudence*, 8.

Retallack, H., Ringrose, J. and Lawrence, E. (2016) '"Fuck your body image": Teen girls' Twitter and Instagram feminism in and around school', in *Learning bodies*. Singapore: Springer, pp. 85–103.

Smith-Anthony, A. and Groom, J. (2015) 'Brandalism and subvertising: Hoisting brands with their own petard?', *Journal of Intellectual Property Law & Practice*, 10(1), pp. 29–34.

Tokeley, K. (2021) 'A call for radical transparency: The regulation of camouflaged online advertising', *Journal of Law, Information and Science*, 25(2), pp. 116–148.

TUC Report (2023) https://www.tuc.org.uk/research-analysis/reports/impact-rising-cost-living-women#:~:text=The%20cost%2Dof%2Dliving%20crisis,less%20insulated%20from%20its%20impacts

Verdin, R. and O'Reilly, J. (2020) 'What future for gender equality policy in the UK after Brexit?', *The Northern Ireland Legal Quarterly*, 71, p. 1.

Chapter 9

Conclusion

Introduction

This book began by analysing the role the EU has played in regulating the use of gender stereotypes in advertising. At first, this was led by the commission in drafting the Goods and Services Directive 2004/113/EC, which sought to incorporate the equal treatment of men and women in advertising. During the drafting process of the directive, this measure was dropped, and subsequently, the commission and Parliament adopted various 'soft law' instruments to pursue the issue and keep it alive. This book then evaluated the divergent approaches from three case studies, Sweden, Spain and the UK, by considering the steps each state has taken, either through the adoption of legislation on harmful gendered content in advertising or by tightening self-regulatory ethical codes that prohibit such problematic adverts. By scrutinising the lack of legislation at the state level and highlighting some of the gaps in self-regulatory codes that govern gender stereotypes in advertising (e.g. the sexualisation and objectification of women and girls), this book has looked towards conceptualising how a future unified code of regulation of gender stereotypes in advertising might look. The analysis of this topic comes at a time when the commission has shown signs of revisiting of the GSD and addressing the issue of harmful gender stereotypes in advertising once more. By drawing on the experiences of teenagers across the three case studies, this book has also provided a deeper understanding of what constitutes harmful gender stereotypes in advertising as well as the more peripheral harms, such as sexualisation and objectification, that are embedded in adverts.

Summary of key findings

By taking a wide-angle view of the issue, the two opening legal framework chapters contextualise the regulation of harmful gender stereotypes in advertising and the EU's endeavours to tackle the problem. Chapter 2 addresses the two interlocking EU competences which the book straddles, anti-discrimination

DOI: 10.4324/9781003336037-9

and media, and explores whether the EU has the competence—and, indeed, the political will—to provide secondary legislation. The chapter maintains that the EU has moved from labour market–oriented equality provisions and has recently moved towards tackling gender equality 'blind spots'. This chapter proposes that since the Lisbon Treaty, the CJEU and the European Parliament have also stimulated a 'hands-on' approach in these areas, particularly where stereotypes are persistently seen as a threat to gender equality. In the final section of the chapter, the CJEU's influence on advertising regulation is discussed and how the court has creatively reshaped the issue as a single-market concern through the free movement objectives of the EU and, accordingly, through the wider scope of goods and services. The chapter concludes that the EU's capacity to provide for secondary legislation is not altogether unimaginable and, indeed, there are instances in which the commission have sought to act, but, due to the underlying free-movement principles, 'soft law' approaches may seem the most realistic tool for accelerating the regulation of gender stereotypes in advertising.

Chapter 3 focuses on the EU's 'soft law' strategy in tackling harmful gender stereotypes in advertising, noting various institutions and organisations that have helped drive the issue forward. Although there is, it would seem, clear political will in the commission and in Parliament to tackle the issue, both the Goods and Services and the AVMS directives have fallen short in delivering regulation of gender stereotypes in advertising. This has been due, in part, to the bulwark market-driven freedom of expression principles that underpin the EU, but also how the lobbying practices of advertising industries and larger and more influential member states can water down the potential of directives. It would therefore seem that the EU is content in striking a happy medium through 'soft law' measures. Amongst these measures, the European Advertising Standards Alliance (EASA), acting as a quasi-regulator, appears to have set a fairly low standard for gender portrayal in the EU27. The chapter reflects that the pursuit of regulating gender stereotypes has been kept alive on the fringes of the EU's agenda, and a refreshed pan-EU regulatory code is required if the EU is to move beyond the status quo. Moreover, the 'soft law' approach precedes substantive law, and it is only a matter of time before the Goods and Services Directive is revisited.

Chapter 4 focuses on the theorisations of gender and the problematic role advertising has in constructing gender. This chapter revisits the work of Erving Goffman to present the subtleties and minutiae of gender stereotypes through the 'gender displays' typologies found in advertising. This chapter argues that such representations in advertising shape the (re)production of gender and distort our understanding of everyday life. Goffman's typologies form the foundation of this book, and testing them this chapter reflects how Goffman's pictorial analysis of gender in advertising is still relevant today. By reimagining Goffman's coding, this chapter applies the 'gender display' typologies to contemporary modes of advertising and, by doing so, updates them to highlight their relevance and importance when deciphering what is meant by 'harmful gender stereotypes'.

Chapter 5 is an exploration of the experiences of teenagers from the three national perspectives. This data underlines the problematic stereotypes present in contemporary adverts. Revisiting and reimagining Goffman's gender display typologies, this chapter gleans themes from the participants: 'mothers', 'women on the verge' and 'objectified self'. Throughout the chapter, it is apparent that current advertising still exerts harmful gender stereotypes and the relevance of Goffman's coding schema and his insistence on 'making the familiar strange'.

Chapters 6, 7 and 8, provide a comprehensive analysis of the legislation and regulation operating in each of the national perspectives. By emphasising the differing approaches that Sweden, Spain and the UK have taken in curtailing gender stereotypes in advertising, the chapter underscores that self-regulation appears to be the dominant and most effective approach in the EU and, indeed, the most palatable—or achievable/practical—in the case studies. The option to self-regulate is what binds the three national perspectives together and reflects the theoretical argument running through the chapter: that states prefer market-driven freedom over a democracy-driven/gender equality version of freedom of expression. Subsequently, a 'light-touch' regulatory organisation and malleable ethical codes serve the interests of the advertising community and consumers alike.

The aim of these concluding chapters has been to examine the significance of legislation, as well as self-regulation, on gender stereotypes and how the two can work together in tackling gender stereotypes in advertising. One the one hand, Spain has used both legislation and self-regulation to tackle the issue, linking the use of harmful gender stereotypes in advertising to increased rates of gender-based violence. This legislation has be proven to be a powerful tool, providing clear guidance as to what constitutes a harmful gender stereotype and the wider ramifications they have in causing harm and violence towards women. The legislation, in conjunction with the self-regulatory organisation Autocontrol, has sought to address the issue head on, intersecting gender stereotypes with the sexualisation, objectification and reification of women in the Ryanair case. On the other hand, the legislation has been deemed excessive for some states, particularly Sweden and the UK, where legislation interferes with the principle of freedom of expression. Or it is deemed far too a blunt instrument; what constitutes a harmful gender stereotypes changes over time, and therefore, these states are content with assigning the issues of harmful gender stereotypes to the more malleable nature of self-regulatory bodies and their flexible ethical codes. Whilst the self-regulation of advertising comes with many flaws, it has so far proven to be at least a relative success, particularly in the last five years in the UK, where the use if harmful gender stereotypes has been incorporated into the self-regulatory code. Self-regulation has a supple personality and allows for elasticity and the changing of social attitudes when tackling the issue; it can react to changes in consumer's attitudes, gauging what is deemed (in)appropriate and what is perceived as harmful, offensive, ironic or humorous. Nonetheless, the self-regulation model contains imperfections in its structure and application.

The findings of this book underscore the importance of a balanced approach to tackling gender stereotypes in advertising, ensuring that legislation and/or self-regulation respects both gender equality and freedom of expression. The scope of this book is not without limitations. The rapid pace of technological advancement and the diversity of legal systems in Europe suggest that ongoing research is essential in this field. Future studies could focus on wider comparative analyses of legislative instruments and self-regulation organisations and their ethical codes, as well as the impact of emerging technologies, such as artificial intelligence and algorithmic (targeted/personalised) advertising.

Recommendations

In this book, I have indicated that legislation can be crucial tool in tackling gender stereotypes in advertising. Whilst such legislative instruments are vital, they are too often insufficient, especially when utilised in isolation. On the one hand, legislation establishes clear standards, providing scope for what types of gender stereotypes are harmful and stating how such harmful stereotypes are linked to wider harms, such as domestic violence and eating disorders. On the other hand, legislation is frozen in time or, as in Sweden and the UK, an unpalatable option for industry and its stakeholders. Therefore, legislation must be complemented with robust self-regulatory organisations and ethical codes that can adapt to the rapid nature of advertising, the ever-evolving changes in society and what consumers perceive to be in good/poor taste, harmful, humorous or ironic. Legislation that is complemented by well-designed and malleable self-regulation code can provide consumers and the advertising industry opportunities to address the shifts in what is perceived as a harmful gender stereotype. The effectiveness of self-regulation depends on numerous factors such as clear and precise ethical codes, supporting guidelines with definitions, examples of harmful gender stereotypes, an effective and transparent complaint process. sanctions such as fines and the capacity to prohibit or withdraw an advert. Based on the findings of this book, the following recommendations are proposed to improve the regulation of gender stereotypes in advertising.

First, the EU must move beyond its current soft law paralysis and show real commitment by revisiting the issue of harmful gender stereotypes in advertising by either updating current legislation (such as the GSD or the AVMSD) or implementing new legislation that sets regulatory standards. Through its international commitments to both CEDAW and BPfA, such legislation ought to encourage member states to prohibit harmful gender stereotypes in advertising through legislation. As discussed in Chapter 3, there have been some indications that the revisiting of preexisting legislation may be in the cards: for example, in 2022, the European Equality Law Network recommended that the commission revisit and recall the exclusion of Article 3(3) of the GSD.

Secondly, at a European level, the EASA should promote and enhance the use of self-regulation organisations and ensure that its members have functioning SROs and ethical codes that include clear and precise measures addressing the use of harmful gender stereotypes in advertising. Mirroring the UK's SRO (ASA), the EASA would benefit from specific examples as to what constitutes problematic or harmful gender stereotypes. Examples of what the ASA considers problematic are comprehensive and discussed in Chapter 8. What is important about the ASA's approach is how gender stereotypes often intersect with objectification, sexualisation, mockery or humiliation. At a state level, SROs should work towards producing bespoke malleable guidelines that speak to the fluid and shifting cultural and societal norms of that country.

Thirdly, the EASA national SROs and their ethical codes (or, indeed, legislation) should provide further guidance on the specific terms 'sexualisation' and 'objectification of women and girls'. These terms are addressed in Chapter 5 and reflect the most problematic and pervasive type of harm in contemporary advertising. Current status quo amongst SROs seems to be fixed on the milder and broader catch-all umbrella term 'gender stereotypes' rather than an explicit categorisation that incorporates and intersects these terms as harms. The Spanish legislation, complemented by its self-regulation and case law, has drawn attention to the legal ambiguity of the terms 'sexualisation', 'objectification' (and, in the Ryanair case, 'reification') and how the legislation and self-regulation can, at times, lack clarity. The Ryanair case proves this point—there is uncertainty as to what constitutes as reification, sexualisation or objectification, and legislation is perhaps not the panacea or silver bullet that will solve the problem.

Fourthly, SROs should promote a more proactive style of self-regulation by incorporating more transparency and accountability and better monitoring. This can be achieved in a number of ways: ensuring that consumers are equipped with the tools to make the initial complaint, including consumer friendly guidance; more transparency through regular reports and statistics; publishing cases of non-compliance; and withdrawing non-compliant adverts. National governments and SROs should create and disseminate public education campaigns to raise awareness of the impact of harmful gender stereotypes and empower audiences to report harmful content.

Concluding remarks

To conclude, regulating harmful gender stereotypes in advertising is by no means a new legal issue, and yet it remains a serious obstacle to the full realisation of gender equality across Europe. As an ever-evolving digital advertising landscape takes shape and, as a society, we become more accustomed to new digital platforms, social media and targeted advertising, tighter controls of and limitations on what we hear and see online and offline are much needed. The urgency for regulation is reflected in both the online world and the analogue world, where audiences carve out new ways to protest or resist pervasive forms of harmful advertising. As this new digital advertising landscape continues to develop, it is crucial that legal scholars, policy makers and practitioners engage in continuous dialogue, gleaning ideas from disparate legal frameworks, ensuring that legislative instruments and self-regulatory standards are simultaneously robust and flexible to protect audiences from harmful gender stereotypes that appear in advertisements. This book aims to contribute to that conversation by providing a foundation for further research and ways in which the EU might advance this vital area of law and self-regulation. The recommendations outlined here provide a roadmap for the various organisations and stakeholders—namely, the EU, EASA, national governments and SROs—to collaboratively dismantle harmful gender stereotypes in advertising. By incorporating these recommendations, states can begin to either provide legislation that includes clear guidance on what constitutes harmful gender stereotypes in advertising or embrace self-regulation and develop malleable ethical codes that encompass a range of harms.

Index

Note: references following 'n' refer notes.

FSC
www.fsc.org
MIX
Papier | Fördert gute Waldnutzung
FSC® C083411

Kolibri 360 GmbH
Ferdinand-Jühlke-Straße 7
99095 Erfurt, Deutschland
produktsicherheit@kolibri360.de